LISTEN

A Guide to the Pleasures of Music

Listen

A guide to the pleasures of music

ROLAND NADEAU
and
WILLIAM TESSON

Northeastern University

ALLYN AND BACON, Inc.   *Boston*

to Beverly

to Jennifer

Contents

ILLUSTRATIONS APPEARING IN THIS BOOK

Preface

THE GOAL of this book and its accompanying workbook and set of recordings is the understanding of music through involvement *with* music. All of the textual material is designed to lead you *to the music itself*.

The three chapters of Part One prepare you for the main body of the book, Part Two and Part Three. In Part One are contained the elements of theory, form, and performance media. Armed with some basic terminology and an awareness of what the aural perception of music is, you will approach Parts Two and Three with confidence.

Of the seven chapters comprising Part Two, the last three are devoted to the music of this century. In Chapter 8, "Early Twentieth Century," the roots of current trends are extensively explored. Realizing that the music of today is increasingly pertinent, Chapters 9 and 10 bring you the latest developments in music on "both sides." Chapter 9, "The Other Side," explores the collective creativity of Folk, Jazz, and Pop. Chapter 10, "Since Webern," investigates the creativity of the individual contemporary composer.

These two chapters show that there is a common concern on both sides for improvisation, pre-determinism, and the new sounds available through electronic technology.

The relevancy of contemporary music as a living, vital force representative of society today is part of a continuum of social-historical arts, the whole of which comprises Part Two.

A special feature of this book—Part Three, SCORE PROFILES (**SP**)—is not basically an original idea. The presentation of the *leading compositional idea* of a musical work as it evolves has been used before for various reasons.

In the field of musical theater or the night club, the conductor often uses a "lead sheet," which is a diagram of the *melody* or the *"leading" voices* at any given moment. Perhaps, in its simplest form, our SCORE PROFILE is really a "lead sheet." But we hope it is more than that. Our idea of a SCORE PROFILE is that it is similar to a topographical map. We try to give not only the contours of the main ideas, but also a little of the elevation. This we try to do in several ways. The first is by showing the manner in which the various instruments are combined. If they are in unison, the instruments are shown on a single line: VL, CL, OB. If they differ in register, the relationships of the registers are shown: VL

    CL

    OB

  Thus, the violin is above the clarinet is above the oboe. Second, the SCORE DETAILS, beginning in Part One, may also be regarded as a "blow-up" illustration. Special details of the original full score are magnified in order to enhance the understanding of a musical work.

  There are many musical examples in addition to the full SCORE PROFILES. It is not necessary to *read* music on the page to perceive important aspects of its meaning. *Following* the SCORE PROFILES, using specific techniques explained in the Introduction to Part Three (p. 303) is enough for the beginning listener.

ROLAND NADEAU

WILLIAM TESSON

Acknowledgments

To Wayne Barcomb, who, as editor-in-chief,
    pointed the way;
to Anne Carlisle, who, as assistant editor,
    enthusiastically took us by the hand, and
to Robert Patterson, editor,
    who saw us through;
to Russell Mead, production editor, who has
    an eye for minute detail,
—— our many thanks for professional guidance.

Thanks are also due to Louise Marsh for research-
    ing the art illustrations; to Michael Bennett
    of Memphis State University, author of the
    workbook accompanying this volume, for
    helpful suggestions; and to Dr. Richard Bobbitt
    for copy-editing of both the type matter and
    the music.

Harmon Diers deserves a word of appreciation
    for suggestions relating to the co-ordination
    of text and recordings.

                                    R.N.

                                    W.T.

LISTEN

A Guide to the Pleasures of Music

PART ONE
ELEMENTS AND MEDIA

MUSIC EXISTED AS a natural expression of man long before it was set down on paper. The notation of music came about only when it was necessary. The theory of music, and learned essays on the art of music all had to wait upon the creation of music. That theory follows practice is now only too well known, but throughout the history of music there have been many times when the theorist forgot he was a theorist and instead thought he was an arbiter of taste, and an authority on what music should be.

The composer is the first authority and the audience is the last authority. Nevertheless, we concede that a body of theory has arisen without granting that it takes the place of the composer's work itself.

The first part of this book is primarily concerned with theory. After grasping the essentials of theoretical knowledge, we will be in a position to appreciate and evaluate what has been done by the composer.

For those who wish to go into the details of musical notation, there is A Short Guide to the Fundamentals of Music, found in Appendix I, p. 391.

CHAPTER 1

Rhythm, Melody, and Harmony

AS NATURAL CREATURES of the universe, we consider some experiences normal and others abnormal. Those that seem normal are those that recur. That seems abnormal which is a distortion or exaggeration of the usual, such as a man eight feet tall or one four feet tall, or which is only occasional, such as an August frost. Those things which occur regularly we take for granted and accept as a normal part of our existence. Our heart, in diastolic movement, is perhaps our closest connection with the movement of life. When we live at a normal pace, it beats regularly and at a certain speed. This is so taken for granted that the doctor uses its regularity and its speed as a check on our health. When we are excited or exert ourselves, it beats faster. When we sleep, it beats more slowly. From these facts of nature has arisen the theory that our heartbeat gives to us the feeling of what is normal in the *pulse* or *beat* of music.

Thus, if a person's pulse beats 80 times per minute, a piece of music with 80 pulses or beats per minute will seem to be the norm or median with which all other pulses may be compared. Slower or faster pulses will seem less normal. Very fast pulses will feel exciting; very slow ones will feel numbing. Pulse in music, the regular recurrence of beats at various speeds, can then be considered as a basic ingredient underlying all musical movement. It is a strong sign of musical life and is the cause of the powerful, energizing force underlying all music—*rhythm.*

RHYTHM

In the broadest possible sense, musical rhythm can be said to include everything pertaining to the duration of musical sound. More specifically, though, rhythm refers to time spans separating successive musical impacts. In effect, it is that element in music that sometimes causes us to tap feet, snap fingers, or set our whole body moving in sympathetic motion.

Note that the first statement uses the term *sound,* not *pitch* or *tone.* Though rhythm is usually inextricably bound up with *melody* and *harmony,* which in turn are themselves dependent on pitch and tone, it can exist without them. In the field of art music, especially that written in our day, pitchless or near-pitchless compositions exist. One example is the *Geographical Fugue* by Ernst Toch, written for speaking *chorus.* And many will have heard a jazz drummer "take a chorus" on his battery of percussion instruments, none of them pitched.

Despite there being no pitch or tone involved, both the above types of music can elicit emotional or aesthetic responses from an audience. If, as we said before, pulse is a strong sign of musical life, the very stuff of musical movement, then rhythm must be its breath and energizing power.

Rhythmic pattern

A rhythmic pattern occurs when a varied group of note values is repeated enough in a composition to become one of its unifying, structural elements. The following rhythmic pattern has been isolated from its melody,

Example 1-1

$$\textleft| \quad \text{♩} \quad \text{♩} \quad \text{♩.} \quad \text{♫♩} \quad \text{♩} \quad \text{♩} \quad \text{𝄾♫} \quad \text{𝄾♫} \right|$$

shown below.

Example 1-2   *Piano Concerto No. 3*, Opus 37, Movt. I, Beethoven

Detail from **"The Wedding Dance,"** by Pieter Bruegel the Elder (*Courtesy of the Detroit Institute of Arts*).

Note that the symbols involved in the raw rhythmic pattern itself (Example 1-1) are those representing durational values only.

Certain melodies are dominated by one rhythmic pattern. One very celebrated theme by Paganini (Example 1-4) —used as the basis for extended compositions in the *variation form* by Schumann, Brahms, Liszt, Rachmaninoff, and Blacher—is based entirely on this rhythmic pattern.

Example 1-3

Example 1-4   *Caprice No. 24*, Paganini

Longer compositions will usually contain several rhythmic patterns. These will contrast with one another and easily be identified as they return in the working out of the composition.

The examples given above are taken from melodies. But it should be remembered that rhythmic patterns also function as supportive elements, particularly in *accompaniment patterns.*

In this *aria,* the rhythmic pattern in the bass staff is repeated constantly

Example 1-5   *Carmen*, Act I, Bizet

and gives the music a dance character, in this case that of the Habanera.

METER

Music is said to be metered when certain pulses are accented on a regular, predictable basis. These accented pulses are felt as primary *strong beats* and distinguished from several intermediary *weak beats.* The two primary characteristics of *meter* are:

1. Alternation of strong and weak beats.
2. Strong beats occurring regularly and often predictably.

Let us examine the song "Clementine," to see how the feeling of meter arises from a simple melody. We assume that whoever first played or sang this melody felt accents on certain pitches, and therefore emphasized them. Anyone can feel the song's natural accent by simply singing it strongly and rhythmically. When he does, he will feel what can be seen below, the arrow

Example 1-6   "Clementine"

over a note indicating a natural accent.

A glance at the rhythmic patterns underlying the melody provides further understanding of why these particular pitches feel as if they should be

Example 1-7

accented. The circled notes are longer than the rest and therefore receive a natural emphasis. The boxed notes are also accented because of their relation to the previous shorter note values. Underlying the whole, of course, is pulse.

If we again sing the song, now accenting sharply every third pulse starting on the first syllable of the word *darling,* we unmistakably feel meter and regular metrical accent. In this instance, because we have felt a regular accent every three pulses, the meter is called *triple.*

The example below shows "Clementine" with an arrow over each note

Example 1-8

of the melody that receives a strong metric accent. The equal-duration values below the melody represent the unit of pulse. These can be counted thus: one—two—three; one—two—three; or tapped.

Note that, between accents, the durational values of the melody itself will vary considerably; *they are not equal.* These *differences* in note duration are absolutely necessary for meaningful rhythmic patterns to occur. The counts or taps representing the beat or pulse, however, are *steady* and *equal* in duration.

Measures and bar lines

A convenient way for the composer to indicate precisely where the first strong metric beat occurs throughout a piece of music is to place a vertical *bar line* on the staff immediately before it. The distance from one bar line to the next is said to be a *measure.* The first beat of each measure is called the *downbeat;* the last beat in the measure, the *upbeat.*

Example 1-9

Bar lines are placed in the score to facilitate the task of reading the music. One is constantly reminded where strong metric beats occur, and specific measures can be easily located.

Time signatures and meter

The performer, in addition to the visual aid he gets from the recurring bar lines, finds further help through the ***time signature.*** We have seen in the song "Clementine" that it has a natural metric accent occurring every three beats.

In addition to this, the notation of "Clementine" contains a double-number at the beginning of the music, telling the performer precisely what the meter will be. This time signature is in effect for the entire composition, or until a new signature is introduced.

Example 1-10

For the purposes of understanding meter itself, only the top number of the signature need be considered. It tells the performer how many beats he will encounter in the music for each metrical group.

$\frac{3}{4}$ —music to be felt in **threes**

$\frac{2}{1}$ —music to be felt in **twos**

$\frac{7}{8}$ —music to be felt in **sevens**

$\frac{5}{16}$ —music to be felt in **fives**

Simple and compound meters

Numbers most often found at the top of the signature are 2, 3, 4, 6, 9, and 12. The first three indicate ***simple meters;*** the last three, ***compound meters.*** In the case of the simple meters, the upper number indicates precisely how many beats there are.

When the upper number in the time signature is 6, 9, or 12, however, the situation is more complicated. Taken at face value, a signature of $\frac{6}{8}$ clearly indicates six beats to a measure. Thus, one would normally expect, in the famous theme from the *Horn Concerto*, K.447, by Mozart, to feel six even

Example 1-11   *Horn Concerto*, K.447, Movt. III, Mozart

Counts: 6   1 2 3 4 5 6   1 2   3   4   5   6   1 2 3 4 5 6   1 2   3   4   5

beats. This is true, and we can indeed feel six beats. However, a metric grouping of six beats tends also to be felt in two groups of three beats rather than the one of six—especially in quick tempo. To experience this one need only count six beats several times over, placing a slight emphasis on the counts one and four. Therefore, the Mozart theme, which moves along at a lively pace, will not only be felt in six very fast beats, as in Example 1-11, but also in two, as shown below.

Example 1-12

Count ⟶ 1   2   1   2   1   2   1   2

Thus, compound meter is aptly named. Beats can be felt and counted in two ways. Meters in 9 and 12 will also subdivide easily into fewer but longer beats per measure. To see this, one simply divides the top number by three. Thus, a 6 meter can be felt in 2, a 12 in 4, and a 15 in 5. The faster the pace of the music, the more easily this subdivision can be felt.

Asymmetrical meter

Meters other than those discussed above are termed **asymmetrical.** We have seen how compound meters can be subdivided into combinations of threes: a 6 meter into a combination of two threes; a 12 meter into a combination of four threes, etc. In all compound meters, the normal subdivided

Example 1-13

(a) $\frac{6}{8}$ Count 1   2   1   2

(b) $\frac{12}{8}$ Count 1   2   3   4   1   2   3   4

grouping is the same—in threes. They therefore feel even. Asymmetrical meters such as 5, 7, etc., can also be subdivided into combinations. But as can be seen below, the groupings are not the same. The whole, therefore, feels uneven.

Example 1-14

(a) $\frac{5}{8}$

or

In the following example we see the time signature $\frac{5}{4}$ as used by Tchai-

Example 1-15   *Symphony No. 6*, Opus 74 ("Pathetique"), Movt. II, Tchaikovsky

kovsky for the second movement of his *"Pathetique" Symphony*. While listening, we can count five beats fairly easily. But without considerable prac-

Example 1-16

tice, it is possible to lose the downbeat and miss the count. We actually feel
more comfortable counting one-two; one-two-three; one-two; one-two-three,
as is indicated in the example below. What we are feeling here, of course, is

Example 1-17

duple and triple meter alternating on a regular basis. It is interesting to note
that both compound and asymmetrical meters ordinarily subdivide into the
two basic meters, duple and triple. In fact, all meter consists of either simple
duple or triple, or their combinations.

Meters with one beat are notated, but do not actually function as such
on a consistent basis. One-beat measures are usually heard in multiples, either in twos or threes.

Suggested Listening: The "General Dance" from Ravel's *Daphnis and
Chloe, Suite No. 2* for asymmetrical meter $\frac{5}{4}$.

Mixed meter and polymeter

Mixed meter occurs when measures in different meter alternate. These will usually be indicated by adjacent time signatures.

Example 1-18   *Variations on a Hungarian Song*, Opus 21, No. 2, Brahms

Polymeter results when two or more meters occur simultaneously (Ex. 1-19). This term is used in the same sense as are the terms *polychord* and *polytonality*. Both of these define different chords or keys sounding simultaneously. Therefore, when discussing simultaneous meters, the term *polymeter* is much more exact than the usual but highly ambiguous *polyrhythm*.

Example 1-19   *Don Giovanni*, Act I, Mozart

Changing meter

Changing meter occurs when time signatures change often enough so that regular downbeats do not come at the same place each time as expected. When this occurs consistently, as may be seen, it can be questioned whether

Example 1-20   Changing Meters in Stravinsky's *The Rite of Spring*

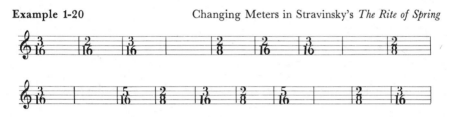

metrical accent really happens at all. Predictability, one of the basic facts underlying the principle of meter, obviously is not present. Though pulse remains, these changing meters serve more to produce varying accent than meter as such.

Syncopation

Syncopation provides momentary deviation from the expected and regular flow of beats. Simple syncopation occurs when expected weak beats are accented. The following example shows an expected weak beat, in this case

Example 1-21   *Symphony No. 44* ("Trauer"), Haydn

the second in a four-beat meter, strongly accented. This is common in music and is often encountered in the music of Beethoven.

Example 1-22   *Variations on a Theme of Diabelli*, Opus 120, Theme, Beethoven

Jazz, perhaps more than other kinds of music, uses much syncopation— especially that produced by accented offbeats. Accents are placed consistently at various points between beats, with the last third of the beat favored. Underlying everything is an unflagging and steady pulse, much of the time organized in the meters $\frac{4}{4}$ or $\frac{2}{2}$. The result of regular but varied offbeat accents, constantly set against an orderly flow of metered beats, can be very exciting and lively.

TEMPO

Tempo deals with the pace of the beats and nothing else. One sometimes hears the phrase ". . . in a fast rhythm." This is incorrect. What is meant is ". . . in a fast tempo," the phrase suggesting that the beats will follow one another quickly. Rhythm includes tempo as one important element, but the term *rhythm* should not be used when *tempo* is meant.

At the beginning of a piece or movement there is usually a **tempo indication,** written in any language. Thus, the tempo direction **Lebhaft** in a Schumann piano piece tells the pianist to play in a lively tempo. The term **Lent** in a Debussy prelude indicates a slow pace. These will apply to the whole piece unless different tempo indications are later introduced.

The tempo given at the beginning of the Score Profile of Beethoven's *"Leonore" Overture No. 3,* on page 357, is **Adagio.** This applies only until measure 37, when the term **Allegro** is seen. Later, at measure 514, Beethoven indicates that the music is to be played **Presto.**

Table of Common Tempo Indications

ITALIAN	FRENCH	GERMAN
Presto—Extremely fast	Animé—Animated	Lebhaft—Lively
Vivace—Fast with vivacity	Moderé—Moderate	Mässig—Moderate
Allegro con brio—Fast with brilliance	Lent—Slow	Langsam—Slow
Allegro con spirito—Fast with spirit		
Allegro—Moderately fast		
Allegretto—Not quite as fast as Allegro		
Moderato—Moderate		
Andantino—Not as slow as Andante		
Andante—Walking tempo		
Lento—Slow		
Adagio—Slow and calm		
Largo—Slow and broad		
Grave—Slow and solemn		

It can readily be seen that terms for tempo are only general indications, helpful though never precise. There have been many attempts to find a system that would be accurate and constant in specifying the speed of a particular piece of music.

Taken on face value, tempo indications would seem to suggest a very steady pulse. This is often true, especially in the Allegros of the Baroque and Classical periods. Obvious, though, is the fact that not all music is meant to be played in strict, inflexible tempo. Music in which the pace of the beats varies considerably is said to be in the **rubato** style, the term *rubato* taken as it applies to nineteenth-century romantic music. In earlier periods, it applied more to deviations from notated durational values than to fluctuations of pulse.

Beats gradually increasing in pace are indicated by the term **accelerando** (acc.) ; **ritardando** (rit.) indicates the reverse.

MELODY

What is melody?

There are many kinds of **melody.** From early times to the present day there have been as many different melodic styles on the part of the composer as there have been different tastes for melody on the part of the listener. But there are structural principles underlying these melodic styles that can be perceived in all periods of music. What, then, is melody? A simple definition would be: *the succession of single tones in time.*

Direction and distance

A tone may be repeated.

Example 1-23   *My Country 'Tis of Thee*

Or, it may be superseded by a tone of a higher pitch, by step;

Example 1-24   **SP m. 88,** Brahms

or change to a lower pitch by step;

Example 1-25   **SP m. 63-7,** Brahms, p. 348

or leap up an interval of a 3rd,

Example 1-26   *Symphony No. 3*, Opus 55, Movt. I, Beethoven

or more;

Example 1-27 *Symphony No. 4*, Opus 36, Tchaikovsky

or leap down an interval of a 3rd,

Example 1-28 **SP m. 222-6,** Brahms, p. 351

or more.

Example 1-29 *None But the Lonely Heart*, Tchaikovsky

Having looked at the several intervallic and directional possibilities of two-note combinations, it is clear that the prospects for variety in a melody lasting through many measures are manifold.

Melodic contour

As a melody spins itself out, it begins to assume an individuality of its own that could not be anticipated from the opening few notes. It now assumes what is variously called shape, profile, or contour. The shape of a melody may be seen by looking at the music as it is printed on the staff. In the well known melody from Tchaikovsky's *Fifth Symphony,* notice the es-

Gradual rise

Example 1-30 *Symphony No. 5*, Opus 64, Tchaikovsky

sentially rising character of the line until the high point, or **climax,** is arrived at in measure four. This type of melodic shape may be seen more clearly below.

Example 1-31

Further abstracted, the shape of the melody looks like this:

Example 1-32

Other melodic shapes often found are:

Gentle rise, gradual decline
Rise and fall of approximate equal length
Fall and rise of approximate equal length

Example 1-33   *Concerto No. 1*, Opus 25, Piano and Orchestra, Mendelssohn

But no matter what the shape, the listener should try to hear the important high and low points of a melody. Further, these shapes may be combined and altered in many ways, especially in melodies of greater length. The greater the length of the melody the more possibilities there will be for variety of contour and for subsidiary climaxes leading ultimately to the high point.

Example 1-34   **SP m. 113-126,** Brahms, p. 349

MELODIC RANGE.   In considering melodic style in relation to *range* it will be noted that melodies that are meant to be sung or based upon the vocal style often stay within a relatively small range. *Gregorian chant,* for example, falls within a very small range.

Example 1-35 *Dies Irae*

The theme that Beethoven used as the basis for the choral movement of his *Ninth Symphony* has a range of only an octave.

Example 1-36 *Symphony No. 9*, Opus 125, Beethoven

In the last movement of Brahms' *First Symphony* the main **theme** is not sung, but is based on a vocal "chorale" style and thus has a relatively small range.

Instruments have more range and flexibility than the voice, and composers have taken advantage of this in expanding the range of melody and in developing greater variety of contour.

Example 1-37 *Symphony No. 2*, Opus 36, Beethoven

CONJUNCT AND DISJUNCT MELODIC MOTION. It will be noticed in the examples given above that vocal music uses step-wise or ***conjunct motion*** predominantly. On the other hand, instrumental melodies more often use leaps or ***disjunct motion.***

HARMONY

Rhythm energizes music; melody and form give it definition; **harmony** provides it with depth and color.

Rhythm sets music in motion. It propels the musical idea forward. Harmony, which provides forward motion through **chord progression,** can be defined as the simultaneous occurrence of three or more tones resulting in **chords,** and the relationships between these chords.

Though music does not actually exist in physical space, it is sometimes useful to think of it in terms of high, low, up, down, horizontal, vertical. When we discuss horizontal aspects, we refer to melodic elements that are represented in notation as going from left to right along the staff. This is also called the linear element of music. Tones occurring *simultaneously* from lower to higher parts of a staff or from lower to higher staves are said to represent vertical aspects.

Homophony refers to the homogeneity of texture that results from the rhythmic simultaneity of the voices. The Greek word *homo,* used as a prefix, means "the same." In homophony the notes of the various parts are articulated at the same time, and therefore sound like a harmonization of the melody and have no rhythmic independence of their own.

It may be shown that when any chords are played in succession, the ear seeks to find the melody in the highest pitched tones, regarding any of the notes lower in pitch as only a reinforcement or thickening of the notes on top. A simple experiment at the keyboard will illustrate. Play several chords on the piano at random:

Example 1-38

The ear hears these notes as the melody.

Example 1-39

The harmonizations found in songbooks or hymnals are usually homophonic. "America the Beautiful" may serve as an example.

Example 1-40   "America the Beautiful," Ward

This is almost pure homophony. The articulations are not in opposition, except briefly in measures 4, 8, and 12.

Chords are enormously powerful agents used by the composer to affect mood and atmosphere. Indeed, the plainest kind of tune can be metamorphasized by the subtle use of chords.

The well known melody, "God Save the King," is harmonized very simply by Beethoven in his keyboard variations of 1804, though not quite as

Example 1-41   *Seven Variations on the National Song "God Save the King,"* Beethoven

simply as it can be heard in its American version, "My Country 'Tis of Thee." In the coda to the variations, Beethoven not only changes the contour

Example 1-42   "My Country 'Tis of Thee"

of the melody, but completely transforms the harmonic scheme from one of routine expectedness to one replete with poignant chords.

Example 1-43   Coda, *Seven Variations on the National Song, God Save the King*, Beethoven

Tertian harmony

Though it is true, as we said before, that *any* three or more sounds occurring simultaneously can be termed chords, it is also true that certain chords are more common than others. One particularly common system of harmony, which has underscored Western music for centuries, is called *tertian*. The cornerstone of the tertian system is the ***triad***.

A triad is a three-note chord built on intervals of thirds. These seem to many to be as eternal and normal as air and clouds, the color spectrum, indeed anything experienced simply but surely in nature itself. The aural comfort and expectedness of tertian harmony may well have a basis in the physical acoustical laws regulating tone itself. It can be shown, for instance, that the three tones of a basic triad

Example 1-44

are derived from the first five tones of the overtone series.

Example 1-45

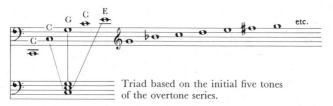

Triad based on the initial five tones
of the overtone series.

If it is true that the overtone series is deeply imbedded in human aural experience, it follows that triads, tertian harmony, and the whole tonal system have been and perhaps for some time to come will be fundamental to musical experience.

Triads may be constructed on any note of the staff, including notes with accidentals.

Example 1-46

We have said that triads are constructed in thirds. Visually, this can be ascertained by noting that all three notes of the triad are either on spaces or on lines. The distance between adjacent lines or adjacent spaces is always a third. The lowest note of the triad is termed its **root,** and the triad takes its letter name from it.

Example 1-47

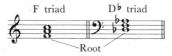

Chord connection

Heard singly, chords can be striking by themselves. But just as a single variety of flower seldom makes a garden, neither does the single chord make music.

The manner in which chords are connected is vital. Harmony textbooks refer to chord sequence as **progression.** The jazz musician speaks of **changes.** But whatever it is called, logical, natural chord connection is as important as syntax is to language. Just as certain ordered words make sense while others result only in gibberish, chords go well together only in certain patterns. These patterns follow principles of chord progression that are consistent and logical.

To see this, one need only examine this example:

Example 1-48 *Old Folks at Home,* Foster

CADENCES. Chords, besides being supportive agents for melody, generators of musical movement through progression, and providers of color and depth, also can be powerful agents in dividing a composition into meaningful, cohesive, inner segments. Just as the eye would find it difficult to isolate phrases, sentences, and paragraphs if no punctuation were present, so would the ear find it difficult to identify intelligible musical statements without *cadences.* A cadence is a short progression of chords that either holds back or terminates completely the flow of music in a composition. Cadences are found at the joints of form; at the end of formal segments such as the phrase, period, part, section, or movement. They signal the ear that a musical statement has either just finished or been interrupted before going on.

MODULATION. The process of transition from one key to another is called *modulation.* Any key, major or minor, may go to another. The modulating passage may be short, long, simple, or complex; the whole depending on the style, the historical period of the composer, and the work at hand. In general, the longer and more complex the composition, the more sophisticated will be the key scheme and the modulation techniques.

The Haydn rondo in the Score Profile in Part Three of this book offers an excellent opportunity for aural and visual recognition of effective use of key and modulation. All key changes and modulations are indicated below the staves.

CHAPTER 2

Structure: Homophonic/Polyphonic

HOMOPHONIC TEXTURES

MUSIC IS THE most abstract of the arts.

Each tone glows, sometimes flames, then perishes to make room for those yet to come. Where has it gone? Time must elapse for music to be. The ear must not only assimilate several tones sounded together, but also remember the ones that came before and anticipate those coming. Otherwise the music is not intelligible. A work may only fill out a few seconds or it may span several hours, but whatever its length, the listener must remember and relate. He *must* abstract.

And beyond this, music, unlike painting or sculpture, must be recreated each time it is heard. Thus, the musical thoughts of the past masters are not directly available to an audience, but must first be filtered through the personality of a conductor, a soloist, or an ensemble. These recreations, or interpretations, necessarily will vary with each performance and with each individual performer or performers. In other words, a performer will not play a piece twice in the same way, nor will different performers play it the same. The listener, then, besides remembering and relating tones that flit by and then vanish, is faced with trying to assimilate and understand the whole composition, which is never heard the same way twice in live performance.

But despite this and without getting into a discussion of musical aesthetics, we will assume that it is patently evident to everyone that there is "meaning" in music; music does make sense. Despite its ephemeral, abstract nature, individual compositions are the vehicles for vivid communication between

composer and listener. This communication can never be completely understood or analyzed, but nevertheless it is unquestionably felt to exist. The
pervading force that makes this communication possible is **musical form.**

Musical form is the organization of tones, progressing in time, into patterns and shapes that the listener may relate and assimilate into a meaningful whole. The myriad formal structural patterns that exist and continue to
be developed articulate the communication—emotional, aesthetic, intellectual—that the composer wishes to express.

Unity with variety

Slowly and painstakingly, forms have evolved such as sonata, opera,
rondo, theme and variations, etc. These are not only treated differently by
different composers, but varied enormously by the individual composers
themselves. Beethoven, for example, in his nine symphonies used sonata-
allegro form for separate movements over and over again, but never in precisely the same way. There is great freedom and transformation in his use of
this formal structure from symphony to symphony.

However, underlying the great diversity in formal structures are certain
principles that operate constantly. Of these, the most important are *unity*
and *variety.* These are present in all music. How this is handled is one test
of the composer.

UNITY.   Unity is provided primarily by repetition. It occurs constantly
and on many levels. **Themes, motives,** rhythmic figures, chordal patterns and
textures, **sections** of movements, etc.—all tend to be heard more than once.

VARIETY.   Variety occurs through **contrast.** The ear needs to hear musical elements again, but it wants to hear them fresh. It also wants to experience the unexpected, the sharply different. A highly unified composition—
for example, one built upon a single motive, a single rhythmic pattern, a single chordal texture—will be stale and uninteresting to the ear unless it is
permeated with strong contrasts or variation.

Contrast comes in a great many ways. To name but a few of the most important, it may occur through change of chord, key, texture, articulation,
melodic contour, range, rhythm, instrumentation, tempo or form.

Contrast also comes with *variation,* the very essence of which lies in identity with change. The substance of this section, in fact, deals with this primary musical function. (See *development* below.) All of the variation tech-

niques described show the manifold ways that have been developed to satisfy the ear's need for identity with change. Variation techniques indeed point up the essential polarity of unity and contrast that exists in all of music.

A composition cannot be successful without both unity and variety operating in some kind of balance. We have said that music that emphasizes homogeneity at the expense of variety will be uninteresting. We now can state that it will be not only dull, but also unsuccessful.

The reverse is true as well. A piece that emphasizes variety at the expense of unity will be unintelligible and meaningless. All effective music mixes unifying and contrasted elements.

Melodic elements

THE MOTIVE. A motive is a short, seminal, melodic idea. It usually includes two or more tones.

Motives are normally striking and graphic, easily recognized and remembered:

Example 2-1   *"Egmont" Overture*, Opus 84, Beethoven

Often they outline triadic shapes.

Example 2-2   *Symphony No. 8*, Opus 88, Dvorak

Sometimes they are very brief,

Example 2-3   *La Tosca*, Scarpia's Motive, Act I, Puccini

other times rather extended:

Example 2-4   *Madama Butterfly*, Love Motive, Act I, Puccini

But even though motives usually spearhead the musical thought, they are only building blocks: vital musical components within a larger design.

It is sometimes possible to divide the motive into a smaller melodic structure called a *figure*. The figure is also at the basis of many non-motivic passages, which then are said to be figurative in character.

THE THEME.   A *theme* is more extended than a motive. It can be a complete musical statement, or it can be neatly tailored and clipped in a symmetrical sixteen-measure frame:

Example 2-5   *Waltz*, Opus 34, No. 2, Chopin

The term *theme* itself is rather loosely used by composers. When the form is labeled "theme and variations," the theme is often extensive enough to display one of several simple forms to be discussed below, such as binary or ternary.

In general, a theme is a melodically striking component of a composition as distinguished from the more figurative, less melodic elements. The motive, usually shorter, will often itself be a component in the structure of the theme.

A *tune* is a simple melody easily played, sung, and remembered. Intervals in its construction are largely diatonic, with limited range, and the whole will be more complete in feeling than either a motive or a theme.

Units of form

Thus far we have dealt with materials—motive and theme—that in themselves do not provide cohesion and definition for musical forms. They are not easily measured. They may be compared to ideas that permeate accepted literary forms. For example, the idea suggested by the title of Emerson's essay "Self Reliance," does not by itself result in meaningful literary communication. Communication only occurs when ideas are developed and made articulate through the author's use of clear language and logic of statement conditioned by the structural principles of the literary form itself.

In the same way, motives and themes—the melodic "ideas" of a musical work—are made articulate in a total work only by the use of certain units of form. For purposes of analysis, these formal units may be measured according to the number of measures they span, and named according to function. From smallest to largest, these units are: phrase and period, part, section, movement.

THE PHRASE.   The *phrase* is the smallest formal unit in music. The phrase varies considerably in measure length according to the style of the music. Asymmetric measure groupings such as 3, 5, 7, etc., are often encountered, especially in folk music and in contemporary works. But very often the phrase's structure will fall into the close-cropped framework of a four-measure unit, as in these examples.

Example 2-6   "Auld Lang Syne"

Example 2-7   "The Chase," Burgmüller

This square, four-measure phrase often leads to another answering phrase, the whole then suggesting a larger formal unit called a *period.*

When the first questioning phrase ends as shown below, it is termed the *antecedent.* Its answer then becomes the *consequent.*

Example 2-8

Small complete structures: part-forms

When we consider small, *complete* forms, we encounter units more extensive than phrase and period. These are **parts;** and the forms themselves, **part-forms.**

WHAT IS A PART IN FORM?   A part consists of few or several phrases often, but not always, organized into periods. These phrases will be homogeneous enough so that they unquestionably stamp the part as *one*. The phrases will often be alike in motive, texture, harmony, instrumentation, accompaniment pattern, key scheme, etc.

ONE-PART FORM.   The smallest possible *complete* form is termed **one-part form** and is simply labeled A:

Example 2-9   *Prelude,No. 7,* Opus 28, Chopin

Though minute, these forms in the hands of masters such as Bartok, Chopin, or Schoenberg can be vivid and satisfying.

BINARY FORM.   Encountered much more often are the **binary** and **ternary** part-forms. A binary part-form, AB, consists simply of two parts usually separated by a double bar. Part A is frequently repeated as is the following section, B. The pattern can be symbolized thus: A :|| : B :|| . The parts may be brief, as seen below,

Example 2-10   *Violin Sonata No. 6*, Movt. II, Haydn

or rather extensive, as in the keyboard *suites* of J. S. Bach. In the more extensive AB forms, the second section will tend to be the larger of the two. Often it will contain at least a portion of the A section. When this happens, though the music may appear visually to be binary, it is at least partly ternary (ABA).

TERNARY FORMS.   The true ternary form consists of three parts, the third being a repetition, either exact or varied, of the first. The returning A section often spans approximately the same number of measures as the first A. Indeed, in *da capo* ternary forms, the returning A is not written out at all. The sign D.C. indicates to the player that he should simply repeat the opening section exactly as before. However, one of the pleasures in aurally tracing small ternary forms, other than da capo, lies in the recognition of the returning A section despite its being subtly transformed through variation techniques. We now can compare and distinguish between five complete small forms.

One-part form:	A
Binary form:	A, B
Ternary da capo:	A, B, A
Ternary with varied return:	A, B, A¹
Hybrid binary-ternary:	A, B + ½ A

Any of the parts within these forms may be repeated *before* the arrival of the following parts without changing the basic formal identity of the music. Forms where successive *different* parts are generated beyond the B part are called *additive:* A, B, C or A, B, C, D, etc.

The complete part-forms discussed thus far are sometimes called *song* or *dance forms.* Though it is true that simple songs and dances easily fall into these patterns, music for other media and purposes also uses them. For example, simple binary or ternary forms underlie a great many of the *character pieces* for piano by Schumann, Schubert, Chopin, Brahms, and Mendelssohn.

Before going on to specifics about structure in the large forms, we will briefly pause to consider a striking facet of form in general. Small formal units are the basis for larger ones. Phrases group easily into periods that themselves are the basis for complete part-forms. Further, all of these small units can be present and integral to larger units, soon to be discussed. Within the large pattern, smaller, often quite different, patterns operate. All are interdependent, and they reinforce and complement each other.

Larger single member forms

We are now prepared to discuss the larger *single member forms* of music, remembering that underlying all of them will be smaller, cohesive formal units. These larger forms can be complete in themselves, or they may represent one member of an aggregate work.

The inner divisions of substantial forms such as sonata-allegro, rondo, theme and variations are termed *sections.* In this text they will be named according to their role in the form, not labeled with letters as are parts. Therefore, part-forms will be labeled with capital letters, while words such as *refrain, exposition,* will describe sections.

THE SECTION. Sections are distinguished from parts in several ways. Usually they are larger. Also, the section allows for greater inner diversity than the part. For example, a development section (see below) may be very extensive and include great musical contrasts. Within the section one or more part-forms may operate, while the part will itself only divide into phrases and periods. The minuet, when found in the symphony or other large forms, frequently shows each section divided into binary and/or ternary part-forms.

Two types of sections may appear in any larger single member form. They are the *introduction* and *coda.*

Introduction. The introduction often immediately precedes larger instrumental forms, which are in fast tempo. It is sometimes fragmentary, like the introduction to the first movement of the *Piano Sonata in B-flat Minor* by Chopin (four measures), or it may be lengthy as in the finale of the *Symphony No. 1* by Brahms (61 measures). The tempo of the introduction is usually slow.

Coda. The coda occurs at the end of the larger forms. Like the introduction, it may or may not be present, and can be of any length. It either continues in the tempo of the main movement or goes much faster, resulting in a brilliant finish.

Thus, the functions of the introduction and coda are similar. Each is optional, and their shape and size is indeterminate. The slow, serious introduction sets the stage; the coda rounds out the form.

TRANSITION.   In contrast to the introduction and coda, the transition is almost always present, but its position in the form varies with the work. Its role is to link relatively stable melodic elements. Its effect is that of considerable musical motion: of "going somewhere." Modulation is likely to be present, especially in the more extensive transitions. So is sequence. Often the music is highly figurative, featuring brilliant scales and arpeggios.

While introduction, coda, and transition occur in any of the larger forms, other divisions are integral to specific forms and will therefore be discussed with them.

The movement

SONATA-ALLEGRO FORM: EXPOSITION, DEVELOPMENT, RECAPITULATION. *Sonata-allegro* is a rather imprecise term used in formal analysis to describe a sophisticated movement prominently featuring development. The term was used to label opening allegros of multi-movement sonatas of the classical period. Because these opening allegros normally employed the formal plan of exposition, development, recapitulation, any form using this plan was called sonata-allegro. Thus, any movement using the above divisions, regardless of tempo or placement within the total work, is labeled *sonata-allegro*.

Sonata-allegro is a most felicitous form, combining the psychological satisfactions derived from ternary principles with the energy and excitement generated by development. The form is ternary because the recapitulation is a restatement of the exposition, but with important modifications. The development bridges the two.

Exposition.   The role of the exposition is to present melodic and rhythmic materials in an orderly but vital manner. In standard works this is realized by themes—contrasted in character and indeterminate in number—appearing in succession, but often separated by transitions.

In the exposition of many works, two keys will prevail—the tonic for the opening theme, and either the dominant or mediant for later themes. Themes are numbered according to their order of entrance.

Development section.   The development section is as free in shape as it is exciting in effect. As the term suggests, its role is to present in a new light the motivic materials already heard in the exposition. These materials are "treated" with an enormous array of compositional techniques, resulting in fascinating new musical shapes. Modulation occurs very frequently, the total effect in more dramatic works being one of growing intensity and excitement until the arrival of the recapitulation section.

Recapitulation. The recapitulation closely follows the pattern of the exposition with but one major change. Whereas the exposition has two contrasted keys, the recapitulation generally stays in one key, the tonic. A typical sonata-allegro form would then follow in this order:

Slow introduction	(optional) .
Exposition	Presentation of themes with transitions and modulation to dominant or mediant key.
Development	Exploration of motives and themes and treatment by various compositional techniques. End of this section built on dominant chord, which leads to recapitulation.
Recapitulation	Return of exposition with all themes in tonic key, and with other minor changes.
Coda (optional)	Usually in same tempo as exposition, development, recapitulation, but sometimes faster.

It should be remembered that the above outline of sonata-allegro applies only to typical patterns. In the hands of the masters, details of structure can and do deviate from the norm. This is indeed true of all forms.

Suggested Listening: Score Profile, Beethoven, p. 356, *"Leonore" Overture No. 3.*

RONDO FORM: REFRAIN AND EPISODE. The *rondo* is often located as the finale in a multi-movement sonata. Its structural pattern is more variable than that of the sonata-allegro. There are two basic sections, the refrain and the episode, but these may be repeated often, and varied considerably. The one constant of the form is that the refrain returns no fewer than two times. Two very commonly seen arrangements of refrain and episode are *small rondo* and *large rondo.* Typical rondo patterns are:

Small, five-section rondo:	Refrain, Episode I, Refrain, Episode II, Refrain.
Large, seven-section rondo:	Refrain, Episode I, Refrain, Episode II, Refrain, Episode I, Refrain.

As we have seen, the distinguishing characteristic in sonata-allegro is the development section with its propulsive, eruptive power. But whereas sonata-allegro animates, the rondo charms. Its principal attraction lies in the refrain, which keeps coming back. Contrasted episodes separate these returns, and the ear delights during the latter portions of these in the anticipation of the refrain's return. In the simpler rondo, the refrain is likely to be repeated exactly as in its first entry. But in more extensive ones it often will appear in delightful mutations, including change of key and considerable variation. Sometimes Episode II itself takes on the character of development as it deals with thematic materials from the refrain. When this happens, the form becomes **sonata-rondo,** a hybrid. Codas regularly appear in rondos, but introductions only occasionally.

Suggested Listening: Small rondo: Brahms, *Symphony No. 1,* Movt. III; Large rondo: Beethoven, *"Pathetique" Sonata,* Op. 13, Movt. III; Rondo-sonata: Haydn, *Symphony No. 88,* Movt. IV (Score Profile, p. 331).

THEME AND VARIATIONS. ***Theme and variations*** as a structural pattern can occur as a member of multi-movement works, but just as often it will be seen as a complete composition, for any instrument or combination of instruments.

As in the rondo, the number of sections in the form is indeterminate. For example, Beethoven gives only three variations in the second movement of his *Piano Sonata,* Op. 14, No. 2, but 33 in the *Diabelli Variations,* Op. 120. In that sense it is an open-end form.

The theme itself, as we said earlier, often consists of a complete part-form. It may be borrowed from outside sources, from another composition by the composer, or be especially written by the composer for the work at hand. Whatever its source, it tends to be of a simple and unadorned nature; thus will it lend itself more easily to expansion and change.

Variations are of two types: ornamental and characteristic. The ***ornamental variation*** is unpretentious. Interest lies in a graceful embellishment of the theme without major alteration of its basic length and shape.

Example 2-11   "Clementine" in Ornamental Variation, Nadeau and Tesson

Indeed, it is sometimes possible to play or to sing the original theme simultaneously with any of the variations. The ***characteristic variation*** uses the theme as a touchstone. From within the theme itself, individual elements, such as motive, rhythmic pattern, and harmony, are isolated and used as the basis for variations of a "character" often wholly different from that of the

Example 2-12   "Clementine" in Characteristic Variation, Nadeau and Tesson

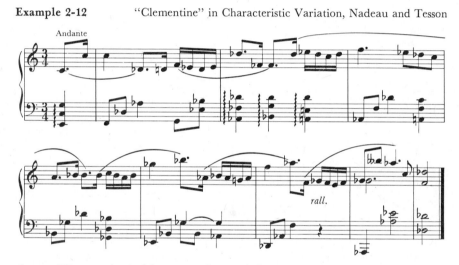

theme. The connection between theme and ornamental variation is physiological; that between theme and characteristic variation is psychological.

    Suggested Listening: Ornamental variations: Mozart, *Variations on "Ah, Vous Dirai-je, Maman,"* K. 265, for keyboard; Characteristic variations: Elgar, *Enigma Variations,* Op. 36, for orchestra.

    MINUET (OR SCHERZO) WITH TRIO. Standard terminology here is confusing, although the actual formal pattern used is very simple. The listener is presented with a form (frequently the third movement of a large structure) called ***minuet.*** However, its inner sections are labeled *minuet* and *trio.*

The contradiction is obvious. How could the first section of the form be a minuet when the entire movement is a minuet?

The pattern used is ternary. The whole form, MINUET, takes its name from Section I, *minuet*. Section II is the Trio. The final section is the repetition of the first. Section I and Section II are frequently quite contrasted. Section II is often in a different key with its clearer texture differing vividly from that in Section I.

The Minuet is also seen with two trios. The plan then becomes similar to that of a small rondo: Minuet-Trio I-Minuet-Trio II-Minuet.

The *scherzo* follows the same formal pattern as the minuet, differing in effect because of its considerably faster tempo.

Suggested Listening: Mozart: Minuet with Trio, Movt. III, *Symphony No. 41* ("Jupiter"); Beethoven: Scherzo with Trio, Movt. III, *Symphony No. 2, Op. 36.*

Aggregate structures

Just as there need be pattern and logic within part-forms and within larger single member forms, so there needs to be some kind of organic unity and balance when two or more of these forms are joined in *aggregate structures.* Some of these are: symphony, concerto, quartet, solo sonata, suite, song cycle, oratorio, and opera.

In instrumental music aggregate forms unite their movements through certain techniques. The standard classical symphony, for example, will often show the same key for three of its four *movements.* The content in each movement will be such that there is follow-through as the work progresses. There will be a four-movement plan with a general tempo scheme of I fast, II slow, III moderate or fast, IV fast. The initial movement is almost always sonata-allegro; the third usually minuet or scherzo, and the last frequently rondo.

Beethoven's *Symphony No. 3,* Op. 55, "Eroica" (1805) is a large aggregate work based on the logical principles of the classical symphony. There are four movements:

Movt. I: tempo—Allegro con brio
            form—sonata-allegro

Movt. II: tempo—Adagio assai (Marcia funebre)
            form—ternary (A, B, A)

Movt. III: tempo—Allegro vivace
             form—scherzo with trio

Movt. IV: tempo—Allegro molto
             form—theme with variations

Beethoven in this symphony works in the traditional four-movement plan, with tempos and structures similar to those used by Haydn and Mozart in their symphonies. Each movement is internally cohesive, but leads to the next movement with convincing musical logic. The instrumental forces used are modest. With the exception of the three French horns, the winds are in pairs; there is the usual string choir and two timpani.

Although this is an *absolute* symphony, showing a rigorous use of rational principles, it is filled with an expressive content that perhaps reflects the composer's spiritual travail at this point in his creative life. Conceived at the time of the Heiligenstadt Testament (see Chapter Six), the "Eroica" symbolizes Beethoven's spiritual catharsis. It is the musical parallel to Beethoven's new personal philosophy resulting from the physical crisis of this time when Beethoven began to lose his hearing.

CYCLIC FORM.   Occasionally two or more movements will be linked physically by a **bridge passage.** Sometimes a kind of formal superstructure, termed **cyclic form,** will firmly relate the movements. This consists of one or more themes recurring in two or more movements, often in addition to the regular themes of the movement.

The Romantic Period is rich in symphonies whose formal superstructure is cyclic. Tchaikovsky's *Symphony No. 4,* Op. 36 is partially cyclic. The dramatic, herald-like theme from the introduction to the first movement interrupts the high spirits of the finale just before the coda. But the cyclic treatment is quite thorough in the same composer's *Symphony No. 5,* Op. 64. The theme from the introduction to Movt. I is heard twice in the lyric second movement, once in the following waltz movement, and several times in the finale.

Both the *Symphonie fantastique,* Op. 14, and *Harold in Italy,* Op. 16, by Berlioz, make full use of cyclic themes. In the *Fantastique,* the cyclic theme—the **idée fixe** representing the beloved—occurs transformed in all five movements. A similar technique is used in the four movements of *Harold in Italy.* The Harold theme is played by the viola soloist and present in all movements. Identity is achieved not only through a unifying cyclic theme, but by the theme being carried by a solo instrument throughout. Cyclic structure provides additional cohesion in an aggregate work. When a program is used, oneness of concept is obviously one of the prime considerations of the composer.

Berlioz, *Harold in Italy*, Op. 16

Program

Movt. I: "Harold in the Mountains"—
            Scenes of melancholy, of happiness and joy

Movt. II: "March of the Pilgrims"—
            Chanting their evening prayer

Movt. III: "Serenade"—
            A mountaineer of the Abruzzi singing to his mistress

Movt. IV: "Orgy of the Brigands"—
            Memories of past scenes

In aggregate vocal forms, such as opera, song cycle, masses, and oratorio, unity is largely provided by the text. In ballet, the plot itself cements the various scenes and dances.

Whether it be the briefest tune or a gargantuan two-hour symphony, unity, organization, logic, balance, and organic development are part of all intelligible music. And all of this is tempered and leavened by the yeast of variety and contrast.

For further information and suggested listening on aggregate forms, both instrumental and vocal, see *Synoptic Listing of Musical Forms* (Appendix II, p. 409).

POLYPHONIC PROCEDURE

The term polyphony, as derived from the Greek, means *many voices*. Its usage, in musical terminology, denotes the combining and blending of two or more melodic lines. These lines may or may not be imitative. Voices or parts are distinguishable as separate melodies in direct proportion to the extent to which:

1. The "rhythmic diagrams" differ: this refers to both the lengths of notes and their moments of articulation.

2. The melodic contours differ.

Melody is linear and harmony is vertical. Therefore, polyphony—as a combination of melodies—is a multiple exposure of lines plus the concurrent tension and release inherent in simultaneous relationships. Polyphony is the most sophisticated of all musical procedures.

Even in homophony there is usually an attempt to keep each voice part somewhat interesting by making its melodic contour different from that of the others. These differences in melodic contour may be seen in "America the Beautiful" (Ex. 1-40, page 21) by inspection of the parts. Note particularly the bass part, beginning with the upbeat to measure 9. Beginning here, and continuing through measures 9, 10, and 11, this part assumes a greater degree of individuality through its imitation of the soprano part in measures 1, 2, and 3. But whatever differences of melodic contour there may be among the four voices, they are of minimal importance in any attempt to achieve a polyphonic style if the rhythmic articulations are simultaneous.

Applied polyphony

COUNTERPOINT. Polyphony refers to music of any age in which the linear aspect is predominant. *Counterpoint* is a more specific term that refers to the *planned setting* of one melodic line against another.

The term counterpoint is derived from the Latin **punctus contra punctum,** point against point, i.e. note against note. The common practice of counterpoint in its early stages was to set another melody, at first note-to-note, against a melody already in existence, the **cantus firmus,** the "established tune." Later, more florid melodies were set against a cantus firmus. The florid melody set above was known as the **descant.** Composers throughout the centuries have been intrigued with the idea of using a theme or melody from sacred or secular literature as a cantus firmus against which to write counterpoint.

Counterpoint, although de-emphasized during various periods of music history, has continued to the present day, achieving a new propulsion in the music of some twentieth-century composers. The styles of counterpoint have changed as the styles of music have changed. Its style is dependent on many factors. For example, the amount of dissonance and the way it is handled; the amount or kind of imitation between the parts; the melodic style, which may be vocal or instrumental, and the attendant amount of conjunct or disjunct motion and rhythmic emphasis. Thus, we may speak of sixteenth-century counterpoint and eighteenth-century counterpoint as related but different *manifestations* within the broad realm of polyphony.

NON-IMITATIVE POLYPHONY. Polyphony can be in two or more parts. Two-part music is the easiest to listen to, but in some ways the most difficult to write. Two-part writing by its very nature cannot have one voice rest for any considerable length of time. Thus, the unity and variety must be accomplished with a minimum of means.

Two-part writing also excludes any extensive use of **parallel** and **similar motion,** as this would tend to reduce the separate individuality of the two parts. The two parts may vary in their comparative importance. In simple two-part writing, one part may consist of basically long notes against which there is a more florid second part.

In the example below we see, in measures 2–4, two-part writing that is mostly note against note. The two parts maintain their identities chiefly through their differing melodic contours.

Example 2-13   *Piano Sonata*, Op. 49, No. 2, Beethoven

QUODLIBET.   *Quodlibet,* which means "as you please," is the name given to the process by which two or more melodies, often popular tunes that originally had separate existence, are made to go together. This practice goes back to early music, and has been a part of popular culture until the present day. The first example of quodlibet combines two tunes of American origin. They are put together with some slight adjustments of the original melodies.

Example 2-14   "Dixie," Emmett
                                       "Old Folks at Home," Foster

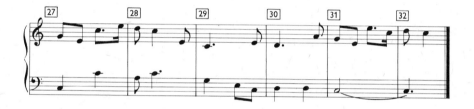

Because they are not only fun, but require some ingenuity, quodlibets are not only found in popular culture but have been explored by the master musicians as well. The more incongruous the borrowings in either tune or text, the more challenging they are. Quodlibets were one of the favorite pastimes of the Bach family through several generations of family get-togethers. Sacred and secular songs were put together, or songs with texts in different languages. Sometimes they were written out; often they were improvised. Quodlibets have found their way into more serious areas as well. Johann Sebastian Bach included a quodlibet at the end of the *Goldberg Variations*. The bass line shown is the basis of Variation 30.

Example 2-15   Bass Line of Theme

Superimposed on this is a popular song of Bach's time, "Ich bin so lang,"

Example 2-16

Ich bin so lang nicht bei dir g'west
I've been so long a-way from you

shown in the second measure in the upper part (Example 2-18), and this is joined by another popular melody, "Kraut und Rüben."

Example 2-17

Kraut   und   Rü - ben   hab - en   mich   ver - trie -   ben
Kale   and   beets   have   driv- en   me   a - way——

These two melodies constantly reappear in different voices throughout the variation.

Example 2-18   *Goldberg Variations*, Variation 30: Quodlibet, J. S. Bach

CANON.   The strictest kind of polyphonic writing is the **canon.** The term *canon* (meaning *rule*) originally was not a title specifying a certain style as does *waltz,* or a certain form as does *rondo,* but was rather an *instruction* by which one voice was to be imitated by another in some specific way. This was the *canon* for that particular piece of music. Therefore, it was necessary to write out one melody only; the other was to be supplied by the performer according to the instruction. It was later that *canon* became a generic term referring to any composition in which the basic principle is *strict* **imitation** *throughout.*

Two things must be known about how the second voice should combine with the first:

1. What note it should start on.
2. When it should start.

One of the simplest two-part canons has intrigued many composers. This is the "Alphabet Song," also known as "Twinkle, Twinkle, Little Star."

Example 2-19   "The Alphabet Song"

If the melody only is given, with the instructions "at the unison," and "with a time-lapse of one measure" the realization will sound as shown below.

Example 2-20   Canon: "The Alphabet Song"

THE ROUND. The simplest kind of canon is the **round**, in which each voice continually returns to the beginning immediately upon the completion of the tune. The round consists of one melody only, but beginning the melody again in other voices sets the melody against itself, creating counterpoint. A round may be in two, three, or four parts, or sometimes more. Most readers of this text have sung "Three Blind Mice" or "Row, Row, Row Your Boat." "Frère Jacques" is another of the best known rounds. Since this is a simple round, each voice entrance is on the same note, middle *C*. The entrances in this case are spoken of as being "at the unison." After the initial start of the tune, the other entrances are successively two measures later. Thus, the entrances are spoken of as being "at a distance of two measures." So, in speaking of this particular round, we say in sum that the entrances are "at the unison at a distance of two measures." The second entry of a round

Example 2-21 "Frère Jacques," French Round

could also begin upon a different tone, such as a fifth above the original entry of the subject. This entry would then be spoken of as "at the fifth."

A round is an *infinite canon* (or *perpetual canon*) because it may go on and on, its close coming about only through the arbitrary decision to allow each voice to drop out in succession, or to come to a stop at some predetermined point wherever the individual voices may be. The process is circular.

A *finite canon* does not return to the beginning but continues on until it is desired to close, in which case the imitation must be broken, the voices concluding in free counterpoint. The process is linear.

THE FUGUE. The *fugue* cannot be considered as a form in the same way that we have defined the structures above. It and many other strictly contrapuntal works are better considered as *procedures.* Such works do not lend themselves easily to analysis in parts or sections. In true formal structures, identification and structural definition come through the balance of parts and sections. For example, a recapitulation section has meaning only in relation to the antecedent exposition that came before. And again, a refrain cannot be a refrain with its own peculiar emotional impact without its antecedent episode or episodes.

A study of form in the purest sense then involves various *horizontal* arrangements of segments, large or small, which make sense only through their relationships with one another.

The process of fugue

The Latin term *fuga,* meaning *flight,* was in use in the sixteenth century in connection with canonic writing. The idea of one voice fleeing from the other is more aptly stated as one voice being the leader and the imitating voice being the follower.

The *fugue* when spoken of today refers to the development that reached its peak in the writings of Johann Sebastian Bach. The fugue differs from the canon in certain important aspects. It is not confined to strict imitation, but rather uses imitation as a "springboard" into areas in which there is a freer "transliteration" of the melodic materials than strict imitation would allow.

THE SUBJECT. The chief characteristic of the fugue is that it "grows" out of one theme called the **subject,** which is of moderate length. The subject may be somewhat shorter or longer than those in the following example, but there are two requirements:

1. It must be long enough to be distinctive as a theme.

2. It must not be so long as to be diffuse.

This single theme becomes the "material" for the entire fugue.

Example 2-22

a. The *Well-Tempered Clavier*, Book I, Fugue 6, J. S. Bach
b. The *Well-Tempered Clavier*, Book II, Fugue 18, J. S. Bach
c. *Messiah*, No. 28, Handel
d. *Requiem*, K. 626, No. 1, **SP m. 49,** "Kyrie," Mozart, p. 371

(a) Subject

The fugue retains one of the basic characteristics of contrapuntal writing, the "overlapping of melodies." A melodic cadence in a single voice does not result in a "cadential feeling," since the melody in another voice is already on its way. In a fugue there are three important areas of interest: *fugue exposition, working-out area,* and *closure.*

Fugue exposition.   In the exposition, the subject is presented at least once in all voices. There is tonic-dominant emphasis.

Working-out area.   The second important area consists of the working out of melodic materials, using various contrapuntal techniques, and exploration of other keys. The working-out area may be any length.

Closure.   In the closure, one voice returns to the subject in the home key; others may follow. There may be homophonic emphasis near the close, and there are one or more cadences in the home key.

STRETTO.   Our English word *strait* has the same origin as the Italian term *stretto,* meaning *narrow* or *tight.* Stretto refers to various entries of the subject in such a short space of time that one statement of the subject is not complete before the next entry is begun. The subject may appear intact or it may be shortened or changed. Stretto creates excitement and tension and thickens the texture. The composer may use stretto anywhere in a work, but because of its inherent dynamism it often occurs in the last half of the fugue. This may be seen in **SP m. 82–85,** p. 376.

CHAPTER 3

Voices, Instruments, and Performance

THE FASCINATION WITH sound itself has beguiled the child in all of us throughout the ages. The wooden whistle made from the tree branch may have been our first introduction to the delight in sound itself— initially without melody, without form. The tinkle of a bell, even the sound of a locomotive in the otherwise quiet night, evokes a memory, dimly felt but enchanting in its resurgence.

By the use of instruments and voices the composer draws upon these sounds in their simplicity and in their sophistication to create in us a new awareness of things as they are or might be—to awaken us to new experiences. Even the electronic composer has not totally abandoned sounds which are imitative of the more natural sounds with which we are acquainted.

How do we designate the various instruments that have served for so long? How do we speak of the differences of tone quality between one singer and the next? How do we fathom the limitless blending of these instruments and voices? And what of the performance experience itself?

VOICES

Singing is a natural and pleasant experience to almost everybody. When music suddenly rises to the surface of our consciousness, nudged there perhaps by a beautiful spring day, we want to sing. Undoubtedly if we carried

49

a flute at that moment and could play it, we would. But for most of us, singing is the most natural and accessible way of making music, and by association, understanding it.

As soon as we can, we repeat nursery songs. At school, one of our first musical experiences is with song. Later on we sing at school gatherings, at rallies, at church, or with a community chorus. We can enjoy singing—on an unsophisticated level, to be sure—without the slightest technical training.

Even at a very sophisticated level of instrumental performance, the concept of song is not far away. The critics speak of a pianist's "singing tone," or we hear of "the eloquent voice" of the cello. And for the very reason that words are usually present, vocal music is easily assimilated. Indeed, we often think of a song in terms of its text, or its textual meaning, rather than its melody or harmony. In short, we easily relate to vocal music because of the words with specific or symbolic meaning. Singing is a natural, familiar way for us to express ourselves. In it are combined the directness and universality of the spoken word and the sensuous appeal of tones produced by the human voice. Thus, the voice rightly has been chosen by the masters as the appropriate medium for some of their most important musical creations.

Voice types

Men's voices differ from those of women primarily in pitch register. The female's total register is one octave higher than that of the male. When a mixed group sings a melody together at a public gathering, the melody is not at the same pitch level, but at the distance of one octave.

Beyond this basic division, men's and women's voices are divided further into voice types corresponding to high, middle, and low *pitch* registers. Thus, for the basic female voices we have, from high to low: *soprano, mezzo soprano,* and *contralto (alto).* For the basic male voices: *tenor, baritone,* and *bass.*

Example 3-1

In mixed *choral music*—most often scored in four parts, soprano, alto, tenor, and bass (SATB) —parts are not often written for middle-range voices

—mezzo soprano and baritone. Thus, if a baritone possesses an exceptionally high range, he may join the tenor section as a second tenor or the bass section as a first bass. In exactly the same way, the mezzo soprano must match her voice either with the altos or sopranos, depending on her range.

In certain vocal forms revolving around several solo parts, middle-range voices are often fully represented with parts written especially for them. For example, Verdi, in his last opera, *Falstaff,* assigned the leading solo parts to voices exactly corresponding to the six mentioned before. The parts are:

Sir John Falstaff, a rotund knight	baritone
Bardolph ⎱ retainers of	tenor
Pistol ⎰ Falstaff	bass
Ford, a wealthy burgher	baritone
Alice Ford, his wife	soprano
Ann Ford, their daughter	soprano
Fenton, Ann's suitor	tenor
Dr. Caius, another suitor	tenor
Mistress Page, a neighbor of the Fords	mezzo soprano
Dame Quickly, servant of Dr. Caius	contralto

THE SOPRANO VOICE. ***Coloratura soprano.*** This is the highest and most agile of the soprano voices. A fine coloratura will negotiate precarious leaps, dizzying high notes, and cascading scales with ease.

Though the music for this voice can be dramatic as in the "Queen of the Night" aria from Mozart's opera *The Magic Flute,* it most often is light, as in this example from Gounod's opera *Romeo and Juliet.*

Example 3-2   *Romeo and Juliet,* Act I, Gounod

It should be remembered that although music for coloratura soprano often emphasizes *virtuosity* and vocal gymnastics, it also can be very melodic and lyric. Also, the term *coloratura* is applied to any voice type when it engages in highly figurative, cadenza-like music.

Suggested Listening: Lucy's "Hello Aria" from Menotti's comic opera *The Telephone.*

A scene from the 1967 Opera Company of Boston production of Verdi's *Falstaff* (*Friedman-Abeles Photographers, Inc., New York*).

Lyric soprano. The *lyric soprano,* as the name suggests, is assigned song-like, sustained melodies. Most of the female leading parts in French and Italian romantic opera are sung by lyric sopranos: Marguerite in Gounod's *Faust;* Violetta in Verdi's *La Traviata;* Mimi in Puccini's *La Bohème.* Just as the coloratura soprano has its lyric moments, so the lyric soprano is called upon often to perform scintillating **runs** and **trills,** and to reach dazzling high notes.

One of the finest lyric soprano parts in opera is that of Violetta in Verdi's *La Traviata.*

Dramatic soprano. A *dramatic soprano* sings in approximately the same register as does the lyric soprano. Like the lyric, she must often sing in an intimate, sustained manner as can be heard in the love song from Act I of Puccini's opera, *Tosca.* But for the most part, and especially in German romantic opera, she must sing with great **volume** of tone and dramatic intensity for long periods of time. Operas using dramatic voices ordinarily feature very large orchestras, sometimes totaling over 100 players, and a dramatic soprano must project all the resonance at her command. Beyond the enormous vocal challenges occurring on almost every page of the score, a full, rich orchestra swells with throbbing sound around the vocal part.

Suggested Listening: The part of Isolde in the opera *Tristan und Isolde* by Richard Wagner.

Boy soprano. Though the *boy soprano* can attain most of the pitches in the female lyric soprano register, the quality of this voice is quite different. It lacks the voluptuous quality often heard in the female soprano. When well trained, it is remarkable for its purity of sound and has little of the **vibrato** often heard in the lyric soprano.

Suggested Listening: The part of the boy in Menotti's *Amahl and the Night Visitors.*

The **castrato,** or male soprano voice, was very popular in seventeenth- and eighteenth-century opera. It was used in church choirs as well as on the operatic stage. Castrati were adult eunuchs who combined the register of the boy soprano voice with the power of the tenor. For obvious reasons, they are not used in our time.

Operatic roles originally done by castrati, such as Idamantes in Mozart's *Idomeneo* and Orpheus in the opera *Orpheus and Eurydice,* are done by a mezzo soprano in modern productions.

The mezzo soprano.   As mentioned before, parts for this middle-register voice are seldom found in music for chorus. But solo mezzo soprano parts in opera abound. As is the case with the baritone voice, however, *leading roles* do not often come its way. Well known exceptions are the flaming roles of Carmen in the opera by Bizet and Delilah in Saint-Saëns's opera *Samson and Delilah.*

Example 3-3   *Carmen*, Act I, Bizet

Suggested Listening: The part of Octavian in Richard Strauss' opera *Der Rosenkavalier.*

Lyric tenor.   The *lyric tenor,* like the lyric soprano, is assigned many of the loveliest melodies in opera and operetta, and often gets top billing. Operatic heroes and lovers are traditionally tenors, while baritones and basses are often cast as villains, fathers, and uncles.

Suggested Listening: The part of Romeo in the opera *Romeo and Juliet,* by Gounod.

Tenore robusto or heldentenor.   Both the terms *tenore robusto* and *heldentenor* refer to the dramatic tenor, whose role in opera is precisely like that of the dramatic soprano.

Suggested Listening: The role of Florestan in the opera *Fidelio,* by Beethoven; the role of Radames in the opera *Aida,* by Verdi.

THE BARITONE VOICE.   Though in opera and elsewhere the leading male role does not often come his way, the well trained *baritone* does have certain advantages. For one, his highest notes often have a brilliance and carrying power close to that of the tenor. On the other hand, the voice tends to have a rich, dark cast usually associated with basses.

When the baritone voice has a pronounced dark cast and approaches the register of the bass, it is then called *bass-baritone.*

Suggested Listening: The part of John the Baptist in the opera *Salome,* by Richard Strauss.

THE BASS VOICE.   The *bass voice* in choral music anchors the total sound. Though it often sallies forth with a melody of its own, especially in contrapuntal music, much of the time it provides a tonal cushion upon which the upper voices depend.

The solo bass, however, is much used in vocal forms and is almost as diversified in tone quality and use as is its opposite member, the soprano. In addition to the quasi-bass, officially called *bass-baritone,* mentioned above, the *lyric bass (basso cantante)* and the *comic bass (basso buffo)* find ample representation in the operatic repertory. These last two voices differ not so much in tone color and in range but in style of performance. The *buffo* emphasizes acting and character portrayal, sometimes to the marked detriment of beauty of vocal sound, while the lyric bass cultivates a singing style where beauty of voice is as important as it is with the lyric soprano or lyric tenor. This example shows a bass melody to be sung in *buffo style.*

Example 3-4   *The Barber of Seville,* Act I, Rossini

Below is a bass melody in the *cantante* style.

Example 3-5   *Don Giovanni*, Act II, Mozart

(Don Giovanni)
Allegretto

Deh   vie - ni al - la   fi - ne - stra,   O mio_____ te -

so - ro,   deh   vie - ni_a con - so - lar   il   pian- to mi - - o.

The ***basso profundo*** is a bass with an unusually low range. An occasional chorus exists where the true basso profundo will be heard underlying the already dark sound of the other basses. Russian choruses often boast many extremely low basses who are able to plumb the depths with ease, thus lending extraordinary solidity and majesty to the choral sound. This subterranean voice is called ***contrabass.***

Suggested Listening: Basso cantante: the part of Mephistopheles in the opera *Mefistofele,* by Boito; Basso buffo: the part of Baron Ochs in the opera *Der Rosenkavalier,* by Richard Strauss.

It should be remembered that all of the various voice registers discussed above are normal-trained, or normal-untrained. Exceptions are often encountered. The tenor Caruso could sing strong low notes ranging down through the baritone register. An exceptionally low chorus alto will sometimes be found who is able to sing all the tenor pitches as well as the ones usual to her voice type.

Vocal performance media

Before advancing to a description of the various physical combinations of voices with one another and with instruments, it is important to distinguish early and clearly between ***vocal performance media*** and vocal forms.

Vocal forms are the various structural patterns inherent in the music to be sung; they exemplify how the music is organized without regard to how many or what kind of voices are involved. (See Chapter 2.) Performance media are the various physical singing forces required to produce music written in these forms.

Thus, the *lied* as a form is a song sometimes cast in a strophic pattern but just as often through composed, using a German text usually of high poetical order. The performance medium used is the solo voice, of any pitch register, sustained by a piano accompaniment. But while the performance medium may change, as when Richard Strauss writes solo *lieder* with orchestra instead of piano, the basic formal structure of the music itself remains.

Vocal forms refer to musical ideas and patterns, vocal performance media to how many and what type voices are used. This distinction applies as well to the instrumental performance media discussed below.

THE CHORUS.   The term *chorus* as understood in the broadest possible sense simply means a body of people singing together. These may be few or many—male, female, or both—divided into parts or singing in unison, accompanied by instruments or not, articulating a text or humming, and singing any kind of music in almost any setting.

In practice, however, choruses are classified and named according to their size, their social function, the kind of literature sung, and other characteristics. These important variations will be discussed after certain basic facts applying to them all are discussed.

Choral music is ordinarily divided into parts corresponding to voice types covering the highs, middles, and lows of music. The most common division is in four parts: soprano, alto, tenor, bass. A chorus thus constituted is called a *mixed chorus,* and the letter symbols used to describe it are SATB.

VARIOUS CHORAL GROUPS.   A *choir* is a chorus that is attached to a church or chapel. Though the normal church choir necessarily is of chamber chorus proportions, it is sometimes large. Also, though its repertoire will be primarily sacred choral music for performance at religious services, it will occasionally include secular music at special concerts or on tour. Church choirs ordinarily are peopled by non-professionals, but the largest church choirs, ordinarily found in large urban areas, will sometimes consist of professional singers.

Secular choruses vary greatly in type and function. They will run the gamut from the polished, disciplined, professional groups heard constantly on radio, on television, and in concert to the informal groups in colleges devoted to the cultivation of student songs.

The *community chorus,* depending on its locale, resources, and the ambition of its members, will vary in quality and number. Some will thrive on slight musical fare, while others each season will mount several magnificent performances of the greatest masterworks with full symphony orchestra.

The term *glee club* usually applies to a collegiate chorus, female, male, or mixed. But such is the interest in choral music at many colleges and universities that several choral groups may flourish simultaneously. There may be a large chorus, a chamber chorus, a men's chorale, a chapel choir, madrigal singers, and other groups. Some of these become so refined and competent that they sing and record with the finest symphony orchestras, tour periodically, sometimes on an international scale, and generally reach a high level of choral art.

Most of the kinds of choral groups mentioned above are rehearsed and directed by a conductor. Whether this person is a professor of music who leads the college glee club after teaching hours, the **chorus master** permanently attached to an opera house, or simply the best musician of the group who dares to stand up and lead, his role is vital—especially if the chorus is a good one. He must rehearse adequately for performances, choose repertoire, draw good overall tone quality from the group, monitor enunciation and pronunciation of words—often in foreign languages—and generally spark the group to produce effective and imaginative performances. Occasionally he will also need to direct a symphony orchestra or other instrumental group along with his chorus.

SMALL VOCAL ENSEMBLES.   Ensembles, with but one voice to a part, are named according to the number of voices involved. Thus, the Brahms *Liebeslieder Waltzes,* for four solo voices (SATB) with piano duet, are written for what is called an accompanied **vocal quartet.** The medium here is chamber ensemble. But while the repertory for such chamber groups is fairly wide, vocal ensembles are more often encountered as a part of other massed vocal media.

Solo ensembles abound in opera, where the several principals join voices in every possible combination. Typical of this is the melodramatic **trio** (STB) heard in the last moments of Gounod's opera *Faust.*

Solo ensembles joining large choruses in the performance of oratorios, cantatas, and other vocal forms are rather conservatively constituted. The usual grouping is in **mixed quartet** (SATB) with the small ensemble sometimes set in dramatic opposition to the massed chorus, and at other times blending in with the whole.

THE SOLO VOICE.   As a performance medium, the solo voice is universally used in combination with a great variety of instruments and in the realization of many musical forms. To name but a few, the solo voice is heard in opera and related forms, sacred and secular choral music, the symphony, with instrumental chamber music, and in the smaller song forms often accompanied by the piano, but also by other instruments and instrumental ensembles.

One of the most rewarding of these forms is the German art song, or *lied,* with piano. Contrary to the view of some, this is really a chamber ensemble and rightly can be considered a duet. As developed by the master German composers of *lieder,* Beethoven, Schubert, Mendelssohn, Schumann, Brahms, Wolf, Strauss, and Mahler, the *lied* as a medium allots as much importance to the materials in the piano part as to those in the voice part. The poems used are generally of a high order. Art songs as developed in several countries are ordinarily heard in solo *vocal recitals,* but may crop up elsewhere.

INSTRUMENTS

The composer, in addition to utilizing the structural elements of music —melody, harmony, and rhythm—is acutely aware of the unique sound of each instrument. Each sound, alone, or in combination with other instruments, can be used to enhance, emphasize, or accent line or texture, or to add spice and variety.

Tone color, or *timbre,* is the quality of sound of an instrument that distinguishes it from any other. Most readers are familiar with the fact that a tuba, which is large, sounds lower than a trumpet, which is small. "Large" and "small," however, are general terms and more specifically include reference to two dimensions: the length and width of the bore. The tuba sounds lower than the trumpet only because its tubing is longer. Its bore is wider, but this affects quality of sound, not pitch.

Tone color is also dependent upon the materials from which the instrument is made, and upon the manner in which the sound is produced, whether by blowing, scraping, striking or plucking.

Ranges

The *range* of an instrument refers to the total number of pitches capable of being produced on that instrument, from the lowest pitch to the highest.

Four basic families of instruments

All musical instruments belong to one of four families: *strings, woodwinds, brass,* or *percussion.* Although there have been more scientific descriptions of instruments, the professional musician—composer, conductor, orchestrator, or instrumentalist—uses this terminology.

violin   viola

double bass   cello

THE STRINGS. In the string family are the violin, viola, cello, and double bass. The tone on each of these instruments is produced by a bow drawn across a taut string. The body of the instrument acts as a resonator and an amplifier. Stringed instruments on which the tone is produced in a different manner—such as the piano, harpsichord, and harp—will be treated separately.

The violin. Because of its extensive range in the upper register, its facility, and its expressiveness, the *violin* may be found in the hands of a Gypsy violinist pouring forth a sentimental melody in a dimly lit cafe, at a country dance playing a spirited jig, in the concert hall as the leading member of a string quartet or symphony orchestra, and in the hands of a great violin soloist.

The violin is held under the chin with the left hand. The right hand holds the bow. The tone of the violin has been described as similar to the human voice. This is a poor comparison. The tone of the violin lacks the basic distinction of the human voice, which is that its sound is the result of a column of air that comes from the lungs of the performer and passes through the vocal cords, setting them in vibration. This method of producing tone is similar to the manner in which the wind player produces tone. The brass player's lips are the "vocal cords." The similarity of vocal tone to that of a wind instrument is well understood by the composer. Examples in the sections on brass and winds will demonstrate this.

It is better to describe the violin as the stringed instrument that it is. No stringed instrument by itself can have the power of the voice or a wind instrument. Instead of power, however, the violin has in its upper range a steely intensity, and in its middle range an insinuating lyricism. In its low range it can be dark, vibrant, and sensuous.

Suggested Listening: Stravinsky, *Firebird Suite* (1919 ed.) , beginning measure 7 of "L'oiseau de feu et sa dance."

The viola. The *viola* has all the appearances of the violin, and is also held under the chin, but it is a slightly larger instrument and it is pitched lower. It is the alto to the violin's soprano, and indeed, *alto* is the French name for the instrument. It has a darker and slightly more full-bodied sound than the violin, and just slightly less flexibility because the distances on the fingerboard from one tone to another are a fraction larger.

The composer not only uses the viola to fill out the middle register of the string section, but, aware of its expressivity and its uniquely introspective tone color, writes for it passages that portray a somber mood or a dark in-

tensity. Sometimes the portrayal suggests a yearning, or possibly an intro-
verted emotional turbulence.

Listen to the enchanting sound of the viola section in the opening bars
of Tchaikovsky's *Sixth Symphony*. The violas enter in the fourth measure.

Example 3-6   *Symphony No 6*, Movt. I, Tchaikovsky

The viola is a regular member of the string quartet and plays a prominent part in much chamber music. Its solo repertoire is not extensive.

The cello. *Violoncello* is the full name of this instrument, but the
shortened version, *cello,* is more often used. Because of its size it stands on
the floor, using an extended end pin, and is held between the player's knees.
This instrument has strings that are not only thicker than those of the viola,
but twice as long. The cello is pitched an octave lower than the viola, and in
its middle and upper range has a rich tenor sound that can be full and
soaring. In its low range, it can be dark or warm as the composer requires.
It can be quietly lyric, or it can give an effect of throbbing.

In addition to its use in the symphony orchestra, the cello is the lowest
member of the string quartet. The solo repertoire for this instrument is
considerable.

Suggested Listening: Dvorak, *Cello Concerto in B Minor.*

The contrabass. The *contrabass* is the largest instrument of the string
family and the lowest-pitched. It is also called the ***double bass*** because it
originally doubled with the cello on the bass line in the orchestras of the
baroque and classical periods.

This instrument stands on the floor as does the cello, but, because of its
size, the player stands or may sit on a high stool. With a deep, sometimes
"gruff" sound because of the length and thickness of its strings, the contrabass is pitched nearly an octave below the cello.

"The Violinist," charcoal drawing by **Degas** (*Courtesy, Museum of Fine Arts, Boston*).

The contrabass differs in certain aspects from the other instruments of the string section. On close inspection it will be noted that its shoulders are more sloping, and its back is flatter. These differing aspects are the result of its descent from the viol family. For this reason the contrabass is still called the **bass viol.** But there are some contrabasses that have incorporated the features of the violin family, not retaining the differences we have mentioned. The contrabass of the symphony orchestra today has an additional fifth string that extends the range of the instrument.

The contrabass is a standard member of the jazz orchestra, having replaced the tuba in the earlier part of the century, and is frequently referred to as the **bass fiddle,** the **string bass,** or simply the **bass.** Its function in jazz is chiefly that of a rhythm instrument, and the manner of playing is usually that of pizzicato, although the bow is used to supply the foundation of the harmony in less rhythmic passages. In the jazz orchestra, the double bass has had a fifth string added to the usual four, but it is a string pitched higher than the other four, rather than lower.

THE WOODWINDS.   The term *woodwinds,* as a classifying name, was first used to differentiate wind instruments made of wood from those made of brass. This was not the only differentiating feature, but it did serve to classify, and it is still in use, in spite of the fact that some of the woodwinds are now made of metal.

Because of some basic differences in construction of woodwind instruments, the woodwind section of the orchestra has many more possibilities for variety of tone color than either the string section or the brass section. Note, for instance, that string instruments are basically the same in their proportions, materials, and manner of construction; they differ chiefly in size. The string section thus presents the most homogeneous sound of any section of the orchestra. The brass instruments, in spite of important differences in their bore measurements, are also reasonably similar in their proportions, materials, and manner of construction. The brass section sound is fairly homogeneous. By contrast, the instruments of the woodwind section are not "all of the same cloth," or even nearly so.

The flute.   Originally of wood, the *flute* often is made of silver, and occasionally of platinum or gold. The instrument is held horizontally to the player's right; the tone is produced by blowing across an open tone-hole in somewhat the same manner as one blows across the open top of a bottle to produce a tone.

With the exception of the piccolo, the flute is the highest-pitched of the woodwinds and the most agile. The flutist can execute long lyrical passages, as well as ones of extreme technical complexity. The tone, acoustically,

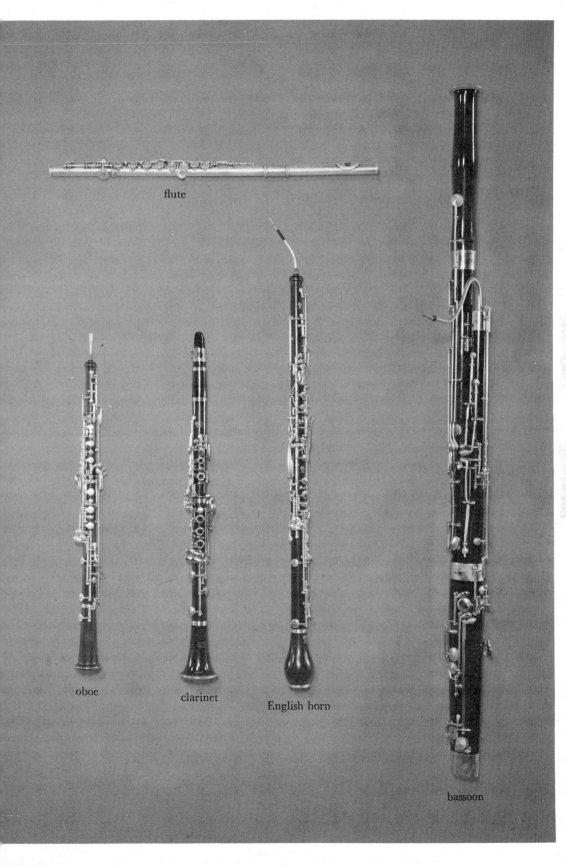

flute

oboe

clarinet

English horn

bassoon

is the "purest" of the woodwinds because so few of the overtones are present in it. As it is the only instrument of the woodwind section that does not use a reed to set the air column in vibration, its tone has more of the quality of "wind" in it than the other woodwinds. Because it is not a reed instrument, its tone is the least insistent of all the woodwinds. In its middle register the flute's quality of tone may be suggestive of calmness or pensiveness. Through association with the shepherd's pipe, it sometimes suggests scenes of a pastoral nature. In its upper register the tone of the flute becomes brighter, and in staccato passages, more bell-like. Aware of the flute's similarity to the human soprano voice in its middle and high registers, composers have often used the flute in duet style with the coloratura in florid operatic writing.

Suggested Listening: Donizetti, "Mad Scene," *Lucia di Lammermoor,* for soprano and flute.

In its low range its tone has a quiet breathiness that can suggest an air of intimacy.

In addition to its use in the symphony orchestra, the flute is also a regular member of the concert band. In recent years it has become popular with jazz performers. This has been made possible with the aid of the microphone, whereas formerly the flute could not compete with the instruments of greater volume.

The piccolo. *Piccolo* is but the short terminology for *flauto piccolo.* The term "piccolo" by itself only means "little." This *petite flute,* as the French speak of it, is pitched an octave higher than the flute and adds not only range but brilliance to the upper register of the woodwind section. Its tone is much brighter than that of the flute and also much more penetrating. It is used in its middle and upper ranges to add sparkle to the orchestration. The tone of its middle range is somewhat comparable to a person's whistle, which is indeed in the same register. In the upper range the tone may be described as shrill or even piercing. The composer uses this range with caution.

In the final pages of his opera *Salome,* Richard Strauss has made interesting use of the piccolo. As Salome carries the silver tray that holds the severed head of John the Baptist, she is about to sing, "I have kissed your lips, Jokanaan." The example shows the piccolo in octaves with the oboe in a figure that is played seven more times at varying time intervals, over trills and tremolos and generally shimmering orchestration. The effect is one of the most eerie in music.

Example 3-7   *Salome*, Strauss

In the concert band the piccolo is used much more often than in the orchestra. In marches the piccolo often plays an ***obbligato*** high above the melody. Well known to many listeners is the piccolo obbligato in the trio section of Sousa's "Stars and Stripes Forever." In the interests of showmanship it is now traditional for the members of the flute section to stand as they play this piccolo obbligato.

The recorder. The ***recorder*** is a woodwind instrument that was in common use from the sixteenth century to the eighteenth. It was finally superseded by the flute for the same reason that certain other instruments lost favor; the flute had a more powerful tone. The recorder is end blown, and has a beaked wooden mouthpiece that fits between the lips in the manner of an ordinary wooden whistle. Its tone is unusually pure and is even more mellow and "hollow" than that of the flute.

To J. S. Bach "flute" meant recorder; when he wished to use the flute that we know today he wrote "flauto traverso." There were several sizes of recorder making up a family, or consort; the most usual sizes were the descant, treble, tenor, and bass. The recorder has been revived in recent years for the proper performance of baroque music, and also as a beginning instrument for children or adults.

The oboe. The double reed of the *oboe* imparts a tone quality to the instrument that is easily recognizable. Sometimes spoken of as nasal, its tone quality can perhaps be better described as reedy and quietly penetrating, as opposed to the clarinet tone, which is more bland. It often alternates with the clarinet in assuming the role of the soprano in the woodwind section, especially in a lyric, cantabile melody. There are many examples of its use as a solo instrument. This well known example by Tchaikovsky shows the abil-

Example 3-8   *Swan Lake Ballet*, Scene I, Tchaikovsky

ity of the oboe to sustain an expressive legato line of quiet intensity in its middle range.

Suggested Listening: Brahms, *Symphony No. 1*, Movt. II.

The oboe tone becomes thinner as it proceeds into the high range and its singing quality becomes less effective, but composers use the high range for special effects.

The oboe has no tuning slide as does a brass instrument, nor has it a mouthpiece that may be adjusted to lengthen the instrument as do the clarinet and flute. Thus the pitch is somewhat fixed, and the orchestra tunes to the oboe.

The English horn. The **English horn** is a double-reed instrument pitched a perfect fifth below the oboe. Larger and longer than the oboe, it is an alto instrument. In addition to its extra length, it may be distinguished from the oboe by the slight curve at its upper end and the globe-shaped bell at the lower. Its sound is darker and fuller than that of the oboe and has a husky plaintiveness that is unique. At times it may sound melancholy, and on occasion, quietly raucous. Broad lyric lines become it. Rarely is it used in passages of a highly technical nature (as are the oboe and the bassoon), being favored by the composer for its interesting tone color.

Suggested Listening: Berlioz, *Symphonie fantastique,* Movt. III ("Scene in the Country").

The clarinet. Not only is the **clarinet** one of the most agile of instruments, but also, in its nearly four octaves, it has the greatest range of all the woodwinds. It also has the largest dynamic range of the woodwinds, varying from the lightest whisper to an impressive forte.

Brought into general use in the symphony orchestra by Mozart in his *"Paris" Symphony,* No. 31, the clarinet remained there as a favored instrument of many composers, chiefly because of the wide variety of tone color of which it is capable. It can produce a wild shriek in its upper range. It can sound hollow or other-worldly in its lower, *chalumeau* register. In its middle range, it can be lyrical and warm, or dry and light. And it can be bland as no other instrument can.

Example 3-9   *Romeo and Juliet*, Tchaikovsky

Suggested Listening: R. Strauss, *Till Eulenspiegel.*

The clarinet is most commonly pitched in B-flat, but there is also the clarinet in A, pitched a semitone lower. Both instruments are standard equipment for the clarinetist in a symphony orchestra.

The clarinet has had wide use in the playing of folk music and dance music in many countries. It has been used in orchestras in the United States ever since the Civil War, when it was borrowed from the marching bands of the day ultimately to become a standard instrument in the early jazz bands. Its use continues to the present day in dance orchestras and theater orchestras, where it is considered a "natural double" for the saxophonist. However, its use in the jazz orchestra has lately decreased.

The B-flat clarinet is a leading member of the concert band, the clarinet section equating in a general way with the violin section of the symphony orchestra.

The E-flat clarinet. A shorter and higher-pitched instrument than the B-flat clarinet, the **E-flat clarinet** extends the upward range of the clarinet section. This instrument has a tone that may be described as thinner and shriller than that of the B-flat clarinet. It is also somewhat more difficult to play in tune. At its worst it is strident; at its best brilliant.

The bass clarinet. The **bass clarinet** is a fairly recent addition to the woodwinds, not coming into general usage until the second half of the nineteenth century. Sounding an octave below the B-flat clarinet, it is curved both at the upper end and at the lower end, with the lower curve turning upward into a bell shape. In its middle and lower range it has a tone color that may be described as "broad, but gentle."

Without the bite and the reediness of the bassoon, its volume is about the same. Therefore its tone can be easily covered by more sonorous instruments. The composer uses it often in exposed passages, in addition to having it supply the bass for quiet woodwind or string writing. In the upper part of the range, the tone of the bass clarinet "thins out." Its upper range is therefore used somewhat sparingly.

The bassoon. Music for the **bassoon** is written in the bass and tenor staves. In rare instances the treble staff is used.

It may be noted that its name in German, *Fagotte,* or Italian, *fagotto,* is equivalent to the English word "fagot," which means several sticks bound together. This was the "look" of the instrument in the earlier stages of its development when the workmanship was less refined. Now, although it retains its original shape, it is a sleek instrument made of maple, with a dark cherry finish brought to a high luster.

The English name, *bassoon,* only refers to the fact that it is a bass instrument. With a range of three octaves or more and a surprising agility for a low-pitched instrument, the bassoon has many uses in the orchestra. In addition to providing the bass to the woodwind section, it is an excellent solo instrument with an expressive, individual sound. Its double reed gives its tone an edge, but it is a tone less penetrating than that of the oboe, its counterpart in the higher range.

In the orchestra of classical dimensions, it often doubles the cello or double-bass part, adding piquancy and verve to a fast-moving line. In its upper range it has a thinner, drier sound that has been used by Stravinsky with remarkable effect in the opening measures of *Le Sacre du Printemps.*

The contrabassoon. Also known as the **double bassoon,** the **contrábassoon** is pitched one octave lower than the bassoon, and it is used by composers to achieve a depth not possible with any other instrument of the orchestra. Its lowest note is but a semitone above the lowest note on the piano, and when the instrument is played in its lowest range, the tone may almost be said to resemble a "rattle." Its use in the symphony orchestra is occasional, although it was used by Haydn in *The Creation* and by Beethoven in his *Fifth* and *Ninth Symphonies.*

The saxophone. The **saxophone** is one of the few instruments that was invented as a complete family covering the registers from soprano to bass. The complete family is still in use today. It is a hybrid instrument. Made of brass, it has a mouthpiece and a single reed like those of the clarinet.

Invented by Adolphe Sax and patented by him in France in 1846, the saxophone did not gain acceptance into the symphony orchestra until the late 1800's, and since then its use has been somewhat sporadic. Richard Strauss introduced a quartet of saxophones into his *Domestic Symphony,* and Ravel wrote for three in his *Bolero.*

Suggested Listening: Debussy, *Rhapsodie for Saxophone and Orchestra.*

The chief use of the saxophone has been in American popular music and jazz. In the early 1900's it found its way into dance bands and jazz bands, and since then it has become the basic section of the large jazz orchestra, supplying the fundamental body of sound as the strings do for the symphonic orchestra. The alto saxophone, the tenor, and to a lesser extent, the baritone, have been the instruments of some of the finest jazz soloists.

Suggested Listening: Recordings by Coleman Hawkins, Charlie Parker, Gerry Mulligan, Stan Getz, and John Coltrane.

The soprano saxophone, pitched in B-flat, has made sporadic appearances as a jazz solo instrument, and has recently been in the spotlight again. The bass saxophone is rarely seen.

THE BRASS. The instruments of the *brass* family include the trumpet, the French horn, the trombone, and the tuba. The symphony orchestra carries a minimum of three trumpets, four French horns, three trombones, and

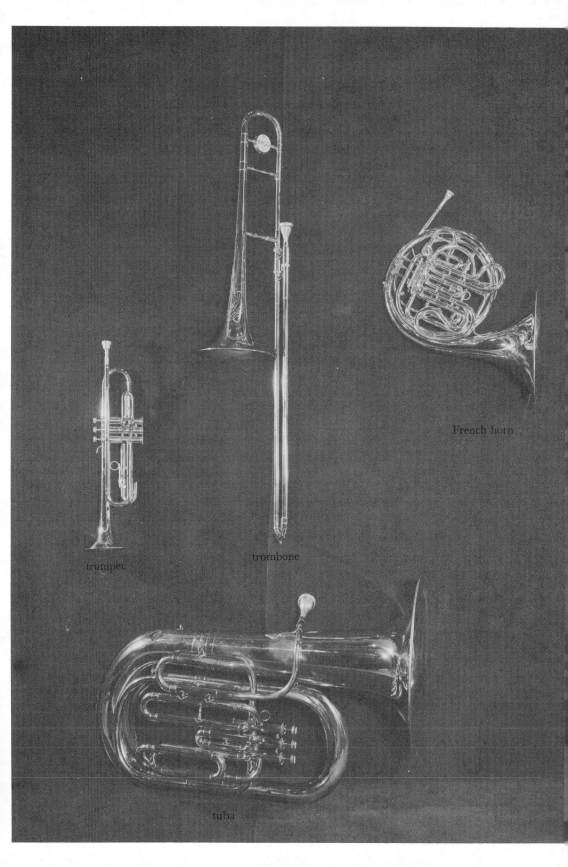

trumpet

trombone

French horn

tuba

one tuba. This is the most sonorous section of the orchestra. Individually and as a section these instruments can produce the greatest volume of sustained sound. In sustained, *tutti* passages the brass dominate.

Listen to the opening measures of the overture to *Die Meistersinger* and look at the first page of the full orchestral score. Notice the predominance of the brass sound in spite of the fact that these instruments are, in number, only 11 out of the entire orchestra.

The sound on all brass instruments is produced by a column of air set in motion. The air from the player's lungs causes the lips to vibrate. The lips control the pitch. The positioning of the player's lips on the mouthpiece is called *embouchure*. Special effects that can be obtained with different degrees of effectiveness on the various brass instruments include *double tonguing, triple tonguing,* and the *flutter tongue.*

Many mutes have been invented for the brass instruments, but there is only one that has become standard in the symphony orchestra. Made of metal or fibre, it is cone-shaped and is known as a *straight mute.* When the part specifies mute, it is understood that the reference is to the straight mute. The mute is fitted into the bell of the instrument, and not only softens the tone but changes its color completely so that it no longer has the basic sound of a brass instrument. The tone changes to one with an edge to it, more similar to the tone of a double-reed instrument. For example, the tone of the trumpet is changed in volume and tone color to such an extent that it is not too unlike the tone of the oboe. The straight mute is used principally in the trumpet and trombone sections, but on occasion even the tuba is called upon to use the mute. This is a huge mute, since it has to fit the upright bell of the instrument, and the free-lance tuba player avoids carrying the mute with him if at all possible. The cup mute, so called because of its shape, is rarely used in the symphony orchestra. It also softens the tone, but it gives the brass instrument a mellow sound more similar to the tone of a flute. The straight mute and the cup mute have long been standard equipment in the large jazz orchestras. The jazz musician has used many devices to change the natural sound of the brass instruments. In addition to the straight mute and the cup mute, there is the harmon mute. This was originally used to produce a "wow-wow" effect (with the aid of the left hand) , but now is more often used without this effect and used instead to produce an intense, soft sound. Some orchestras, such as that of Duke Ellington, have long used a "plunger"—this is actually the rubber end of a bathroom plunger—to produce a somewhat hollow sound, and in the hands of an expert trombonist it sounds oddly imitative of the human speaking voice.

The trumpet. The *trumpet* is the soprano voice of the brass section. With tubing that is narrow-bored and mainly cylindrical, the trumpet has a brilliant, commanding tone that can "carry" above the entire symphonic orchestra playing at full volume.

The cornet. The *cornet* is occasionally called for in a symphonic score, but its chief use is in the concert band.

The tubing of the B-flat cornet and the B-flat trumpet is exactly the same length, in spite of the fact that the cornet looks shorter. The cornet appears to be shorter only because its tubing is coiled differently. In addition to their length being the same, both instruments have the same valve system, and are playable by both cornetists and trumpeters. The tone of the cornet is mellower than that of the trumpet because its bore is larger and more conical. The bore of the trumpet is basically cylindrical, which accounts for its more brilliant tone.

It has sometimes been said that the cornet is easier to play than the trumpet. This is true in a very limited way; the more conical bore allows for a certain "easiness" in making the instrument speak and in the playing of a legato line. However, the chief reason that has always been advanced for its use as a leading member of the concert band is its mellowness of tone, the trumpet tone being regarded as too brilliant.

The French horn. The ***French horn,*** usually called simply the *horn,* is the alto instrument of the brass section. It has a natural tone that is somewhat mellower than that of the trombone. Its tone is further mellowed, or darkened, by a practice that is unique in the playing of brass instruments, i.e., the normal method of playing the horn is with the player's right hand inserted into the bell, and the hand is "cupped" so as to somewhat muffle the tone.

The horn is also the only brass instrument in which the valves are played with the left hand. Before valves were invented, the horn was held with the left hand, the right hand being inserted into the bell in order to "manipulate" the tones by changing the air column enough so as to affect the pitch. This practice is known as "stopping," and continues today as a special effect. When valves were invented, horn players were already accustomed to using the right hand in the bell.

The mellow tone of the horn enables it to blend with the woodwinds as well as the brass in the symphony orchestra. It is an excellent solo instrument, as this example shows.

Example 3-10   *Till Eulenspiegel,* Richard Strauss

The range of the horn is exceptionally large, and the example from Strauss shows use of this large range. However, since horn players sometimes specialize in "high horn" and "low horn," on occasion the last two notes of the solo above have been played by another horn player in the section.

The trombone. The *trombone* is a tenor instrument pitched an octave below the B-flat trumpet. Because its bore is narrow and mostly cylindrical, it has a tone brighter than that of the horn, and more akin to the trumpet. Its name, which is Italian, actually means "large trumpet."

The trombone historically is the oldest type of brass instrument in wide usage that still exists in its original form. Because of its slide, which can elongate the instrument through seven positions, thus supplying seven different fundamental tones, it has always been able to play the chromatic scale. Playing a prominent part in early music, it did not come into use in symphonic writing until Beethoven introduced it in the last movement of his *Fifth Symphony*.

Although the trombone had not been accepted in symphonic circles in Mozart's time, Mozart made notable use of it in certain of his operas, often for the representation of the supernatural. In *Idomeneo* the trombones accompany the voice of the oracle speaking from the waterfall. This is their only use in this opera and the sounds come, not from the pit, but from backstage, accompanying the voice. In *Don Giovanni* Mozart again uses the trombone as part of a supernatural effect. He reserves their use throughout the entire opera until the appearance of the statue (or ghost) of the Commendatore whom Don Giovanni killed in a duel at the beginning of the opera. The trombones here also are backstage.

A unique piece of trombone writing is to be found in Mozart's *Requiem* in the "Tuba Mirum." This is a part written for the tenor trombone in duet with the bass soloist. The first 13 measures are considered to be by Mozart,

Example 3-11   *Requiem*, K. 626, No. 3, "Tuba Mirum," Mozart

with the following written by his amanuensis, Süssmayr. The solo is found in the second trombone part, because in that day there existed the true *alto,* tenor and *bass trombones,* and Mozart wanted the tone color and range of a tenor trombone.

The trombone has had wide usage throughout all periods of jazz. In the early days of jazz it was borrowed from the marching bands to play the bass line in Dixieland, or "tailgate" from the back of a truck. It was one of the instruments of the blues, and went from there into the large dance bands and jazz orchestras. Its lyric voice was made prominent by Tommy Dorsey, and continues today in big bands, television studios, and in many jazz groups. The trombone has also been a constant in the band, from the front line of the marching band to its position in the concert band, which is basically similar to its position in the symphony orchestra.

The tuba. The *tuba* most commonly used is the BB-flat (the double B-flat), pitched an octave below the B-flat trombone, and with tubing twice as long. The tuba has an extremely wide bore—wider in proportion to the length of its tubing than that of any other brass instrument—and thus has a very broad, sonorous sound.

The tuba, with no history prior to the invention of valves, was the last of the brass instruments to become a member of the symphony orchestra. The predecessors of the tuba were the *ophicleide,* which was the bass instrument of the *keyed bugle* family, and the *serpent,* so named because of its shape.

Suggested Listening: Mendelssohn, "A Midsummer Night's Dream," Overture.

Symphonic tuba players use a tuba in C, pitched one tone higher than the BB-flat. This instrument provides a slight advantage in the upper range, and also "manipulates" just a bit more easily. Its tone is slightly less obtrusive. More rarely, smaller tubas pitched in E-flat and F are used in the symphony orchestra.

In the concert band, the BB-flat tuba is the standard instrument; but the tuba in E-flat is very common. The chief reason for the E-flat tuba in the band is its smaller size and lighter weight, which is more practicable for high school or college students who may not have the "heft" necessary to handle the large instrument. This is especially true when the instrument must be carried while marching. A further aid to the tuba player in marching is the use of the model known as the *sousaphone.* This is an instrument of the *helicon* type, in which the bell faces forward, and was the innovation, although not the invention, of John Philip Sousa. The instrument encircles the player and "sits" on his shoulder.

The tuba has been in and out of orchestras in the popular and jazz fields since the late 1800's. Before the turn of the century the most accessible and the least expensive instruments were those that had become "army surplus" after the Civil War. Thus it was only natural that the clarinet, trumpet, trombone, and "brass bass" (or tuba) were instruments of the early jazz orchestras. The tuba's position was gradually usurped by the bass fiddle, and by the mid-thirties it had become a rarity.

THE PERCUSSION. The basic instruments of the percussion section have a history that precedes that of the other families of instruments that have been discussed. The bass drum, the snare drum, and the timpani are but variants of the ancient drums of different sizes that were used in primitive cultures as an integral part of festivals or religious ceremonies, as signals in time of danger, or to set the rhythm for the dance. The ancient drums were made by stretching the dried and treated skin of an animal over one end of a hollowed-out tree trunk or gourd.

Timpani. The most refined of the membrane percussion instruments are the *timpani.* They are the only instruments of the membrane type that are tuned to specific pitches. There are hand screws on the upper rim that

Example 3-12

control the tension of the head (the membrane). The tension of the head must be uniform around the upper rim. Adjusting the tension may be compared to tightening the nuts on the wheel of an automobile consecutively and uniformly—except that it is a far more delicate operation, and the adjustment depends entirely upon the ear of the timpanist.

The classical orchestra usually employed two timpani (performed by one player), one tuned to the tonic of the key and the other tuned to the dominant. As noted in the section on the trumpet, the timpani and the trumpets were often used in conjunction with each other.

The timpanist is the principal player of the percussion section. With the bass drum and the snare drum, the timpani are often employed in performing passages of a pronounced rhythmic nature, but in producing a definite pitch the timpani are often the foundation of the harmony. Because of these

timpani

snare drum

bass drum

cymbals

tambourine

two attributes of the timpani, it has been said, "If you don't have a good timpanist, you don't have an orchestra."

The snare drum. The *snare drum* differs from every other kind of drum in that it has a set of coiled wires strung across the bottom head of the drum. These coiled wires are known as *snares.* When the top of the snare drum is struck, the snares add a crispness of sound that is useful in rhythmic passages requiring a dry, distinctive staccato effect.

A well known use of the snare drum in the symphonic orchestra is this example from Ravel's *Bolero,* which is repeated throughout the entire work in a constant crescendo to the end.

Example 3-13 *Bolero,* Ravel

The snare drum is familiar to all as the instrument that plays the "street beat" in the marching band when other instruments are not playing. The snare drum is a basic part of the equipment of the jazz drummer.

The bass drum. The *bass drum* hardly needs to be explained or described, but it may be said that it consists of two heads of stretched membrane, each stretched over opposite ends of a barrel-type wooden (or metal) structure. Although bass drums vary in size, they are always the largest drums in either the band or the orchestra.

The bass drum has hand-screws on both rims that control the tension of the heads. Although of indefinite pitch, the best *tone* for the purposes of the symphony orchestra or the concert band is that which is between the one extreme of a "boom"—which is too reverberating—and the other extreme of a "thud"—which has too little reverberation.

The importance of the bass drum cannot be overemphasized. As correct tempo is the first requisite in performance, the rhythmic function of the bass drum is vital.

Cymbals. *Piatti,* which is the Italian term for *cymbals,* literally means *plates.* The term well describes the general shape of cymbals. Made of spun brass, they come in all sizes. The cymbals used in the symphonic orchestra and the concert band are eighteen inches or more in diameter, and are capable of a large dynamic range, from a whispered "z-z-z" to a resounding crash.

A pair of cymbals is played by one man. They are sounded by being struck against each other with a technique that might be described as "striking together obliquely."

There are also smaller cymbals, in various sizes, that may be played in different ways. The single cymbal may be struck with a felt-headed mallet, or a drumstick, or a roll may be played on a cymbal. In fact, the possibilities are many, and the twentieth-century composer often goes to great lengths to explain in the player's part just how he wants special effects produced. In the orchestra of the theater pit, the television studio, or the jazz orchestra, the suspended cymbal (or several of them in different sizes) is preferred to the larger "concert" cymbals.

The tam-tam. The **tam-tam**, or **gong**, is of Chinese origin. A giant cymbal, sometimes as large as four feet in diameter, it is struck with a round, soft-headed mallet to produce a reverberating tone that spans a range in volume from the softest whisper to a thunderous roar.

The lowest sounding of all the cymbals, it has a lip at its outer edge, facing away from the player. Because of its immense size it is hung on a free-standing frame. The player on certain occasions starts the vibrations ahead of time by hitting it very lightly.

The xylophone. The modern **xylophone** is of comparatively recent origin, and because of its hard, dry, staccato sound it is used in the symphony only in special passages. Its keyboard resembles a portion of the piano keyboard. The xylophone bars (keys) are made of wood.

Set horizontally on a stand, the xylophone is normally played with two mallets, but on occasion three or four mallets are used.

Suggested Listening: Stravinsky, *Petrouchka.*

The marimba. The **marimba,** which is a larger version of the xylophone, has the added feature of resonance, which the xylophone does not have. Rare in its appearance in the symphony orchestra, it is used when the composer desires a deeper sound than the xylophone, and a continuation of sound, which the xylophone cannot produce.

Also resembling the piano keyboard in its four-octave range, its bars are of wood. Set horizontally on a stand, it also is played with from two to four soft rubber mallets. Under each bar there is a resonating tube that gives it its unique deep, hollow sound. The player also has a foot-pedal, which may damp the tones or allow them to ring.

The marimba has occasionally been used in dance orchestras, but is more commonly associated with the performance of the solo night club entertainer who performs on all of the "mallet" instruments.

Orchestra bells.   The keyboard of the *orchestra bells* resembles that of the xylophone, but the instrument is smaller and its lowest *C* is pitched an octave higher. The bars are made of metal and, when struck with a hard-headed mallet, give off a sound similar to actual silver bells. Orchestra bells are also well-known by their German name, *glockenspiel.* They are standard equipment in today's symphonic orchestra, although their use is only occasional.

Suggested Listening: Mozart, *The Magic Flute.*

The use of the orchestra bells is far more common in the band, as they are often given passages that accent a melody played in the brass or winds. They are also used as a solo instrument. Fast passages are not usually written because of the carry-over of the sound: one tone will blur into the next, as there is no damping system on the instrument.

The orchestra bells, or glockenspiel, when used with a marching band, are referred to as the *bell-lyra,* as the bells are then in a vertical position, contained within a lyre-shaped frame.

Chimes.   The *chimes* are long metal tubes, one and one quarter or one and one half inches in diameter, suspended vertically from a rack. They are struck at the top with a wooden hammer, and give out a sound that resembles that of church bells.

There is a foot pedal mechanism, which may damp the tone or allow it to ring.

The triangle.   The *triangle* is a round metal bar, about one half inch in diameter, bent at two points to form the triangle shape, and open at the end. It is struck with a small metal bar, and gives off a sound, indeterminate in pitch, which may best be described as a "ting."

The triangle was first used by Gluck. One of its more familiar uses is in Beethoven's "Turkish" variation of the choral theme in the *Ninth Symphony.* Here it is used simultaneously with the bass drum and cymbal to produce the "Turkish" effect.

It is a standard part of the percussionist's equipment in symphony, theater, and studio orchestra.

Suggested Listening: Beethoven, *Symphony No. 9,* Movt. IV; Liszt, *Piano Concerto* in E-flat.

Other instruments

THE **piano**. The *piano* is probably the most well-known of all musical instruments. According to the American Music Conference, 22,300,000 Americans play the piano. With the exception of the organ, it has the largest range. Its 88 keys arranged in semitones serve as a reference chart in designating the ranges of all other instruments.

The piano is actually a percussion instrument. Each tone is produced by the striking action of a felt hammer against the strings. And although the task of each pianist in playing a lyric or legato passage is to make the tone as sustained as possible, each tone begins to die away immediately after it is begun, in the same manner that the sound of a cymbal dies away after being struck.

The dynamic range of the piano is considerable, from crashing chords to a feathery wisp of sound. The piano has three foot-pedals that add certain features to the expressivity of the instrument. When the damper pedal, on the right, is depressed it releases the dampers from the strings. This allows the strings to sustain the sound. The pedal on the left, the soft pedal, moves the hammers so that one less string produces the tone. The pedal in the middle (not practicable on some upright pianos) is the sostenuto pedal. This sustains the sound of selected tones during the playing of others that are not to be sustained.

Almost every major composer has written important works for the piano as a solo instrument, or in combination with other instruments.

The name *piano* is in reality an abbreviation of its former full name, *pianoforte,* which was its original designation, signifying that it could play both softly and loudly from touch alone, in contradistinction to the harpsichord, which it superseded.

Invented in Italy in 1709, the piano was in general use by Mozart's time, but it had a much lighter sound than does our piano of today. It is interesting to note that Johann Christian Bach, an older contemporary of Mozart, wrote keyboard works in which he specified "harpsichord or forte-piano."

Suggested Listening: Schubert, *Piano Quintet in A* ("*Trout*"), Op. 114; Stravinsky, *Petrouchka.*

THE HARPSICHORD. The *harpsichord,* usually in a shape similar to the grand piano, has a smaller range. The tone of the harpsichord, softer than that of the piano, is produced by a plucking action. When a key is depressed, a plectrum is moved upward, plucking the string as it passes. A harpsichord often has two sets of manuals (keyboards), and these are often played in combination to achieve various nuances of sound. A system of foot pedals also permits coupling of the two keyboards in various ways, including octave doublings, which allows for a variety in expression that some find more interesting than that of the piano.

With the renewed interest in music of the Baroque period in recent years, there has been a resurgence of interest in the harpsichord, and it now makes its appearance quite regularly on the concert stage.

Suggested Listening: J. S. Bach, *Well-Tempered Clavier.*

THE VIRGINAL.   The tone of the *virginal* is produced in the same manner as that of the harpsichord. Its shape is rectangular, and its much smaller size permitted it to be carried from room to room and set on a table. Indeed, it might be thought of as a "portable harpsichord." However, it did not have the potential for expression that the harpsichord had, being limited to one keyboard and having a smaller range. It was a favorite instrument for the home in sixteenth-century England, and much harpsichord music was performed on it. The best known collection of music written specifically for the instrument is the Fitzwilliam Virginal Book.

THE CLAVICHORD.   The *clavichord* is the earliest of the keyboard instruments with strings. In the baroque period the clavichord was a sister instrument of the harpsichord. Of earlier origin, its tone was softer but nevertheless more expressive. The manner of producing the tone differed from that of the harpsichord. The tone is produced by a brass wedge (called a tangent), which touches the string. The force of the tangent may be varied by the pressure on the key that sets it in action. Thus, the control of volume is similar to that on the piano, although on a smaller scale. Also, since the tangent maintains its contact with the string while the tone is sounding, an expressive vibrato may be produced by the action of the player's fingers on the keyboard.

Music written for the *clavier* (keyboard) in the baroque period was performed on either the harpsichord or the clavichord, the choice being dependent upon the music's character and style.

THE HARP.   The name *harp* derives from the Italian term for the instrument, *arpa*, which suggests the natural aptitude that the instrument has for playing arpeggios, broken chords. This natural aptitude is likewise, to some degree, its limitation.

"Lady Playing the Virginal," etching by Wenceslaus Hollar (*Courtesy of Prints Division, The New York Public Library—Astor, Lenox and Tilden Foundations*).

The strings are arranged, not in semitones, but in diatonic scale steps in the key of C-flat major. By a system of foot pedals the player can raise the pitch of each string by one semitone, or by one whole tone. There are seven foot pedals, each standing for one note of the scale in all octaves. There are three separate notches for each foot pedal. When all of the pedals are in the highest notch the instrument is then in C-flat. Placing all of the pedals in the middle notch shortens each string so that the instrument is then pitched in C. Placing each pedal in the lowest notch pitches the instrument another semitone higher. Various combinations of the foot pedals allow for a limited amount of chromatic writing, but in anything but slow tempos, the harp is essentially a diatonic instrument.

The harp is one of the oldest instruments, but it did not make its way into the symphony orchestra until the nineteenth century. It is now a regular member of the symphony orchestra. In large orchestras there are two harps. The solo and chamber music literature for the harp is not large.

Suggested Listening: Ravel, *Alborada del Gracioso,* for orchestra (score includes two harps) .

THE ORGAN. The **organ** is the most complete single instrument in its range of volume and by virtue of its possibilities of registration. *Registration* refers to the various combinations of tone colors that may be produced by the operation of the organ *stops*. These stops, which may be adjusted by the player ahead of time or during the course of the music, change the quality of tone. The number of stops varies with each organ, and therefore the variety of tone color differs with each instrument. Some of the stops are designated by terms such as *trumpet* or *oboe*. But to the organist these stops are not so much an imitation as (with the other stops) they are a means of differentiating the array of colors available on the organ.

The organ is one of the most ancient of instruments, and was known as the *hydraulis* by the Greeks and Romans. Its golden age ended with the Baroque period, but the nineteenth century French composers showed much interest in the instrument.

In recent years there has been a renewal of interest in reproducing the smaller instrument that was used in the baroque period. This baroque organ may be a single instrument, or it may form a part of the design of a large organ. The return to the sound of the baroque organ parallels the return to the use of the harpsichord, both the result of a constantly burgeoning interest in the authentic performance of baroque music.

The solo literature for the organ is vast, and it often makes its appearance with the symphony orchestra.

Most organs have at least two manuals and one pedal keyboard, allowing for possibilities of polyphony and contrast of color not available on any other keyboard instrument. The registration of the manuals may be kept distinct or they may be combined by the use of couplers.

The sound of the organ is produced by wind, which is forced through pipes that are of a whistle type (such as a recorder) or a reed type (such as a clarinet). The wind was at one time generated by hand pumping, and this chore often was performed by choirboys. The wind is now usually provided by an electric blower.

THE CELESTE. The *celeste* (also called *celesta*) is a small keyboard instrument with a range of four octaves. The tones of the instrument resemble the sound of small silver bells. The sound is produced by a hammer action on small steel plates, similar to those of the orchestra bells, or glockenspiel, but the added feature of resonators enhances the sound.

Its first use in the symphony orchestra was by Tchaikovsky in the *Nutcracker Suite*.

Example 3-14   *Nutcracker Suite*, "Dance of the Sugar Plum Fairy," Tchaikovsky

The symphony orchestra

When the Pilgrims arrived in the New World in the year 1620, the piano had not yet been invented; the viol family of stringed instruments had not yet been superseded by the violin family; the brass instruments did not have valves; there was no such instrument as a tuba, and the beginnings of the symphony orchestra were over a hundred years away.

In the second half of the eighteenth century, the symphony orchestra, far smaller than now, was being shaped into an effective vehicle of expression which was to reach a peak in size at the end of the eighteenth century. New instruments were added to expand the tonal palette of the orchestra. Tone color in all its variety became the goal of many composers.

The size of the orchestra has been increased from 30 to 40 players to sometimes well over 100, although the usual symphony orchestra of today is now standardized at about 80 to 100 players (the chief differences being in the size of the string sections). The orchestra continues to evolve as composers constantly search for new modes of expression.

A glance at the orchestra at different periods will point up the orchestra's expansion from the classical period to the present day.

Figure 1

Possible Seating Plan of the Full Symphony Orchestra

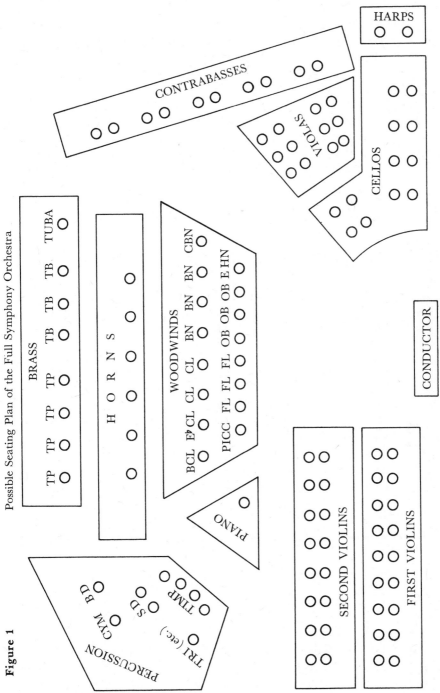

The Mannheim orchestra, which Mozart visited and which influenced him to add clarinets to his later symphonic works, was considered at the time to be the finest orchestra in the world. According to one of Mozart's letters, the instrumentation of the orchestra consisted of the following: two flutes, two oboes, two clarinets, four bassoons, two trumpets, two timpani, ten or eleven first violins, ten or eleven second violins, four violas, four cellos, and four contrabasses. The score of Beethoven's *Fifth Symphony* calls for the following instrumentation: one piccolo, two flutes, two oboes, two clarinets, two bassoons, one contrabassoon, two horns, two trumpets, three trombones, two timpani, first violins, second violins, violas, cellos, and basses. The instrumentation of two well known symphony orchestras presently stands as shown in the following listing:

	NEW YORK PHILHARMONIC	BOSTON SYMPHONY ORCHESTRA
VL 1	17	18
VL 2	16	16
VA	12	12
VC	12	11
CB	9	9
FL	3	3
PIC	1	1
OB	3	3
EHN	1	1
CL	2 B♭, 1 E♭, 1 bass	2 B♭, 1 E♭, 1 bass
BN	3	3
CBN	1	1
HN	6	6
TR	4	4
TB	4	4
TU	1	1
TIMP	1	1
OTHER PERCUSSION	3	4
HARPS	1	2

Chamber orchestra

The term **chamber orchestra** most often means an orchestra small enough in size to play in a room for a more intimate gathering than would be found in a symphony hall. It is not possible to be precise about numbers. More to the point is the intent of the composer and the manner in which he handles the instruments. At the heart of the matter is the concept of treating the instruments more individually. Thus, there is often only one player on each type of instrument, for example, one clarinetist or one French horn player rather than a clarinet section or a French horn section. The strings are somewhat exceptional, and may or may not be reduced to one player per instrument.

The term *chamber music* may specify music written for a chamber orchestra, but actually it is a more encompassing term and generally refers to music written for perhaps six or more players up to the limits of a chamber orchestra. The term also may refer to music with parts for voices as well as instruments. Some examples of chamber music are: Richard Strauss, *Serenade,* for two flutes, two oboes, two clarinets, four horns, two bassoons, and contrabassoon or bass tuba; Stravinsky, *L'Histoire du Soldat,* for clarinet, bassoon, cornet, trombone, percussion, violin, and contrabass; Stravinsky, *Octet,* for flute, clarinet, two bassoons, two trumpets, and two trombones; Stravinsky, *Cantata,* for soprano, tenor, (small) female chorus, two flutes, two oboes (oboe II doubling on English horn), and violoncello.

Smaller chamber ensembles and solo performance

Also falling in the category of chamber music is music of a more soloistic character. Rather than being spoken of by the generic term, *chamber music,* however, music in this category is more often referred to by the specific traditional groupings of the instruments written for. These are the *woodwind quintet:* flute, oboe, clarinet, horn, bassoon; the *brass quintet:* usually two trumpets, horn, trombone and tuba; the *string quartet:* two violins, viola and cello; *string trio:* violin, viola, cello.

When the strings are joined by another instrument the group is specified by the distinguishing name of this instrument. Thus when a piano is added to a string quartet the ensemble is called a *piano quintet.* But the *"Trout" Quintet* of Schubert is an exception to this; the instruments are piano, violin, viola, cello and contrabass. A *piano quartet* is a string trio plus a piano: piano, violin, viola, and cello.

Works written for two players are not spoken of as duets. Because of the soloistic nature of such works the two instruments are mentioned specifically, for example, *Sonata for Violin and Piano.* Within this category fall works written for two pianos.

There are many works for solo instruments, but the instrument with a superabundance of such literature is the piano. Compositions for other solo instruments are much more unique, as well as often being a considerable challenge. On opposite sides of the spectrum are J. S. Bach's *Sonata in A Mi-*

nor for flute unaccompanied and Leonard Bernstein's *Elegy for Mippy II,* for trombone and foot.

Suggested Listening: Francis Poulenc, *Trio for Oboe, Bassoon, and Piano.*

The concert band

Although the **concert band** is often questioned as a performance vehicle for serious music, it actually has the potential for the presentation of the highest expression of any composer. The reason for the supercilious attitude toward the concert band is usually based not on its potential, which is great, but on the quality or type of music that has been performed by it in the past, and in many cases, on the quality of the performance itself.

At the turn of the century the Sunday band concert in the park was a diversion for the average family, a light-hearted presentation of popular songs of the day, potpourri of well known operatic selections, and usually some very "flashy" solo work by a cornet or trombone soloist, often in the form of variations on a theme. The soloists were outstanding technicians, and the well known bands of Sousa and Pryor contained some of the best musicians of the day, but the musical fare was geared to the tastes of the average. In short, it was a commercial venture, rather than an artistic one. The concert band did not intend it to be otherwise, except perhaps in the presentations of transcriptions of symphonies. But this was only borrowed glory.

And here is the nub of the matter. In an attempt to play works of a more artistic nature, the band of necessity borrowed from works written for the symphonic orchestra, and although it might be said in some cases that the attempt was laudable, any attempt to perform a work originally intended for orchestra can only be a miscarriage if played by a musical organization that is distinguished by the fact that it contains no stringed instruments.

The era of the concert band first began to decline with the advent of radio. With so many forms of entertainment now available at the turn of a dial, the band today exists mostly as a social outlet for students in high school or college. These are obviously not intended to be professional organizations, and since professional levels of performance cannot be obtained here, the composer does not have the incentive to write music for concert or symphonic band. However, there are notable exceptions in certain colleges, and several professional symphonic bands do exist. For example, the symphonic band at the Massachusetts Institute of Technology now performs original works for band exclusively, and often commissions composers to write for it.

The concert band—or **symphonic wind ensemble,** as some prefer it—consists entirely of wind instruments, with the exception of the percussion section. As suggested above, there are no stringed instruments. The concert band evolved from the marching band, which of necessity used instruments that had the advantages of volume and portability. However, since the concert band has divorced itself from the marching band concept and moved into the concert hall, it has now made some exception to the concept of "wind instruments only" and has added string basses and timpani, as well as tubas.

The basic sound of the symphony orchestra relies upon the strings; the basic sound of the concert bands is winds. The concert band lacks strings, but in its woodwind section it has a far greater potential for variety of tone color than that of the symphony orchestra because of its greater number and variety of woodwind instruments.

In this century composers have written for the concert band as a normal vehicle for serious artistic expression.

Suggested Listening: Milhaud, *Suite Française;* Hindemith, *Symphony in B-Flat for Band;* Persichetti, *Divertimento for Band; Psalms for Band;* Holst, *Suites Nos. 1 and 2 for Band;* Vaughan Williams, *Folk Song Suite.*

PERFORMANCE

The composer as performer

In the past, composers who were merely competent as performers were rare. In fact, many were the supreme virtuosos of their time. J. S. Bach was perhaps better known for his technical facility and improvisations at the organ than for his compositions, while his contemporary in Italy, Domenico Scarlatti, electrified audiences with digital acrobatics at the cembalo. Mozart, Clementi, and Beethoven were legendary virtuosos of the keyboard. And, of course, Paganini, Mendelssohn, and Liszt were leading virtuosos of the romantic period. Berlioz and Wagner, though indifferent as players, yet managed to remain in intimate contact with performance and performers. They were leading conductors of the nineteenth century and performed their own as well as other composer's works. Wagner's *On Conducting* remains to this day an indispensable handbook for aspiring students of the art.

The composer remained in direct contact with his audience, whether his listeners formed a church congregation, a circle of aristocrats in a gilded salon, a coterie of intellectuals gathered around a piano, or a massed audience in a large opera house. The composer/performer learned at first hand exactly how his listeners reacted to his music. The audience for its part saw and heard the composer present his own music in authentic performances. There was not the problem of the middle man/performer *interpreting* the composer's expression. The audience received the sense of the music directly.

During the 19th century, however, the unity that was composer/performer gradually disintegrated, and ultimately they were no longer one. As a specialist, the concert artist became a new force in the world of music. Pianists such as Carl Tausig, Isidore Philipp, Ignacy Paderewski, Leopold Godowsky, retained certain credentials as composers but were of far greater significance in the musical world as concert virtuosos. At the beginning of this century the composer no longer felt the pressing need to mount the concert stage. For example, Debussy and others were less than matchless pianists. However, many 20th century composers took to the podium. The post-romantics, Mahler and Richard Strauss, were internationally known as conductors. Schoenberg as a young man played the violin in cabarets, but never espoused the concert stage as a player. However, Schoenberg, Stravinsky, Hindemith, Boulez, Bernstein, Copland and many others have devoted much of their time to conducting.

Hindemith, perhaps lamenting the loss of the composer/performer as total musician, excelled as a violist and made it a point to play tolerably well most of the instruments for which he wrote. And the precedent of composer/virtuoso set by Paganini, Mendelssohn, and Liszt was not entirely lost. The Russian composers Rachmaninoff and Prokofiev, and the Italian composer Busoni attained great virtuosity at the piano and established world reputations as concert artists.

Interpretation

Once the disengagement of composer from performer was a reality, a tremendously important concern arose: interpretation. If it is the role of the performing artist—pianist, violinist, conductor, singer—to transmit the composer's idea to the concert public, how is he to interpret the composer's wishes? When there is intimate communion between player and composer, as with the pianist Soulima Stravinsky and his father Igor Stravinsky, the task is less difficult. Piano rolls, or recordings made by composers of their own works also help. But, essentially, the artist has to find for himself the musical voice of the composer. It goes without saying that he must attain great physical skills, and develop a powerful technique to enable him to conquer the most taxing compositions, but more important, he must steep himself in the life and work of the composer. He must analyze assiduously the composer's score,

Igor Stravinsky and his son, Soulima (*Photo by John Brook, Boston*).

seizing upon its every detail to achieve as closely as possible the composer's intentions. He must consider matters of tone, *dynamics,* tempo, phrasing, and balance of melodic lines and harmonies. And he must know the tenor of the times in which the composer wrote. In other words, the challenge to the concert artist is enormous. He spends much of his life perfecting his interpretations of the masters.

Precisely because of this enormous technical and interpretive challenge many artists specialize in the music of one or two composers. For example, Wanda Landowsky made a specialty of the harpsichord and clavichord music of J. S. Bach. Alfred Cortot, an extraordinary pianist of the early 1900's, was renowned for his Chopin playing. At present Rudolf Serkin excels at Beethoven and Brahms, Artur Rubinstein at Chopin, and Vladimir Horowitz at Liszt, Scriabin, and Prokofiev. In the world of opera, virtuoso singers have always been associated with certain roles and with certain composers, such as Joan Sutherland's *Norma,* Renata Tebaldi's *Violetta* and *Tosca,* and Jon Vickers' *Florestan.*

Two important developments in the twentieth century have tended to shake the privileged position of the concert artist. One of these is the growth of jazz as an improvisatory art; the other is the recent surge of interest by composers in electronic media. The jazz artist again is a composer as was the harpsichordist, organist, violinist, in earlier ages. Sometimes using a basic pattern such as the blues, or a well known song or dance, but more and more using his own material, the jazz player improvises a statement that is uniquely his. With pure electronic music it is something else: the performer becomes obsolete. A thing—tape recorder or synthesizer—totally replaces him.

Eugene Ormandy, conductor of the Philadelphia Orchestra (*Photo by Authenticated News International, New York*).

All that needs be done is that the machine be switched on. A recreative artist, the middle man, is not needed; nor are traditional instruments, the tools of his trade. The composer is assured that his message will reach his audience exactly as he wrote it, and the medium becomes the message.

The conductor

What has been said of the performing artist's interpretive challenge applies as well to the conductor. He also searches for the meaning of the music as represented by the score. His pitch perception must be highly developed for he must be always aware of his players' intonation. He needs to be extremely sensitive to good balance between choirs, sections, and solo instruments.

What agile fingers, sensitive embouchure, controlled breath are to the soloist, baton technique is to the conductor. In its most basic aspect *conducting technique* refers to certain gestures traced by the right hand of the conductor which represent groups of beats. Following are three of the basic ***beat patterns:*** *

Patterns in two beats: Down, up

Patterns in three beats: Down, right, up

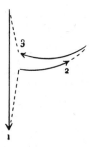

* From *Conducting Choral Music*, Robert L. Garretson. Third Edition. © by Allyn and Bacon, Inc., Boston, 1970, pp. 6–8. Used by permission of the author.

Patterns in four beats: Down, left, right, up.

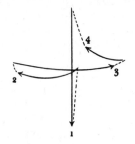

Other, more complicated rhythmic groupings resulting from compound or asymmetrical meters result in comparable complexities in the conductor's gestures. This visual analogue of the beat is really not much more than a safeguard for the player, since he counts anyway to insure correctly timed entrances and exact ensemble. It is of much greater importance to the orchestra that the conductor also *controls the tempo*. Through his patterned rhythmic gestures he establishes a basic tempo, changing it when there are several different tempos within one composition. For example, a piece may begin in a *largo* tempo, switch to *allegro,* and end with a *presto*. Also, within a basic tempo, a pushing ahead (*accelerando*) or falling back (*ritardando*) of the beat is sometimes required by the composer. All of this is indicated by the conductor's right hand. The left hand has its own, interdependent role. With it the conductor either cues for entrances or elicits dynamic effects and good balance. And, perhaps more important, the conductor must establish a rapport with his players, drawing out their best efforts while applying judicious discipline when necessary. The music director/conductor also plans programs and chooses guest artists over his entire season, and often tours and makes recordings.

The listener's part

The roles of composer and performer are very clear; the composer creates and the performer recreates. What then of the listener? What does he bring to the musical performance? Obviously he brings his attention and interest. This may be expressed by a quiet demeanor or by many sorts of active physical responses—depending on the kind of music heard. He may bring with him considerable listening experience sustained by extensive knowledge of the composer's cultural background and aesthetic outlook, or in the instance of folk music, he may understand its social or ethnic roots. But there is something much more important that the listener must bring to all serious musical expression, whether that expression is in the area of the "classics" or the avant garde of jazz, folk, pop, or rock. The serious listener of music must have an attitude that is as conscientious as that of the composer and performer. In its deepest, most universal essence, music is the expression of the self. It voices the manifold aspects of human selfhood through the creativity of composer and performer. This self-expression is as unlimited as there are human modes of feeling and perception. Thus there are musical expressions reflecting states of nature, romance, philosophy, religion, humor, irony, sarcasm, optimism, pessimism, and intellectualism. Every listener, precisely because he is human, possesses a spark of creativity himself, no matter how latent or submerged it may seem to be. It was Freud who said that the poet or artist "forces us to become aware of our inner selves in which the same impulses are still extant even though they are suppressed." And Kant stated that the aesthetic experience "is represented as *universal,* i.e. valid for every man." The necessary conscientious attitude then is that of taking serious music seriously; of dredging from within oneself a creative responsiveness that will reverberate vividly to the sounds of genius. The listener must lend both his mind and heart to serious music. He must listen, not just hear.

The critic's role

The music critic is no more than a practised and informed listener. As a professional he articulates his musical reactions which are then disseminated via the communications media. However, he often has become the arbiter and conditioner of mass taste, and the damnation or salvation of both creative and recreative musicians. Properly he should give the particulars, the what-where-when-who of the musical occurrence, and then follow with his opinion of the work, the performer, or both. Unfortunately, many critics either pass judgment as if in a court of law, or their opinion *is taken* as authoritative judgment. The absurdities indulged in by overly opinionated critics can readily be seen in the following excerpts from Slonimsky's *Lexicon of Musical Invective:* "Beethoven, this extraordinary genius, was completely deaf for nearly the last ten years of his life, during which his compositions have partaken of the most incomprehensible wildness. His imagination seems to have fed upon the ruins of his sensitive organs." * One assumes that these comments applied to the last piano sonatas and string quartets, the *Missa Solemnis,* and the *Ninth Symphony,* now universally recog-

---

* *Lexicon of Musical Invective,* Nicolas Slonimsky. Second edition. ⓒ by Coleman-Ross Company, Inc., N.Y., 1965, p. 46 (W. Gardiner, *The Music of Nature,* London, 1837) .

Maxim Gorky (*Courtesy of Tass from Sovfoto, Moscow*).

nized as some of the most profound music ever written. And one can only marvel at the lack of musical perception by the great Russian novelist and dramatist, Maxim Gorky, as he reacted to a jazz concert:

> An idiotic little hammer knocks drily: one, two, three, ten, twenty knocks. Then, like a clod of mud thrown into crystal-clear water, there is wild screaming, hissing, rattling, wailing, moaning, cackling. Bestial cries are heard: neighing horses, the squeal of a brass pig, crying jackasses, amorous quacks of a monstrous toad . . . This excruciating medley of brutal sounds is subordinated to a barely perceptible rhythm. Listening to this screaming music for a minute or two, one conjures up an orchestra of madmen, sexual maniacs, led by a man-stallion beating time with an enormous phallos.*

Readers who follow critics closely should note Hume's astute epigram: "Although critics are able to reason more plausibly than cooks, they must still share the same fate." Critics are not infallible, nor do they represent ultimate authority. The listener will do well to read the critics. Whether or not he has heard the performance himself, he should learn from and enjoy the critic's viewpoint, but only as another private, though informed, opinion. The listener's ultimate judgment should come only from hearing the music itself. Music means as many things as there are people to hear it.

* *Ibid.,* p. 25.

PART TWO
HISTORY

ACH AGE IN history is, in fact, an age of transition. But in retrospect it seems that certain periods more than others were periods of stabilization. Tendencies, although sprung from different sources, lead toward the same focal point and finally merge. Though these merged tendencies seem clear enough now, it is often doubtful that during these periods the figures who now loom large to us as leaders would have thought of their times in terms of stability. To the philosopher, to the statesman, to the artist who is in the middle of the stream of thought or action, it is always a time of transition, a time of trying to reach some landing point that cannot yet be seen.

From our vantage point now, however, the smaller details blur and the large outlines remain, showing us the more important trends and their culmination points. Through hindsight we can check the truism that "every man is the product of his age." The age he lives in is the age he knows. "We sleep, but the loom of life never stops, and the pattern which was weaving when the sun went down is weaving when it comes up in the morning." And we are part of the texture. It is not more true of the artist than it is of the common man, but it is more important. It is more important because the artist leaves us an expression of his age.

In recognizing that each artist is a product of his age we should not attempt to equate the expression of one artist with that of another—to equate the output of the musician, for example, with the output of the architect. The inspiration of the painter and the musician, the author and the architect may all be triggered by the same environment, but their manners of expression will be individual. Similarities may be found in the ethos, but not necessarily in the expression of it. The uniqueness of the "comment" or expression of each artist will depend upon two things: the degree to which his expression is original, and the manner in which he handles his material.

Attempts to correlate the various expressions of artists have taken us to many a dead end. These attempts have resulted in describing baroque music as though it were baroque architecture; in characterizing impressionistic music in the terms of impressionistic painting; in equating the rhythms of jazz with the rhythms of certain twentieth-century paintings. Similarities and relationships are certainly apparent in these various pairings, but the similarities are in the original concept, not in the expression. Each one in the pair may complement the other, but they are not of the same kind. Comparisons have gone even farther, reaching the ultimate in vapidity in the phrase, "Architecture is frozen music." Neither music nor architecture can benefit by this. None of this is to say that it is not illuminating to compare the arts within a period. But the comparisons should not result in facile phrases.

No, each art form, each specific work must be considered as something unique. Instead of forcing superficial relationships upon the arts we should try to see how the same influences resulted in different expressions. Similarities will exist, but they will be of mood or style, not of design or form.

Each art will flower on its own branch. Thus we must look for the growth, the evolutionary progress, of music basically within its own historical perspective as an expression of the happenings of each age.

CHAPTER 4

Pre-Baroque: before 1600

Sing joyously of God our strength;
Shout aloud of Jacob's God.
Raise the chant and beat the drum,
Both the pleasant harp and the lute.
Blow the trumpet at the new moon,
At the full moon on our festal day.

Psalm 81 *

THESE LINES FROM the 81st Psalm are reminders that singing and the playing of instruments in religious ceremonies date back to early times. There are many other references in the Old Testament that testify to the Hebrews' long association with music. It was only natural that the early Christians were influenced by the music and the ritual of the synagogue.

During its first three centuries, Christianity was expanding, but its followers were constantly persecuted by the powers in Rome, and many meetings had to be held in secret. In the fourth century certain things happened, affecting both the church and its music. In the year 312, Constantine, Emperor of Rome, embraced Christianity and gave it legal sanction. The Christians could now come above ground and conduct public services. Greek, the language of the New Testament and until this time the language of the church, was replaced by Latin. A vestige of Greek still exists in the language

* Smith, J. M. P., ed. & trans.: *The Complete Bible: An American Translation.* © 1939 by the University of Chicago. (The Apocrypha & the New Testament translation by Edgar J. Goodspeed.)

of the Mass. In the latter part of the century, Ambrose, bishop of Milan, gathered together a large number of hymns and antiphonal psalms for use in the church service. It is conjectural whether Ambrose contributed as a composer to this collection, but in any event this large body of work has come to be known as Ambrosian Chant.

Inspired by the writings of Augustine, and with the foundations of the Roman Empire beginning to crack, more and more of the people turned to the church and away from the state. When the Empire disintegrated in the fifth century, the church became the dominant authority for many. The church grew and the body of its music grew, borrowing from various sources. These sources included Eastern as well as Western culture, pagan as well as religious, secular as well as sacred.

In the sixth century Gregory, who was Pope of Rome from 590 until his death in 604, felt it was time to draw together the loose ends of the heterogeneous—or, perhaps better, miscellaneous—collection of church music; to make choices out of the large abundance of materials that were in existence, to "purify" in some cases, and to establish an ideal of what the main body of sacred music should be.

That he was successful is only too well established. Gregorian Chant, as this body of music came to be known, has served the church to the present.

THE MIDDLE AGES

Gregorian chant (Plainsong)

Gregorian chant may be sung by a solo voice or a chorus singing in unison. It may be responsorial—alternating from solo to choral singing, or antiphonal—alternating from chorus to chorus. The range of chant is not large, very often being contained within an octave.

Gregorian chant, in the quiet undulating motion of its melody, sung by male voices only, conveys a feeling of purity and otherworldliness that lends itself well to the Catholic liturgy. The serene quality of this music is uniquely refreshing to ears accustomed to the more turbulent, emotional expression of later days.

The melodic style of the chant may be *syllabic,* one syllable to each tone; or *neumatic,* in which two, three, or four tones are sung to one syllable; or *melismatic,* in which an extended series of tones are sung to one syllable.

GUIDO. Guido d'Arezzo, a monk and a theorist of the eleventh century, must have had the sense of frustration that all trainers of choral groups often have in trying to teach singers how to remember pitch relationships. There was no table of reference for relative pitch names. It can only be imagined that when something went wrong in the learning of a new piece of music, Guido would often have to work from the beginning again. How long he searched for a system we do not know, but one way or another—and perhaps accidentally—he discovered that the beginning tone of each of the phrases of the *Hymn to St. John* was related to the other tones by step, and in an ascending pattern. As a memory device he decided that the Latin word or syllable sung to these tones could serve as the names of the tones, and thereby be used to designate the relations of the pitches.

Hymn to St. John

	DERIVED SYLLABLES		DERIVED SYLLABLES
Ut queant laxis	**Ut**	Solve polluti	Sol
Resonare fibris	**Re**	Labii reatum	La
Mira gestorum	**Mi**	Sancte Iohannes	—
Famuli tuorum	**Fa**		

Ut has since been changed to *Do,* except in France. The syllable for the seventh scale step, *Si,* was added later (by the sixteenth century). One theory has it that *Si* was derived from the first letters of the last two words of the hymn.

Organum

The first deviation from the prevalent unison singing occurred sometime before the tenth century. There is only speculation as to how this started. It may have been in secular music, or in music of the church. At any rate, a second part was added, which was sung in fourths or fifths along with the basic chant. This parallel motion, called ***organum,*** in which the

Example 4-1   Organum

lower voice was a coupling of the upper, must indeed have sounded exciting after centuries of unison singing. The theory of organum was first described in *Musica Enchiriadis,* written in the ninth century.

In time the two voices of organum were doubled at the octave above. This is called ***composite organum.*** A further development, referred to as ***free organum,*** allowed more freedom of parts, especially at the beginning or end of the chant.

The next step shows the added part above rather than below the plain chant, and the intervals varied so that the two parts show differing melodic contours. Here are the seeds of polyphony. But one step more is needed to attain the true aspect of polyphony: to the differing contours of the separate melodies must be added rhythmic distinction. By the twelfth century this had been achieved. Against the plainsong the upper part is a weaving, florid line.

The setting of a florid part against the chant necessitates holding the tones of the chant longer. As the lower tones became stretched out, this lower part became known as the *tenor* (from the Latin, *tenere,* to hold) .

Notre Dame

In Paris, in the twelfth and thirteenth centuries, the church of Notre Dame was the fountainhead of new developments in polyphony. Late in the twelfth century, Leonin, organist and composer, and his successor, Perotin, contributed many works. The thirteenth-century motet evolved out of their work, to become one of the most important forms of this period. To a melismatic portion of a plain chant, used as the tenor (and the basis) of the musical work, two upper parts (usually) would be added.

Unlike organum, which was mostly rhythmically free, the motet was organized into rhythmic patterns, but with the tenor part in longer note values. The melismatic portion taken from a plain chant as the basis for the motet would be changed into a fixed rhythmic pattern. This, in many cases, would be played by instruments. Above this would be added two or three parts with words of secular origin. The term **motet** arose out of the French *mot,* or word. In addition to the mixture of music derived from both sacred and secular sources, a polytextual element was also introduced. One part above the tenor might be in French, another in Latin.

A further development toward rhythmic regularity can be seen in Latin songs of this period. The **conductus,** for example, consisted of a tenor part not derived from the chant but composed; thus the complete work is now original. The parts are mostly homophonic.

Secular music

During the first ten centuries the systematic preservation of church music resulted in a body of music that is available to the musicologist. But there

---

Cathedral of Notre Dame, Paris (*Photo by William Tesson*).

is no equivalent with respect to the secular music of these centuries. The church took great pains to preserve its music, but the preservation of music outside of the church was mostly ignored. Only in the last 100 years have scholars realized that the music of a people is an important part of their culture, and therefore made intensive studies in these directions. There is little secular music extant that precedes the tenth century. The largest body of secular music that has been preserved is from the eleventh and twelfth centuries. In southern France in the twelfth century we find the **troubadour,** usually of noble birth, singing songs of love and of chivalry. The troubadour songs were in a style meant to communicate easily and directly.

Travelling about from town to town the troubadour (and later in Northern France, the *trouvère*) would often have in his company a *jongleur,* a man of many talents but not of noble birth. The term **jongleur** originally meant jester or juggler, and to these talents the jongleur added singing, and often dancing or playing an instrument.

In Germany the art of the troubadour was carried on by the *minnesinger* and the *meistersinger*. The meistersingers eventually formed guilds, and awarded prizes for composition within specified "rules and regulations." This was actually a surrender of the original freedom of improvised song. An excellent illustration of the guild movement may be seen in Wagner's opera, *Die Meistersinger.*

Sumer Is Icumen In

The oldest example of a six-part polyphonic style that has been preserved now resides in the British Museum. Termed a *rota,* "Sumer Is Icumen In" is an infinite canon (or round) for six men's voices. It is written so that

Example 4-2   Sumer Is Icumen In, Rota

four voices form the canon, accompanied by two others that sing a bass line as a double ostinato. The canon is at the unison at a distance of four measures. "Sumer Is Icumen In" is believed to be from about the middle of the thirteenth century.

A free rendering is given of the old English, so that the round is practicable for singing. For the original text see the *Historical Anthology of Music.*

> Summer is a-coming in,
> Loudly sing cuckoo.
> Groweth seed and bloweth mead
>   and springeth woodland new.
> Sing cuckoo.
>
> Ewe now bleateth after lamb,
> Low'th after calf, the cow,
>
> Bullock starteth, buck he grazeth,
> Merry sing cuckoo.
> Cuckoo, cuckoo.
> Well sing'st thou cuckoo,
> Nor cease thou never, now.

Pre-Renaissance

The flowering of an age is a fascinating display, and perhaps the most fascinating age of all is the Renaissance. Before the Renaissance, common man, when not worshipping God, had his eyes on the ground. On his shoulders were the burdens of tradition and superstition; feudalism dominated his way of life. His moral choices seemed to be for the most part between God and the devil; he was the victim of diseases of society as well as of the body; he was circumscribed by important limitations of the mind as well as those of his physical universe. He had yet to look beyond the horizon, not only of the western ocean but of his limitations of knowledge. Perspective was yet to be found not only in painting, not only in the relation of the earth to other astral bodies, but in the relations of man to men.

There have been many attempts to pinpoint a single date as the beginning of the Renaissance, but no flower has a single root. The roots of the Renaissance are many and go back to the beginning of the fourteenth century. It was here that the sense of restlessness, the desire to become loose of the shackles, the itch to move out of the restrictions of manner and mode of thought and its expression were first most noticeably apparent.

The travels of the Crusaders had awakened many to the worlds that lay beyond their borders—worlds of other cultures and customs, of other moral and political beliefs. The desire for the expression of the individual led to the beginnings of a middle class society, and serfdom began to fade.

Roger Bacon, who died about 1294, was an English monk in the Franciscan order. In his experiments in chemistry, optics, and astronomy we find the modern concept: the scientific method of inquiry as opposed to belief based on tradition. Dante, although in other respects a medieval man, made the greatest impress toward the use of a modern language in his writings, and is the first representative figure of the new language of the new age. Latin continued to be spoken and written in the universities in Italy. In 1305 Dante writes, and encourages others to write, in the best vernacular of the time. Not only Italy, but England and France as well, were at the beginnings of a national language and a national culture. In Chaucer's greatest work, *The Canterbury Tales,* the stories were medieval, but the language was new. And late in the fourteenth century, we have Wycliffe's translation of the Bible into the common tongue.

In the century that followed, the voyages of Columbus opened the way for further explorations and also established avenues for international trade and commerce, which ultimately freed man not only from his physical insularity but from his insularity of thought, preparing him to acknowledge the existence of ideas and customs that could differ from his own.

More constantly questions were raised about the individual's position in society. Dante had written, "We must now determine what is the purpose of human society as a whole. . . . There is . . . some distinct function for which humanity as a whole is ordained, a function which neither an individual nor a family, neither a village nor a city, nor a particular kingdom has power to perform. . . . The specific characteristic of man is not simple existence, . . . it is rather the possible intellect, or capacity for intellectual growth."

Ars nova

The restlessness was apparent in the world of music as well. Early in the fourteenth century a treatise ascribed to Philippe de Vitry was titled "Ars Nova," to describe the new styles in music, as opposed to those of the earlier century. The music of the earlier century became then known as "Ars Antiqua." The treatise was essentially a discussion of notation and rhythm, and advanced an argument for the use of duple as well as triple meter. The prior concept that triple meter was the "pure" meter stemmed from the traditional concept of three as the perfect number, the trinity being at the center of Christian theology. The title of the treatise was felt to express the spirit of the times, and it was taken up and adopted as a label to symbolize the new freedom of expression that was arising in France, and—a little later—in Italy.

The "New Art" of the fourteenth century, as contrasted to the musical practices of the previous century, shows a greater use of thirds and sixths in part writing and a freer use of dissonance. The new interest in rhythm resulted in new means of expression. Regular rhythmic patterns had become, during Ars Antiqua, a part of the final development of organum and had been firmly established in Latin songs such as the *conductus,* which was mostly homophonic. Also, dance forms such as the *estampie* had carried this rhythmic regularity even further. The modal rhythms that had been in effect were now cast aside as being too restrictive. Now there was to be an interesting combination of a free polyphony that nevertheless carried within its framework repetitions of rhythmic patterns. The leading composer of this period was Guillaume de Machaut. Born around 1300 in Champagne he was to dominate French music in both sacred and secular works. In addition to setting the music to his own poetry in *Remede de fortune,* he established an important body of repertoire in his ballades, rondeaux, and virelais as well as his polyphonic chansons. There are also motets and a complete mass. He was the first composer to singly set the ordinary of the mass.

In Machaut's mass as well as in most of his motets we see examples of the new rhythmic concept, **isorhythm.** This term refers to the repetition of *similar rhythmic patterns* within what is nevertheless a polyphonic flow.

Also in the Machaut Agnus Dei, from the mass, is seen the **hocket** ("hiccup"), which had appeared in the thirteenth century but was much used in the fourteenth. The term refers to the interruption, by a short rest, of the syllable being sung. During the rest the singer would take a quick breath and then return to singing the interrupted syllable. Often during the rest another voice would insert itself, creating an "in-and-out" effect that added rhythmic variety and accent to the texture.

Another development of the fourteenth century was the use of chromat-

ics, not written in the music, but introduced by the performer. Termed *musica ficta,* these would often occur at the end of a phrase in a melodic cadence, 7–8; or they might occur during the piece to make a smoother melodic line.

Burgundian school

In the early fifteenth century important developments in music sprang chiefly from a group of composers working for the court of Burgundy. We now see developments in polyphonic style taking place that will ultimately lead to the refined style of Lassus and Palestrina. The Burgundian school was influenced by the writings of John Dunstable in England whose use of imitation represented the beginnings of contrapuntal style. His interest in setting words in their "conversational" usage resulted in an expression the opposite of the melismatic. And the use of vertical structures emphasizing thirds and sixths was to lead to a greater appreciation of the triad as a building unit.

In the music of Guillaume Dufay, leading composer of the Burgundian school, we see the use of imitation. In the tenor part we may still have the cantus firmus, but the other parts are beginning to "loosen" into a flowing, expressive style.

Finally, the restriction of the lowest part to a cantus firmus was done away with, at first by putting another part below the tenor. This lowest part became ultimately the *bass* part, and the part above the tenor became the *alto.* The voice above the alto, tenor, and bass (in the superior position) ultimately became the *soprano.* Thus, about the middle of the fifteenth century, the basic four voice parts were established that have remained as the norm for choral writing to the present day.

THE RENAISSANCE

Josquin

The roots of the Renaissance were in the fourteenth century. The Renaissance itself is most conveniently designated as the period from 1450 to 1600.

"Singing at a Funeral Ceremony" (**from a 14th Century manuscript**) (*Courtesy of Historical Pictures Service, Chicago*).

The first outstanding musical figure of this period is Josquin des Prez. He has been spoken of by some writers as the "first genius of modern music." His music is the first that registers with us as being of the musical language that we know. His melodic lines have continuity and coherence as we understand it, his harmonies are colorful and expressive, and his phrases and cadences have the rise and fall that are familiar to us.

Born about 1450 in the Netherlands, his name was Josse. The diminutive, Jossekin, became Josquin. He traveled widely, spending much time in Italy, at one time in the service of the ducal court at the Sistine Chapel in Rome, and at other times serving as court composer in Milan and France.

From Ockeghem, and from the influence of Obrecht and Busnois, he learned not only the highly complex devices common to contrapuntal writing at the time, but the art of musical expressiveness that goes beyond the devices and uses them as a means rather than an end in themselves. Riddle canons had been the delight of composers of the time, but some of the composers had become lost in the presentation of the puzzle, losing sight of the musical end. The oft-quoted statement of Martin Luther bears repeating: "Josquin is a master of the notes; they have to do as he wills, other composers must do as the notes will." Naumann, in speaking of the Netherlands school in general, said, "Henceforth counterpoint was but a means to an end, and art-music began to assume for the first time the characteristics of folk-music, i.e. the free pure and natural outflow of heart and mind, with invaluable addition, however, of intellectual manipulation." The way was opening for a musical expressiveness that was to find its culmination in the fugal style of Bach.*

Luther was enchanted with polyphony. He speaks of how "other voices at the same time cavort about the principal voice in a most wonderful manner . . . They seem to present a kind of divine dance, so that even those of our day who have only a most limited amount of sentiment and emotion gain the impression that there exists nothing more wonderful and beautiful. Those who are not moved by this are indeed unmusical and deserve to hear some dunghill poet or the music of swine." †

---

* *Famous Composers and Their Works*, Vol. I, ed. by Paine, Thomas, and Klauser, © 1891 by J. B. Millet Co., Boston, Mass., p. 16.
† Quoted in *HiFi/Stereo Review*, Dec., 1966, "Martin Luther, Musician," by William Kimmel, p. 50.

"La Dame et Licorne," tapestry (*Archives Photographiques, Musée de Cluny, Paris*).

"Martin Luther in His Home" (*Courtesy of Culver Pictures, Inc., New York*).

Lassus and Palestrina

Longfellow's statement, "In character, in manners, in style, in all things, the supreme excellence is simplicity," is an overemphasis and thus not quite true, but as applied to the style of a work of art it does point up that certain great masterworks have a simplicity that is disarming. Disarming because this certain kind of simplicity is the resolution of many complexities. The complexities the artist has already dispensed with—whether through thought, or experiment, or previous works—and what is left is the pure simplicity. The "supreme excellence" that is simplicity may be found in Lincoln's Gettysburg Address, in the beauty of a gem, in a *haiku*, or in Da Vinci's Mona Lisa. It may be also found in the music of Lassus and Palestrina. Lassus and Palestrina, one Flemish and the other Italian, both died in the year 1594, and it is this date that is usually taken to denote the close of the "golden era" of polyphony.

Lassus was born Roland de Lattre, in Mons, and was the last of the great masters of the Netherlands school. He is known by the Italian form of his name, Orlando di Lasso, or the Latinized version, Orlandus Lassus. Like Josquin, he travelled widely, but his travels began under circumstances that are somewhat unusual. Because of the excellence of his voice as a boy, he was kidnapped three times. The first two times he was recovered by his parents, but the third time marks the beginning of his journeys, which took him first to Milan and Naples and then to Rome, where he became a chapel master. At various times he visited France and England, and ultimately he married and settled in Munich. The profound "Penitential Psalms" are of this period. Writing constantly, both sacred and secular music, he became famous throughout Europe. Contrary to the experience of many composers, he received the rewards of an adoring society, he was knighted, and he received the order of the Golden Spurs from the Pope. He was one of the most prolific composers of all time. For example, he left over 500 motets.

Giovanni Pierluigi was born in the town of Palestrina, not far from Rome. He has been called the greatest of the church composers, and his music is also considered to be the "purest expression" of the polyphonic school of the sixteenth century. Whereas Lassus travelled widely and wrote in all forms, both secular and sacred, Palestrina spent most of his life in the service of the church. As a result almost all of his large output is music for the church.

Palestrina at once represents the close of the Flemish school and the beginning of the Roman school in music for the church. He is considered to be the greatest composer of the Catholic church, and in him we find a purity of expression that seeks not to let earthly passion obtrude in the service of worship but to express the serenity and the other-worldliness of a hushed chapel. Versed in all of the compositional techniques of the Netherlands school, Palestrina sought a "purer" expression. As the Lutheran chorale later would be the foundation for the music of Bach, so the Gregorian chant was the foundation on which Palestrina built.

In the interest of purity, he reduced in his music the amount of chromaticism and dissonance that was common in the works of other composers. His musical lines are more conjunct and less disjunct. When he does introduce leaps, they are often counteracted by a returning conjunct movement, which fills in the interval of the leap. Thus each voice is a gently undulating line, intended to propel the listener on quiet waves of sound.

The words of Palestrina will show his earnestness in striving for the essence of purity in his music:

> Music exerts a great influence upon the minds of mankind, and is intended not only to cheer these, but also to guide and to control them, a statement which has not only been made by the ancients, but which is found equally true today. . . . anxiously have I avoided giving forth anything which could lead anyone to become more wicked or godless. All the more should I . . . place my thoughts on lofty, earnest things such as are worthy of a Christian.*

---

* *Famous Composers and Their Works*, Vol. I, ed. by Paine, Thomas, and Klauser, © 1891 by J. B. Millet Co., Boston, Mass., p. 31.

The madrigal

One of the very special achievements of the late Renaissance was the development of the *madrigal* in Italy. It was a secular expression parallel to the sacred motet of the 16th century. It began to come into prominence early in the 16th century when musicians became more and more interested in the extremely expressive writings of the contemporary poets.

The madrigal grew out of the *frottola,* which was an Italian secular stanza song in chordal style, first in vogue near the beginning of the 16th century. In their musical settings of the poems each madrigal composer tried to express the emotional content of important words or phrases. This developed into a kind of picture-writing that at times (in the hands of certain composers) was somewhat cloying, but at its best evoked a kind of writing that was extremely powerful in its effect.

Where the frottola had been essentially homophonic, the madrigal grew more and more polyphonic until it was a felicitous combination of homophony and polyphony, the changing texture occurring as a result of the proper expression of the text.

The madrigal was freely composed, its length dependent upon the length of the poetic text. In the works of 16th century madrigal composers such as Adrian Willaert (c. 1490–1562), Jacob Arcadelt (c. 1505–c. 1560), and Nicole Vincentino (c. 1511–1572), there is a charming use of word-painting as part of the new attitude toward expressive writing. If the text referred to sighing, the music would "sigh" with the text through a downward curve of the melodic line.

Chromaticism beyond the uses of *musica ficta* was prominent by the time of Luca Marenzio (1553–1599), who set the final stamp on what may be called the mature Italian madrigal.

One other composer cannot be ignored, however; Carlo Gesualdo (c. 1560–1613), considered to be outside the mainstream of composers of this time, carried the ideas of lyric expression and word-painting to the ultimate, in harmonies which foreshadowed both Wagner and Debussy.

With the publication, in 1588, of a collection of Italian madrigals titled *Musica Transalpina,* the madrigal passed to England. The collections, mostly Italian madrigals with Italian and English words, contained many of the compositions of Marenzio, de Rore, Palestrina, and others, including, as well, William Byrd of England, who had previously seen the Italian madrigals in manuscript and had recognized their significance.

William Byrd was the first of a long list of English composers, who, influenced by the madrigal of Italy, made the madrigal their own, and thereby established a musical culture of their own. The seed had landed in fertile ground, and a whole body of literature began to spring up.

Important composers of the madrigal in England, in addition to William Byrd, were: Thomas Morley (c. 1557–1603), Thomas Weelkes (c. 1575–1623), Orlando Gibbons (c. 1583–1625), John Dowland (c. 1562–1626), and John Wilbye (c. 1574–1638).

Along with the madrigal in England there was a development of the solo *ayre* with lute accompaniment. Most English madrigalists also wrote ayres or songs with lute accompaniment, but among the chief lutanist song composers of the late 16th century were: John Dowland (1562–1626), who was responsible for *The First Book of Songs or Ayres* (1597); Thomas Campion (1567–1620), doctor, musician, and poet; and Francis Pilkington (c. 1562–1638).

Many of the ayres or songs also lent themselves well to accompaniment on the virginal, which was the popular household keyboard instrument of 17th century England. Here again we come upon the name of William Byrd, the chief composer for the virginal. One of the most important early virginal books was *My Ladye Nevells Booke* (1951), which contains nearly three hundred works.

Thus, as the 16th century turns into the 17th, we have seen vocal polyphony come to its full glory, we note the rise in the importance of instruments, we approach the combination of instruments and voices in a new form—opera—and ultimately we will become aware of a surge that encompasses the development of instruments—and the writing for them—that will culminate, in central Europe, with the emergence of one of the most dramatic expressions of man: the symphony.

CHAPTER 5

Baroque/Rococo

T O THE UNTRAINED listener, the music of the Baroque (approximately 1600–1750) is frequently perplexing. He searches hard but scarcely catches a tune. Sometimes so many tunes assail his ears at once that he cannot distinguish between them. The ones that he does isolate from the thick web of sound strike him as either jagged and spiky or rambling and diffuse. However, he does feel rhythm, indeed, sometimes a very insistent, steady beat. But he is likely to consider it to be monotonous, like the clacking of an old fashioned treadle sewing machine. And what bothers him more than anything else is a kind of formidable facade of dignity and reserve that seems to keep his emotional responses at arm's length.

Thus, before musical enlightenment comes, he gives only part of himself to the fugues, concerti grossi, cantatas, and passions that he encounters from the period. This he does despite perhaps what we might call unconscious appreciation of the best known pieces from the period. He glories in singing the carol by the great baroque master, Handel, "Joy to the World." He is touched by *Messiah,* and he dearly loves the romantic composer Gounod's "Ave Maria" without realizing that it is based entirely on a prelude from J. S. Bach's *Well-Tempered Clavier.*

The contrast that exists on the purely musical level between the Baroque and the following periods is very pronounced. The prevailing texture in musical composition in the Baroque is polyphonic, while that in the classical and romantic periods is primarily homophonic. We who have been weaned on homophony in our immediate social activities with hymns, folksongs, and patriotic songs, take very readily to the clearly marked leading melodies buttressed with the colorful harmonies of Haydn, Mozart, Beethoven, and Tchaikovsky. But we are puzzled at the thick tangle of melody lines and rich luxuriant detail of the Baroque. Thus, to enter into the beauties of much of the music in the Baroque we must undergo a certain amount of aural reconditioning. We must learn how to perceive and truly experience simultaneous melodic lines.

Similarly, the forms of the seventeenth and eighteenth centuries are not those with which we feel most comfortable. For example, the many elegant dance forms of the Baroque and earlier periods are quite foreign to us as living dance vehicles. On the other hand, the waltz, which flowered in the nineteenth century, is still danced extensively today. The minuet, gavotte, and sarabande, are emblems of a munificent, luxuriant society only encountered now in films. The instruments of the period—the harpsichord, clavichord, tracker organ, recorder, viola da gamba—have only recently been the object of renewed interest.

THE AGE OF REASON

Pascal said, "All the dignity of man consists of thought." The meaning of these words is germinal to most of the philosophical and scientific thought of the seventeenth and eighteenth centuries. Man had come into the security and certainties of rationalism. It was the Age of Reason.

Galileo and Kepler destroyed geocentric thinking and, as a fortuitous by-product, flattened the fossilized theories of the time. Chemistry replaced alchemy, and Harvey discovered that blood travels constantly throughout the entire body. Rational, comprehensive explanations were found for phenomena that had puzzled men from the beginning of time.

Newton, the author of the monumental *Principia Mathematica,* hoped to explain all material occurrences with mathematically expressible rules. He said, "I wish I could derive all phenomena of nature by some kind of reasoning from mathematical principles. . . ." Thinking baroque man then believed that his world could be reasoned out, could be fully understood, and perhaps even fully controlled by the use of logic and the new methods as outlined by Newton and Descartes.

As in every musical period, it was inevitable that pervasive and compelling ideas such as these were reflected in the arts. Thus it is that the music of Vivaldi, Handel, Corelli, J. S. Bach strikes us as being so solid and rational. It seems to be suffused by iron bonds of logic. Once the musical thought in a Bach fugue—say the "Kyrie Eleison" of his B-Minor Mass—has taken root in our consciousness, the music's direction and plan seem self-evident, completely right and logical. The ideas follow naturally and surely.

On the technical musical level this sense of permeating, comprehensive order can be illustrated many times over. It will suffice to point out the prominence of **figured bass** (or **thorough-bass**) in the Baroque. Figured bass was simply a system of numbers placed on the score itself. These numbers indicated with considerable precision the vertical interval combinations to be realized by the keyboard player. The analogy between musical notation and the mathematical bias of baroque philosopher/scientists is obvious. Relationships of tonality, chord, interval, scale, and modulation had become so systematic and general, so logical, that they could now be represented by numerical figures.

Besides this orderliness, there is also the feeling of luxuriance and richly decorative detail in many of the works. Again this reflects a very important aspect of baroque life.

There existed at that time an enormous social and economic gap between the masses and the aristocracy. Despite the mid-seventeenth-century republican insurrection of Cromwell in England and that in the Netherlands earlier, it was a time of splendid yet despotic monarchies in Europe.

We can clearly perceive this social cleavage by looking at some of the facts surrounding the life and manners of Louis XIV, the Sun King, who reigned in France for nearly three-quarters of a century.

He thought that, "As he [the king] is of a rank superior to all other men, he sees things more perfectly than they do, . . . occupying, so to speak, the place of God, we seem to be sharers of His knowledge as well as of His authority." "L'état c'est moi." Indeed! His official residence, the chateau of Versailles, housed ten thousand inhabitants and consumed 6 out of every 10 francs collected in taxes.

The pomp and splendor of the court extended even to the most quotidian functions. The noble chosen as the official bearer of the king's chamber pot was considered fortunate indeed.

H. G. Wells, in his *Outline of History,* mentions the ". . . sculpture in alabaster, faience, gilt wood-work, metal work, stamped leather, much music, magnificent painting, beautiful printing and binding, fine cookery, fine vintages. Amidst the mirrors and fine furniture went a strange race of gentlemen in vast powdered wigs, silks, and laces, poised upon high red heels, supported by amazing canes; and still more wonderful ladies, under towers of powdered hair and wearing vast expansions of silk and satin sustained on wire. Through it all postured the great Louis, the sun of his world, unaware of the meagre and sulky and bitter faces that watched him from those lower darknesses to which his sunshine did not penetrate." *

---

* *The Outline of History* by H. G. Wells, Vol. II, Garden City Books, N.Y. 1949, pp. 825–826.

Most of the master composers of the period either were in the "employ" of this gilded aristocracy or were church musicians. Very few, like Handel, or John Gay, became entrepreneurs, appealing directly to a paying, theater-going public.

It followed then that baroque secular music, written expressly for the aristocracy should clearly reflect the sumptuous qualities of court life in general. In the music of the court—secular and sacred—there is much melodic ornamentation, and exquisite detail of texture is paramount. Dances are those from the glittering ballrooms of court life.

For many years the great master Lully, founder of the French school of opera, was court composer for Louis XIV, writing masques and ballets in which both he and the king actively took part. Having glimpsed at the splendor of this court life it is small wonder that another side of the Baroque should exemplify panoply, dignity, pomp, luxuriance.

The third influence in baroque music was undoubtedly that of religion and the church. Many of the greatest works in the Baroque are religious in nature: cantatas, passions, oratorios, masses, Te Deums, and Magnificats. Though outwardly these religious structures tended to be ostentatiously elaborate, the music itself often represented the composer's innermost subjectivity. It was here that he could appropriately air his innermost sentiments.

There is a fourth quality in baroque music—its aliveness. Not so long ago it was fashionable to speak of baroque music as being dry, and arid—even academic. This was partly due to performers who considered the music of the early masters little better than finger exercises. Needless to say, their playing of J. S. Bach, Corelli, and Handel was deadly and antiseptic.

All of this was partly due to the tremendous power and influence of Romanticism in the nineteenth century. Many musicians felt that music without the intense subjectivity and overt passion of Wagner, Chopin, and Schumann simply was dry. Accordingly they played baroque music badly.

We now know differently. The music of the Baroque, especially in its late phases, is extremely vital, especially in the area of rhythm. Sometimes it is as raucous and colorful as the satirical paintings of William Hogarth (1697–1764). John Gay's enormously successful *The Beggar's Opera* is the perfect counterpart to the work of Hogarth. And the high spirits in Henry Fielding's novel *Tom Jones* (1749) finds a perfect match in the finale of J. S. Bach's *Sixth Brandenburg Concerto*.

But from whatever impetus or for whatever purpose, individual movements, dances, choruses, arias, etc. in baroque music show great homogeneity of mood and expression. The baroque doctrine of the affects as a basic approach to composition dictated that all structural elements—rhythmic, harmonic, melodic—be representative of a single affection or mood. Thus, within individual items, there is strong continuity bordering on the uniform.

For example, in the "Crucifixus" from J. S. Bach's *Mass in B Minor* (see below), all inner materials are continuously consistent with the mood to be established, in this case one of intense pathos. A single subject, one rhythmic pattern and tempo, and a consistent texture underlie many of the single forms of baroque composers.

GENERAL CHARACTERISTICS

Melody

Viewed from the standpoint of basic shape and type, baroque melody shows an interesting dichotomy. On the one hand, it is frequently highly expansive, personal, even romantic. At other times the "melody" is a mere fragment, a wisp of a tune that becomes important only through its elaboration and working out.

Example 5-1   *Well-Tempered Clavier*, Book I, Fugue 4, J. S. Bach

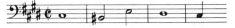

These few notes, followed by their blossoming into great music, remind us of the rationalistic philosopher Descartes' raising enormous edifices of wisdom on his simple yet potent idea: "I think, therefore I am."

Baroque melody frequently has an angular, rather jagged contour. Often it takes on life only through the poignant ornamentation dotting its surface.

Rhythm

There is a certain expectedness to baroque rhythms which to some people is disconcerting. Especially in many of the allegros we hear repeated rhythmic patterns, propelled by an unflagging beat. And we do not hear a great variety of tempos, as we do in Beethoven, Chopin, or Tchaikovsky. All of this is apparent when we compare the dreamy, flexible chant from previous periods with the straight-gaited beat of a chorus in the late Baroque.

This rigidity, however, occurs only on the surface of baroque music. Underneath the rather plain rhythmic exterior exist perhaps the most subtle and sophisticated rhythmic structures of any period.

Among the many rhythmic riches, perhaps the most exciting is that of syncopation. A great many baroque compositions make astonishing use of syncopation. If played with a steady, motoric underlying pulse, and if the

"The Enraged Musician," engraving by William Hogarth (*Courtesy of Prints Division, The New York Public Library—Astor, Lenox and Tilden Foundations*).

melodic line is accented according to its natural beat, the music shown in this example is surprisingly close to jazz. Indeed, fine jazz artists of our day are increasingly admiring and playing baroque music.

Example 5-2   *Invention No. 6*, J. S. Bach

Harmony

The Baroque is particularly interesting in the area of harmony. Of course, some impetus from the Golden Age of Polyphony remained; contrapuntal structures such as fugue, chaconne, and canon evolved and indeed tended to predominate. But, simultaneously, homophony came to the fore, with the musical center of gravity shifting to a single commanding melody. And although much of the music is either primarily polyphonic or homophonic, often there exists a masterful blend of the two. Thus, the Bach chorale not only is considered to be the fountainhead for all later tonal developments in vertical relationships, but also represents an ideal model for organizing four separate, but cooperating, melodic parts.

This development of massive polyphonic structures side by side with the homophonic, and the potent mixture of the two, could not have happened without the emergence of the two diatonic scales, the major and the minor. These were the foundation of a powerful homogeneous tonality. In the pre-Baroque the major scale (formerly Ionian mode) and the minor scale (formerly Aeolian mode) were only two of several possible scales underlying the structures of the Renaissance and earlier. But the hardy, homogeneous system of major-minor tonality was so satisfactory to many baroque composers that it must have seemed as eternal and fixed to them as the basic mathematical principles established by Newton and Descartes were to contemporary philosophers.

As early as 1602, figured bass can be seen. Later it had become so universal that Rameau in his several treatises, including the *Treatise of Harmony,* incorporated the whole into a comprehensive harmonic system. The principles of figured bass are not difficult to understand. Accompanying a bass line are certain numbers, either one or several, which indicate notes to be added above each bass note. These notes always were "figured" up from the bass, and were meant to be played by the keyboard performer. He would often use the resulting chords for extensive extemporaneous elaborations, accompanying the principal melody or melodies. In effect, this was a shorthand system that saved the composer much time and also allowed for interesting personal contributions from the player involved.

Example 5-3   *St. Matthew Passion,* Recitative, J. S. Bach

Figured bass served a purpose similar to that of the chord system used in the popular music of our day. The player "realizes" a lead line accompanied by a special system of chord letters and figures. And though baroque harmony did become extremely solid, rational, and self-contained, it should

never be thought that it was dull and colorless. Operating within the limits of major-minor tonality and figured bass were vertical sounds and progressions that are as trenchant and voluptuous as the vibrant colors in a Rubens painting.

Range and dynamics

As might be expected, both range and dynamics in baroque music were limited in scope. Most of the music of the period fits comfortably within a range of four or five octaves.

Because so much of the music of the Baroque is polyphonic, it is obvious that every voice—bass, tenor, alto, soprano—will at times carry leading melodic parts. But the favored register is decidedly the high soprano. Instruments with the ability to climb very high, such as the clarin trumpet (*clarino*) and soprano recorder, were much used. The baroque organ is distinguished by the many "mixture" stops, which often highlight the brilliant upper soprano register. Many of the **trio sonatas** by Corelli are written for two violins, which frequently criss-cross and hang high in the soprano. Beneath is the continuo part in the bass, realized by cello and keyboard. The rather bare middle register area was left to be "filled" by the keyboard player reading the figured bass.

Dynamics were most conservatively used. A modest forte or piano sufficed for most of the music. Significant crescendo and diminuendo was impossible on some keyboard instruments and sparingly used in general. It was not until the classical period, particularly with the orchestra at Mannheim, that colorful, graduated dynamics came into strong favor. Indeed, the mere fact that Rossini was called "Signor Crescendo" attests to the novelty of this effect.

Baroque masters were not unaware of the emotional impact derived from artfully utilized dynamics. But rather than rely on crescendo and diminuendo, or on extremes of dynamic levels, they preferred to use the sharp juxtaposition of forte with piano.

Performance and instruments

Performance standards were rather high in the Baroque, and the gulf that exists today between performer and composer was largely absent then. Many master composers were also brilliant performers. Daquin astonished all who heard him because of the brilliance of his passage work at the keyboard. Corelli, Torelli, Locatelli, and Vivaldi all were renowned violinists. Domenico Scarlatti astounded the courts of Italy, Spain, and Portugal with his digital gymnastics at the harpsichord. J. S. Bach was perhaps better known for his playing at the organ than for his compositions.

Of the 381 instruments owned by King Henry VIII in sixteenth-century England, 272 were winds. Only 109 were strings, including keyboard instruments. Winds certainly predominated in the Renaissance; strings were emphasized in the Baroque. The seventeenth and early eighteenth centuries saw the flourishing of the master instrument builders at Cremona: Stradivari, Amati, Guarneri, and others. There is no question that the finest literature of the period is written for strings. The string family formed the backbone of many of the orchestras of the day.

Keyboard instruments—clavichord, harpsichord, organ—also were prominent. The piano, though existing in the late Baroque—J. S. Bach is known to have played on Frederick the Great's new Silbermann pianofortes—did not displace the harpsichord in the affections of musicians until the time of Mozart and Haydn.

Forms

Opera, cantata, passion, the liturgical mass, the chorale, and many forms occupied a vital position in the musical thinking of baroque masters. In both vocal and instrumental music, polyphonic structures predominated. Bach felt so challenged by the fugue that he wrote 24 preludes and fugues spanning all possible major and minor keys in a volume known as the *Well-Tempered Clavier*. Then, 22 years later, he wrote 24 more. In this effort, however, he was anticipated by Johann Caspar Fischer who, in 1715, published 20 preludes and fugues covering 19 different keys.

There is no question that the enormous technical challenges found in polyphonic composition appealed to the rationalistic facet of the baroque composer's personality. The miracle of it all is that these ultra-sophisticated contrapuntal structures manage, in the hands of the masters, to achieve great emotional impact.

At the same time that traditional approaches to compositions were employed, many forms appeared that were destined to achieve dominance in later periods. Thus, we see early forms of the concerto, symphony, sonata, suite, aria, and overture. Each achieved ascendancy later in the classical and romantic periods. These early forms only anticipate in a general way the actual dramatic structures of the late eighteenth and nineteenth centuries. The baroque solo concerto, though it and the later Viennese concerto both follow the fast-slow-fast pattern, is vastly different from the structures developed by Mozart and Beethoven.

For example, the typically classical sonata-allegro structure was not used in the baroque concerto. The baroque concerto employed a considerable degree of polyphonic texture, while the later form is predominantly organized with loose homophonic textures. And, most important, the dramatic juxtaposition of soloist as protagonist with orchestra only occurs in the later variety.

THE COMPOSERS

It was a long time from the days of Monteverdi, at the turn of the seventeenth century, to the ripe musical days of J. S. Bach. There is even more contrast between the works of the early baroque masters and those of Bach and Handel than there is between early Haydn and late Beethoven. It will follow, then, that no single, overriding aesthetic outlook will permeate all of the figures in this period. There was tremendous variety of style during these many decades. For example, a comparison of Antonio Vivaldi and J. S. Bach, contemporaries writing in similar idioms, uncovers tremendous differences. Among these are the closely cropped textures and complexity of Bach's rhythms, as opposed to the near-folk-song simplicity of Vivaldi. Despite huge contrasts in their respective styles, Bach so admired Vivaldi that he transcribed (among other Vivaldi works) a concerto for four violins by the Italian into one for four claviers.

Early Italian composers

There are six major figures at the outset of the Baroque. Each had deep roots in the Renaissance period, and wrote many works clearly in the sixteenth-century style. Yet each was an innovator, breaching reactionary defenses and catapulting music into a new age. All were Italian: Giovanni Gabrieli (1551–1612), Don Carlo Gesualdo, Prince of Verona (1560–1613), Giulio Caccini (1546–1618), Jacopo Peri (1561–1633), Claudio Monteverdi (1567–1643), and Girolamo Frescobaldi (1583–1643).

Peri and Caccini collaborated on the first opera ever written, *Daphne,* but to Caccini alone goes the honor of writing the first opera published, *Euridice.* These men were in the artistic-intellectual group revolving around Count Giovanni Bardi, scholar and patron of music. This group, called the "Camerata," wished to bring back the simplicity and directness of expression that they associated with ancient Greek culture. This resulted in the *monody* of Peri and Caccini, which might seem rather bland and anti-lyric now. In fact, much of it consists of little but a recitative-like single line sustained by block chords. But to these men, accustomed to the thick, clustered web of ecclesiastical polyphony of the renaissance style, this new, direct mode of musical expression seemed the perfect tool for the humanism that they advocated.

Gesualdo is an interesting figure, not only for his music, but in the de-

tails of his private affairs. The color and excitement generated by the extreme chromaticism of his madrigals is only surpassed by the romance of his
life. He is the only major composer with the distinction of being a murderer. He is positively known to have arranged for the assassination of his
wife's lover. If one is slightly disturbed at the thought that such noble
sounds were created by a murderer, one need only read Machiavelli's (1469–
1527) *The Prince.* There he will find an eloquent advance apology for the
murky backgrounds of brilliant men such as Gesualdo, the great sculptor
Benvenuto Cellini (1500–1571), and others.

Monteverdi in his operas such as *Orfeo,* through the immensity of his
genius, outstripped by far his predecessors in the field. Though he did not
write instrumental music as such, he greatly expanded the role of the orchestra in vocal music. Novel effects introduced by him, such as pizzicato and
tremolo in the strings, startled the music world. In his unique way with harmony he anticipates much of modern usage. Unprepared dissonances and
trenchant juxtaposition of chords usually not heard side by side can be heard
in his madrigals, operas, and songs. If Peri and Caccini were the founders of
monody and opera, Monteverdi must be considered the founder of modern
harmony.

Frescobaldi and Giovanni Gabrieli were both renowned organists. Both
were vital in the development of instrumental forms. Frescobaldi in his
ricercari anticipated one of the late Baroque's most important structures,
the fugue. Gabrieli created pieces for grouped instruments such as the *Sonata pian e forte,* where the winds are juxtaposed to the strings in the antiphonal style. He reveled in the color possibilities of antiphony, sometimes
dividing his massed voices into four choirs singing back and forth.

Giovanni Gabrieli is a particularly pertinent example of a great transitional figure. His uncle, Andrea Gabrieli (1510–1586), of whom he was a
reverent disciple, was a grand figure in the Renaissance. His pupil, Heinrich
Schütz, is considered to be of major importance in the development of the
German Baroque.

Following closely on the heels of the composers discussed above came
Giacomo Carissimi (1605–1674), who was instrumental in the creation of
oratorio. That form at first was distinguished from early opera only by its
sacred text. But with Carissimi's masterful balancing of choral and soloistic
forces, and the addition of the narrator, the oratorio took on tremendous
meaning for the future.

Violinist-composers

Shortly after the blooming of the new vocal forms of opera, oratorio, and
others, there developed an extensive and long-lived school of composers

whose primary interest lay in music for the violin. It was quite fitting that Italy, the mother of *bel canto,* should have produced this brilliant group of player-composers, and that the Italian city of Cremona should have produced the finest stringed instruments that the world has yet known. With many magnificent instruments by Nicolo Amati (1596–1684), Antonio Stradivari (1644–1737), and Giuseppe Guarneri (1681–1742) available, Italian composers set about composing a multitude of sonatas, concertos, and single pieces of singular grace and lyric elegance. This long line of composers included Archangelo Corelli (1653–1713), Tommaso Antonio Vitali (1665–?), Antonio Vivaldi (1680?–1743), Francesco Geminiani (1687–1762), Giuseppe Tartini (1692–1770), and Francesco Veracini (1685–1750). As can be seen, this line of composers spanned the better part of 100 years and included several pre-classical composers.

Corelli and Vivaldi

Perhaps the two outstanding figures in Italian baroque music were Corelli and Vivaldi.

Corelli, besides having systematized bowing on the violin, is said to have been the first to introduce **double stops.** But much more important than his fame as a player and innovator of violin technique is the nobility and profundity of his works. The solo violin pieces are still much esteemed by concert audiences, but it is with the *concerto grosso* and the *trio sonata* that Corelli's true greatness is apparent.

Vivaldi was an extremely colorful figure. Perhaps his music now is beginning to rival that of J. S. Bach and Handel in popularity with concert audiences. Called the "Red Priest" because of the color of his hair, Vivaldi was a clergyman whose pedagogical excellence matched his prowess with the violin and genius in composition. For 36 years Vivaldi directed a music school for indigent girls. One cannot better the quote from De Brosses in *Grove's Dictionary:* "Indeed they sing like angels, play the violin, flute, organ, oboe, cello, bassoon—in short no instrument is large enough to frighten them. . . . I swear nothing is more charming than to see a young and pretty nun, dressed in white, a sprig of pomegranate blossom behind one ear, leading the orchestra and beating the time with all the grace and precision imaginable." *

His output was enormous: the 447 concertos for a wide range of instruments including guitar, mandolin, and piccolo represent a stupendous achievement. Particularly intriguing is the set of four violin concertos called

---

* *Grove's Dictionary of Music and Musicians,* Vol. IX (New York: St. Martin's Press, Inc., 1960), p. 27.

The Seasons, each representing a different time of the year. They are studded with appealing moments of imagery, such as a summer storm and bird calls.

Not especially associated with the school of violinist-composers were two other masters, Alessandro Scarlatti (1659–1725) and Giuseppe Sammartini (1693–1770). Both wrote instrumental music that anticipated the classical symphony. In addition, Scarlatti was a great master of late baroque opera, and is credited with the perfection of the oratorio form.

Lully

Underlining the influence of Italian masters in the early Baroque is the fact that the first truly great French composer of the Baroque, the founder of French opera, the creator of the disciplined court orchestra of Louis XIV, was a violinist from Florence by name of Jean Baptiste de Lully (1632–1687). He was a tremendous force in the music world of his time. Even the English acknowledged his luster. Roger North, a lawyer-turned-composer, in his *Memoires of Musick,* said, ". . . during the first years of Charles II all musick affected by the beau mond run in the French way; and the rather because at that time the master of the Court Musick in France, whose name was Baptista (an Italian frenchifyed) had influenced the French style by infusing a great portion of the Italian harmony into it, whereby the air was exceedingly improved." *

Lully's temper was said to match the power of his music. He died from an infection caused by striking his foot with his enormous baton while in a rage with his orchestra.

Other French masters

Francois Couperin (Le Grand) (1668–1733), the most illustrious of a family of musicians rivaling the Bach family for longevity, wrote much charming music for the clavecin (harpsichord). His colorful pieces, replete with delightful titles, are still extremely popular with keyboard artists. Some of the finest of these are "Le Moucheron" (anticipating by two centuries the famous *Diary of a Fly* by Bartók), "Soeur Monique," and "L'Anguille," whose wiggling figurations charmingly suggest the slithering of the eel.

Jean Philippe Rameau (1683–1764), in addition to systematizing har-

---

* David G. Weiss, *Samuel Pepys, Curioso* (Pittsburgh: University of Pittsburgh Press, 1957), p. 49.

mony, had a great influence on the theoretical thinking of composers after him. More important, however, is his music, especially the novel and majestic operas, such as *Castor et Pollux.* His pieces for clavecin rival those of Couperin for clarity, sophistication, and color.

Claude Daquin (1694–1772), the composer of the familiar keyboard piece, "Le Coucou," was a rival of Rameau's and famed for the clean articulation of his playing at the organ.

Other important composers of French baroque music are Jean Baptiste Loeillet (1680–1730); Louis Marchand (1669–1732), the player who defaulted in the famous proposed organ playing bout with J. S. Bach; Marc Antoine Charpentier (1634–1730); and Jean Marie Leclair (1697–1764), a famous violin virtuoso.

The English

The English, after the luminosity of their many magnificent Renaissance composers such as Byrd, Dowland, and Morley, produced only a few masters in the Baroque.

John Blow (1648–1708) was organist at Westminster Abbey before Purcell. John Christopher Pepusch (1667–1752), the collaborator with John Gay in the fabulously successful *Beggar's Opera,* was really a transplanted German. Dr. Thomas Arne (1710–1778) lived into the classical period.

Without question the leading personality of the English Baroque was Henry Purcell (1659–1695). In his short 36 years, he managed to produce a great many profound works. In the geniality of his melody, the copiousness of his output in so short a time, and the richness of his harmony, he is much like Schubert. Purcell's best known works are the operas *Dido and Aeneas* and *The Fairy Queen,* adapted from Shakespeare's *Midsummer Night's Dream.*

German masters

Heinrich Schütz (1585–1672) is justly called the father of German music. He is a major figure in the early Baroque, occupying a position of equal importance to that of Monteverdi in Italy. His opera, *Daphne,* now lost, was the first in the German language. The many sacred choral works such as the *Seven Last Words of Christ,* the *Passions,* and the *Christmas Oratorio* show a Bach-like power and intensity. There can be no doubt that the sacred choral works of this master were the cornerstone and inspiration of much of the work of J. S. Bach and Handel.

If the favorite instrument of the Italian Baroque was the violin, that of the German Baroque was the organ. The violin was the perfect instrument for the transmission of Italian bel canto; the organ, with its power and diversity of tonal color, was the ideal instrument for German complexity of polyphony. Just as the violin, in the hands of the master craftsmen at Cremona, became highly perfected, so did the great baroque organs, especially in Germany.

These great organs, with their utter clarity and substantial body of tone, were the ideal instruments for the fugues, toccatas, passacaglias, and chorale preludes so intrinsic to German baroque music. There are many who feel that these great organs by Schnitger and others have never been surpassed.

An illustrious line of organist-composers accordingly arose beginning quite early in the seventeenth century. The student of Frescobaldi, Johann Jakob Froberger (1616–1667), was one of the first. Among many others were Johann Pachelbel (1653–1706) and Dietrich Buxtehude (1637–1707). Buxtehude's playing and compositions so attracted J. S. Bach that he walked 50 miles to hear him. Bach overstayed his leave from his church position by three months in order to hear and study the master's music.

George Philip Telemann (1681–1767), whose fame much eclipsed that of J. S. Bach in his day, wrote many facile and entertaining suites, concertos, trio sonatas, and vocal pieces. Such was his technique as a composer that he was said to be able to dash off an eight-part motet as easily as another would write a letter. Schumann quoted him as saying, ". . . a proper composer should be able to set a placard to music."

Handel and Bach

The German Baroque culminated with two majestic names in music: Georg Friedrich Handel (1685–1759) and J. S. Bach (1685–1750).

In some ways the lives of these two men parallel those of two later German masters who summed up the romantic period, Johannes Brahms and Richard Wagner. Brahms was a gentle, rather parochial conservative who worked mostly with the instrumental classical forms, while Wagner espoused opera and assailed the whole world with his "music of the future."

J. S. Bach, much like Brahms, stayed in Germany, and developed to a high level of perfection the sacred vocal and organ forms that he inherited from his predecessors. Opera was not part of his output, although it inundated the stages of the civilized world. However, Handel, like Wagner, was much more of an entrepreneur, and much of his most important work was in the field of opera.

Johann Sebastian Bach was a member of a distinguished family of com-

"The Organ," engraving by M. Engelbrecht (*Courtesy of Prints Division, The New York Public Library—Astor, Lenox and Tilden Foundations*).

posers and players that thrived in Germany for 200 years. Strong roots in the craft of his fathers and his own inclinations towards sober hard work kept him, perhaps, from wandering much in the world or from urgently seeking recognition. However, he did challenge the great French organist Marchand to a musical duel at the keyboard, and was happy enough late in his life to visit and play for Frederick the Great at Potsdam. He held posts as Kapell-meister at important churches, and as court composer.

Bach's musical style is matched by an interesting dichotomy. On the one hand it is super-sophisticated at almost every level. The polyphony is of such intricacy and such pervasive power of musical logic that it staggers the mind. The rhythms are more advanced by far than anything in Mozart or Haydn. His unique handling of dissonance anticipates the music of our times. In short, Bach's music is highly intellectual, showing the highest flights of which the musical mind is capable. On the other hand, his music is never dry. No matter how cerebral it may be, it always is suffused by a warmth, a uniquely human quality. For example, the "Crucifixus" from the *Mass in B Minor* represents the highest kind of technical thinking in music. It is a chaconne, with utterly refined use of polyphonic variation over the repeated chromatic bass figure.

Example 5-4   *Mass in B Minor*, "Crucifixus," J. S. Bach

Yet, despite the formal intricacies, the effect is sublime. The sounds emanating from the voices are as rich and satisfying as anything from Beethoven or the Romantics.

In this connection—where the intellectual is matched by the emotional—Bach is again very much like Brahms. Bach's best known works are the *B–Minor Mass*, the *St. Matthew Passion*, the *Well-Tempered Clavier*, the *Brandenburg Concertos*, the concertos for single or multiple instruments, the chorale preludes for organ, and the cantatas.

Analysis and Commentary: "Wachet auf, ruft uns die Stimme" Chorale Prelude by J. S. Bach

This piece is particularly rewarding for analysis and study. It illustrates the highest kind of music by the master who is conceded to represent the very essence and culmination of the baroque style, Johann Sebastian Bach. It is rewarding from the historical point of view in that the form used, the chorale prelude, is of major significance, with a long line of ancestry in German music.

The Lutheran chorale, which is at the foundation of the form itself, was very important in the German Baroque. Also important is that this piece is found in two versions: as an organ piece (from the Schubler Chorale Preludes) and as the fifth number from *Cantata 140*. Thus, the music not only illustrates Bach's habit of setting the same music for different performance media, but offers an excellent opportunity to contrast the effect of the same music presented in different timbres. The chorale will already be familiar to many, for it is included in many modern Protestant hymn books.

Example 5-5   Chorale, "Wachet auf," third verse, J. S. Bach

This chorale illustrates another important facet of Bach's genius. The tune is actually by an earlier composer, Philipp Nicolai (1556–1608), but

the beautiful harmonization by J. S. Bach only adds to the luster of his genius.

The form of the chorale prelude as used here by Bach is one of several possible. Bach creates soprano and bass lines of exquisite sensitivity. At certain points in the flow of these are heard successive phrases of the chorale itself. Thus, the whole consists of three-part counterpoint, the chorale acting as a cantus firmus somewhat in the fashion of music of the pre-Baroque. Each melodic part contrasts rhythmically with the others: the upper quite active, the lower more stately, using primarily quarter-notes and eighth-notes, while the chorale is quite plain.

It begins with an idea, with the typical jagged intervals found in so much

Example 5-6

Bach. This rugged contour is explained by the fact that not one but two

Example 5-7

melodic parts are suggested within one line. In measure 5 another, comple-

Example 5-8

mentary, idea begins, which leads to an interesting syncopated figure.

Example 5-9

At measure 13, on the third beat, the chorale enters. The miracle of this mo-

Example 5-10

ment is that it is so natural an entrance. The first 12 measures of two-part counterpoint are so absolutely satisfying in themselves that one marvels at the arrival of a third melodic part which suddenly seems an indispensable addition. We wonder if Bach might very well have been able to add a fourth and a fifth part with perfect ease and natural effect.

The first phrase of the chorale is heard with its accompanying counterpoint. Then the music thins to a two-part texture again, where we hear a firm modulation to the dominant key, B-flat major:

Example 5-11

After a repetition of this material a new phase begins and the music shifts to another tonal area, this time to the key of C minor:

Example 5-12

The two-part counterpoint touches briefly on G minor, and soon after sinks back into E-flat major, the home key. At this point the last phrase of the chorale is heard. After it is completed, the last part of the prelude is taken up by the final spinning out of the florid melody of the beginning, the whole gradually coming to a majestic repose with a cadence in E-flat major on a simple, reverent tonic octave.

Example 5-13

Handel was much more volatile and enterprising than Bach. He once fought a duel with the organist-composer Johann Mattheson and survived to enter the lists later in England with his bitter rival for operatic supremacy, Bononcini (1670–1747). He traveled early to Italy, met both Scarlattis, and quickly ascertained that his fortune lay with the stage. In his later years in London, where he was much celebrated, he wrote a great many operas in the Italian style, and oratorios, including the famous *Messiah*. The effect of his music is much more immediate than that of Bach's. The texture is more open, with much less dissonance. Though counterpoint is the cornerstone of his style, it is much less compact than Bach's. The harmony, though occasionally astonishing in its chromaticism, usually is rather bland. The rhythms are seldom as intricate as those in Bach, and his melodic lines are more fluid and lyric.

Handel is supreme in massed effects. Pieces such as the *Te Deum* are monumental in scope. In this respect Handel's music sounds well when sung by large choruses of 150 or more voices (though much of it was written for smaller groups), while that of Bach becomes almost unintelligible when done by anything larger than a chamber chorus.

Beethoven esteemed Handel above all others in the field of vocal music and asked for a complete Handel edition near the end of his life.

Handel, like Bach, was almost blind for his last few years, though he managed to play the organ in his own oratorios until his death in 1759.

IN TRANSITION: THE GALLANT STYLE
OF THE ROCOCO

The next major period to be encountered after the Baroque will be the Classical, encompassing the lives of three giants: Mozart, Haydn, and Beethoven. The stylistic gulf that separates the densely intellectual, massively ornate Baroque from the directly expressive Classical is huge.

The music that fills this gap is called **Rococo.** The word is derived from the French, *rocaille,* meaning "rockwork," and refers particularly to the ornate arrangements of rocks in the gardens at Versailles. As it applies to music it means an emphasis on the elegantly embroidered, graceful, and charming. Its purpose is simply to please. It is purposely shallow, reflecting the hedonism so apparent in the court of Louis XV.

Rococo music frequently is saturated with melodic ornaments, called *agréments* by the French. Homophony predominates, with the harmonies simple and affecting. Frequently, as we saw earlier with Couperin, catchy titles were used.

The exquisite hedonism of the Rococo is reflected in the polished paintings of Watteau, where grace, sheen, and elegance reign supreme. The many scrolled mirrors at Versailles also reflect this accent on decoration, and the heightening of the pleasures of life. So does the exterior of the clavecin, the leading instrument of the gallant style.

Attendant to the new simplicity of the French Rococo were parallel developments throughout Europe. Mentioned above was Gay's extremely popular *Beggar's Opera* (1728), which routed the conservative *opera seria* (serious opera) from the boards of the English stage. In the Paris of 1752 an Intermezzo, *La Serva Padrona,* by Giovanni Pergolesi (1710–1736) ran for one hundred performances. This frothy piece in the new Italian *opera buffa* (comic opera) style precipitated the "War of the Buffoons." Through a series of polemical pamphlets, many of the finest minds in Paris debated the merits of the new popular *buffo* style versus the traditional *opera seria.* As could be expected, the philosopher Rousseau, as the champion of "natural man," favored the fresh expressive tide brought in by Pergolesi's masterpiece. In 1752, the same year that marked the sensational debut of *La Serva Padrona* in Paris, Rousseau wrote his own opera buffa, *Le Devin du village.* And the pre-classicism of the newly emerging orchestral symphony at several European cultural centers clearly pointed away from the dense severities of

The Hall of Mirrors at Versailles *(Courtesy of Rapho Guillumette Pictures, New York).*

the Baroque. The general term, *gallant,* denotes the common tendency in the late Baroque towards a sensual, direct, and immediately appealing kind of music. Much of the music of Couperin, Pergolesi, the sons of Bach, D. Scarlatti, and others is spoken of as being in the *style galant.*

Of the French composers discussed above those often associated with the *style galant* are Couperin "Le Grand," Rameau, Daquin, and Leclair. In Italy, Domenico Scarlatti concerned himself much with music for the cembalo (harpsichord), on which he was as renowned a virtuoso as was Liszt on the piano in the nineteenth century. His sonatas, numbering over 500, are frothy, piquant, and elegant, often displaying qualities similar to those of the French Rococo.

But, one of these, the *Cat's Fugue,* shows how very much rococo masters were rooted in the true Baroque. This piece, built on a subject supposedly originating from notes played by the household cat jumping up to the cembalo keyboard, is cast as a perfectly correct, baroque fugue.

In Germany the counterpart to the French rococo gallant style was the *empfindsamer stil.* This musical expression can be heard in the slow movements of the keyboard sonatas of C. P. E. Bach (son of J. S. Bach and court musician to Frederick the Great). There is subtle nuance, varied expression, and a touching sensitivity throughout. C. P. E. Bach's own directions for realizing this style at the keyboard point up the emphasis placed on effective representation of emotion in the *empfindsamer stil:* "In languishing, sad passages, the performer must languish and grow sad. Thus will the expression of the piece be more clearly perceived by the audience."

CHAPTER 6
Classicism

MONTAIGNE UNDOUBTEDLY EXAGGERATED when he said of man's progress in history, "We do not go; we rather run up and down and whirl this way and that; we turn back the way we came." * Certainly it is true that history repeats itself, at least in part. Nothing is all new. There simply does not exist a totally new style of painting or musical composition. This is particularly apparent in successive musical eras. A new period or style may well have evolved in an atmosphere of violent reaction to the "artistic establishment" immediately preceding it. The development of spare and simple monodic forms by the Italian Camerata near 1600 as a strong protest to the elaborate polyphony of renaissance music is a good example of this. Yet that which is new—and worthwhile—is always powerfully rooted in the past and especially in the near past. Classicism is no exception to this.

Classicism sits squarely on the foundation built by baroque masters. In the field of harmony, Rameau and others had solidified chord structure, chord progression, and major-minor tonality to such an extent that it sufficed basically unchanged for Haydn, Mozart, and Beethoven, and lasted until the twentieth century. Lyric homophony, which is the prevailing texture throughout the classical era, actually was fully developed in the Baroque, though it shared the attention of composers with polyphony. The masters of Classicism took full advantage of the enormous growth of instrumental music, as well as the refinement of the instruments themselves in the Baroque.

The music of the classical masters often shows strong atavistic traces.

---

* Robert Maynard Hutchins, ed., *Great Books of the Western World*, Vol. 25, Montaigne (Chicago: University of Chicago Press), p. 439.

The slow introduction of Beethoven's last *Piano Sonata,* Opus 111, shows an unmistakable resemblance to the typically somber French overture of the Baroque.

Example 6-1   *Piano Sonata*, Op. 111, Introduction, Beethoven

Beethoven's predilection for the fugue in his later years is well known. Mozart, besides writing many sterling fugues himself, arranged five fugues from J. S. Bach's *Well-Tempered Clavier.* His writing additional accompaniments to four choral works of Handel—including the *Messiah*—shows an involvement in the Baroque beyond simple homage to the past.

Yet, aside from these obvious and necessary connections with the Baroque, classical music is strikingly original in sound. We have seen in Chapter 5 what distinguishes baroque style. In it can be seen a splendid display of energy, drive, and passion tempered by utter dignity, and a luxuriance of detail made convincing by complete logic of structure. Briefly, baroque music can be said to display an intense but thoroughly ordered musical expression.

In contrast to this, typically classical music emphasizes symmetry, reserve, a profound simplicity. Emotion is present—indeed sometimes it seethes to the surface as in the Symphony No. 40 by Mozart—but it seldom is as obvious as in the Baroque. Its goal is balance; a blending of form with content. Hellenistic simplicity, purity, symmetry, universality were the ideals in all the arts of this time.

Jacques Louis David produced paintings such as "The Death of Socrates" and "Brutus" whose content and form were directly influenced by Greek and Roman aesthetic attitudes.

Palladian architecture, with its emphasis on early classical symmetry and just proportion, permeated England and, of course, the North American colonies. The University of Virginia, designed by Thomas Jefferson, is a particularly fine example of early American use of Palladian architecture.

In the music of the Classicists, symmetry, purity, and simplicity can be heard. One beautifully chiseled phrase will be answered and balanced by another very much like it. There is much expectedness. Nothing is done in excess. The music is seldom hotly passionate. Textures are open, simple, and pellucid. Everything is as functional, simple, and dignified as the Roman toga, woven of a single piece of undyed wool. Rather than the kingly dignity found in much baroque music, classical music shows controlled equanimity.

Though polyphonic forms continued to be used—especially in sacred music—cleanly chiseled, diaphanous single melody, supported by logically structured chords in various guises was predominant in the classical period. Lyric homophony was easier to understand, representing perhaps plainer, more direct expression. Therefore it was ideal for a serene, classical style.

Summing up, the transition from the Baroque was one from complexity to simplicity, from a luxuriant vivacity to a serene, generally buoyant simplicity. Rhythms became simpler, melodic contours smoother, textures more open, forms easier to perceive. Homophony largely replaced polyphony. All of this was effected with the help of a bridging period, the Rococo.

What, then, were some of the forces at work in society that conditioned musical thinking of the last half of the eighteenth century?

We have already seen in the Baroque how Europe was divided by the Great Powers: France, England, Spain, Germany. A gilded, pampered aristocracy yoked and abused the great mass of suffering humanity. Imperialism, mercantilism, absolutism, reigned.

Many courts had become corrupt. The longer their princes and kings reigned, the sillier and more unrealistic they became. Samuel Pepys in his diary noted, "On the night when our ships were burnt by the Dutch, the King did sup with my Lady Castelmaine, and there they were all mad, hunting a poor moth."

But counterbalancing this were many free, independent souls, products of the Enlightenment, disgusted at the excesses of the courts and at the pitiable state of the poor masses. John Locke with works such as *An Essay Concerning Toleration*, deeply influenced the American libertarian revolutionaries. In France, Rousseau, Diderot and the Encyclopedists, and Voltaire raised loud cries of protest. And then, within a span of 20 years, two revolutions occurred on different continents which were destined to shake the very foundations of existing social structure. The American Revolution of 1776 and the French Revolution of 1789, occurred at the height of what is considered to be the classical period in music.

To some it may seem strange to link together the graceful, somewhat detached music of this period to the terror in France during the revolution. The picture of hundreds of patrician heads rolling into baskets, or gracing elevated pikes throughout bloodthirsty, raging Paris, does not harmonize well with minuets, romances, and serenades. However, there is a connection.

The French and American Revolutions signaled a fundamental change in world history and attitudes. Throughout history, there had been talk and theory of the fellowship of man; of democracy and equality for all men.

The Greeks and Romans had eloquently spoken for it, but in practice it turned out to be a democracy for those only who happened not to be slaves. The Cromwellian Republic in England lasted but a few years, despite the magnificent proclamation of the Rump Parliament, "that the people are, under God, the original of all just power."

In America, after the Revolution, four million people consciously set out to see if democracy could work. In France, despite many regressions, a similar experiment had begun. This had enormous repercussions throughout the world. Whether democracy succeeded or not in Europe and America was not as important as its existence in practice. The dike, holding back the perfection and happiness of mankind had finally been breached, though imperfectly.

We shall see in the next chapter how revolution in art, philosophy, science, medicine, and industry is the very hallmark of Romanticism. And who can doubt that, in our own day, revolution is the single most important factor in the world?

The essence of this constant social revolution beginning in the late 1700's and intensifying in the twentieth century, is the importance of man—of Everyman. Music somehow had to reflect emerging truths about the nobility of common man, of the essential dignity of his reason and emotions.

In the Renaissance, music was apt to reflect the serenity and repose of an ideal world—another world accessible only through a churchly, pious life. Baroque music mirrored an expanding, vital, growing world on all levels. It is enormously energetic, the lavish sonorities of its secular music reflecting the high gloss of aristocratic life. Its sacred music mirrored the depth and passion of the Protestant Reformation, or the sincerity and brilliance of the Counter-Reformation. Rococo music, emphasizing expression, sensibility, and ultra-refinement of the sensual, reflected the jaded ennui of a fast decaying aristocratic society. In this process it strove for simplicity and directness. Here it began to approach what was to come in Classicism. Jean-Jacques Rousseau, who with his opera *Le Devin du village* (1752), wrote in an extremely direct, simple homophonic style, said of polyphonic devices that they "reflect disgrace on those who had the patience to construct them." The very fact that Rousseau, the champion of "natural man" and of total democracy, propagandized and publicized the new gallant style is highly significant. It shows that the new, non-contrapuntal, melodic style dovetailed exactly with the revolutionary ideas about sentiment, importance of emotion, and the value of the individual.

The effect of this new, simple harmonic style on the sophisticated listen-

---

The Parthenon at Athens, Greece (*Photo by Elizabeth H. Burpee; Design Photographers International, Inc., New York*).

ing public must have been like the figure of Benjamin Franklin as an envoy to France during the American Revolution. His public appearances, in plain clothes and without ceremonial wig, did much to win French hearts to the Republican cause.

In sum, the atmosphere of the time was conducive to an establishment of a direct, more personal style of musical expression. Through its emphasis on simplicity, reason, and directness of sentiment, it paved the way for a truly *personal music*. This subjective, intimate factor began to appear in late Mozart and Haydn and finally flowered with Beethoven. It was then—at the turn into the nineteenth century—that music became the magnificent medium for the expression of the essence and nobility of all men. Thus, Classicism is a most significant era in the history of music.

GENERAL CHARACTERISTICS

We have already touched on some of the basic characteristics of classical music, its perfect lucidity and ideal proportion. Content—melodic and harmonic ideas—is perfectly matched to structure. Though there are serious moments in the secular music, replete with tender pathos, the tendency is to-. ward good humor, toward sparkle and zest. The classicists aimed to please. They had to, if they wished to retain their princely patrons.

Sometimes the humor achieved rather robust proportions, as in the *Musical Joke* by Mozart. Here the composer flashes one tonal jest after another. For example, after a perfectly innocuous beginning in the Menuetto, the horns are required to play this passage:

Example 6-2   *A Musical Joke*, K.522, Movt. II, Mozart

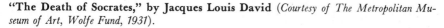

"The Death of Socrates," by Jacques Louis David (*Courtesy of The Metropolitan Museum of Art, Wolfe Fund, 1931*).

Monticello, Thomas Jefferson's home (19th Century wood engraving by Pierson) (*Courtesy of Historical Pictures Service, Chicago*).

The finale ends with a cadence in five keys at once.

The third movement ends with a tongue-in-cheek whole tone scale, gracing a terribly obvious cadenza for the first violin.

In addition to Mozart's *Musical Joke,* there is also his delightful multilingual round, *Bona Nox,* which is pure frolic.

Melody

Mozart had declared, "I compare a good melodist to a fine racer, and counterpointists to hack post horses."

With the acceptance of homophony as the basis for much classical music, attention turned strongly toward melody, especially in its lyric aspect. Now that a single, predominating line received much of the compositional thrust, it had to be constructed so that it would instantly fix and hold the listener's attention. It therefore became simpler than either rococo or baroque melody. Though ornaments continued to grace classical melodies, they were used much more sparingly than before. Melodic contour was "smoothed out": intervals used caused the melodies to be less jagged than in the Baroque. Because of the tremendous emphasis of symmetrical phrase and period structure, melodies seemed neatly trimmed and tailored. They seemed blocked out more, segmented, conforming to the inner divisions and dimensions of balanced classical forms.

Another striking contrast in classical melody relative to that in the Baroque is in the area of melodic rhythm. In the earlier period, melodic syncopation was commonly used. Sometimes rhythmic patterns were so diffuse and irregular that they seem to be entirely independent of the established meter in supporting elements.

Classical melody on the other hand is quite metrical. Underlying rhythmic patterns are simple, often built upon a single rhythmic idea. Patterns usually coincide with strong beats.

Harmony

A powerful yet flexible system of major-minor tonality underlay the tunefulness, clarity, and elegance of classical music. Mozart and Haydn inherited a system of chord structures, consonance-dissonance, and chord progression that had been systematized by Rameau and refined by J. S. Bach. The Bach chorale is the paragon of harmonic usage. This the classical masters knew and enjoyed.

The prevailing key and scale was major. Of the symphonies attributed to Mozart, only two are in the minor mode: No. 25 and No. 40 are both in G minor. Only two of the piano sonatas and two of the piano concertos are in the minor. The minor was used for music in the *patetico* style, and with Haydn and Mozart it was quite subjective and personal. But though the usual overall key scheme tended to be major, episodes or secondary themes in minor could be striking in effect.

The Andante cantabile from the *Sonata in C major* by Mozart is a good example of this. The first section is dominated by a theme in major.

Example 6-3   *Sonata in C*, K.330, Movt. II, Mozart

The second section, in F minor, begins as shown below.

Example 6-4

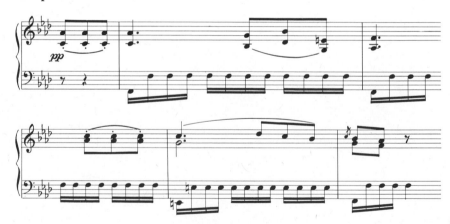

The sudden poignancy achieved through the intensity of the harmony is wonderful—especially after the serenity of the beginning.

One curious facet of classical harmony is that dissonance is encountered significantly less often than in the Baroque. At first thought, this would seem a regression, especially if increased dissonance is equated with heightened expression as it sometimes is. It is a fact that the sinewy counterpoint and colorful chromaticism of J. S. Bach produced many more dissonant intervals and chords than in following years. This certainly points to the greater emphasis placed on emotion and expression in the Baroque.

Equanimity being more important than pathos to the classicists, it is expected that dissonance would be at a lower level.

Register

In one area, that of register and tessitura, Classicism was quite similar to the Baroque. Both favored the soprano. If one considers the string choir in Mozart symphonies, it becomes apparent that the violins consistently have the better of it melodically. Cello and contrabass are largely supportive.

The same can be said about the other forces of the classical symphony. The most important winds were flutes, oboes, and trumpets. Bassoons were the only winds to anchor the total sound in the bass. Trombones did not come into steady use until the nineteenth century. Neither did the tuba, bass clarinet, or the contrabassoon.

Of course, there are many striking pieces emphasizing bass instruments or voices. One thinks immediately of the Mozart bassoon concerto, or the buffo parts in classical opera such as that of Leporello in Mozart's *Don Giovanni*. But, perhaps, because of the classical masters' penchant for lucidity with brilliance, high registers were primary.

Dynamics and tempo

We have already noted the tremendous stir caused by the systematic use of crescendo and diminuendo by the composers of the Mannheim School in the pre-classical period. Unquestionably, these surging dynamic effects stirred mightily the emotions of audiences of the day. Indeed, a well managed crescendo or diminuendo even today is a powerful tool for creating excitement and mood. In the time of Mozart and Haydn the resulting expressivity was precisely in line with the developing need for a more personal music. With Beethoven it became a major tool for achieving searing dramatic effects.

Along with the traditional use of *forte* and *piano* in juxtaposition, the *fp* and the *sf* attained some prominence. This last effect was especially useful in music for the pianoforte, which, in contrast to the harpsichord, could effectively manage sudden louds followed by sudden softs within the body of a phrase or period.

However, a medium-loud forte and a gentle piano were the usual. It was not until Beethoven that *fortissimo* and its opposite, *pianissimo,* consistently came into use.

In a similar way, tempos were moderate. The Mozart presto was probably no faster than a Tchaikovsky allegro. The plain truth is that the wealth of detail, marvelous juxtaposition and combination of ideas cannot be perceived adequately by the listener if tempos in this music are excessive.

Performance and instruments

Performance standards were quite high. With the development of many resident orchestras, at Mannheim, in Paris, at Esterhazy, and elsewhere, players took pride in their profession. Virtuosity became common. Mozart had his Leutgeb, sometime cheese monger and brilliant player of the horn, and four concertos were written for him.

And there was the brilliant Anton Stadler who did much to spur Mozart's interest in the clarinet. His playing was the inspiration for the *Clarinet Concerto,* the *Clarinet Quintet,* and many others.

The travels of the boy Mozart and his sister, Nannerl, throughout the continent as prodigies of the keyboard are well known. In maturity, Mozart was an incredible virtuoso at the keyboard. The performances of his own concertos were renowned. In like manner, young Beethoven was celebrated as a fiery, brilliant pianist; much more so than as a composer. His passionate improvisations affected audiences to such a degree that everyone in his audience wept.

Virtuosity on any of various instruments was much in vogue throughout the last half of the eighteenth century. Attesting to the public's hunger for any sort of instrumental virtuosity were the scintillating careers of two ladies, the English Marianne Davies and the German Marianne Kitchgessmer. Both were famed for their performances on the glass harmonica, an instrument perfected by Benjamin Franklin.

Forms

The shift of emphasis from the polyphony of the Renaissance and the Baroque to the homophony of Classicism had many results: changes in melody, harmony, and rhythm were enormous. But most important of all was the new outlook on form. The most important relationships in renaissance and baroque contrapuntal composition are parallel or oblique. The vital structural feature in an invention or a fugue is how the parts fit together on top of one another, how they invert and how imitation comes into play.

Here energy, vital dynamism, come through the interplay of simultaneous melodic parts.

In contrast to this, because there is often only one leading melodic part in classical homophony supported by variously arranged chords, parallel considerations are not of primary importance.

To be sure, the way in which a melody is colored and enhanced by chords affects its style tremendously. But just as important as the way things *sound together* is the way things *sound side by side*. In other words, the horizontal connection of themes, parts, and sections is the most important principle in classical form.

Balance, symmetry, proportion become powerful factors in these forms: four measures balanced by four more; exposition matched by recapitulation; statement answered by restatement. The most important forms were those dependent on the Viennese sonata principle: the solo sonata, concerto, symphony, string quartet, and, in addition, opera. Sacred choral music continued to be prominent.

Chapter 2 in the first part of this book dealt primarily with forms first developed by the classicists. A re-examination of the Haydn rondo in Score Profile at the end of the book will show how juxtaposition and balancing of all formal units on a horizontal level is the single most important structural feature. However, the magnificent double fugue from Mozart's *Requiem,* p. 371, shows that contrapuntal sophistication was still very much present in certain kinds of classical writing.

THE COMPOSERS

No other period in the history of music is represented by so few major composers as is that of Classicism. Beyond Joseph Haydn (1732–1809) , Wolfgang Amadeus Mozart (1756–1791) and Ludwig Van Beethoven, composers of absolutely first rank, there is Christopher Willibald Gluck, who revolutionized opera but did not essay very much in other musical forms. But, though only few, these composers had tremendous impact. The essentials of their art—harmony, form, rhythm, melody—persisted as the foundation of music until the twentieth century.

Chronologically, the adult creative lives of the great triumvirate are separated by 20 years more or less. Thus, there occurred a rather neat line of descent, spanning the whole period. One generation separated each. Haydn came into his adult artistic powers in the early 1750's, shortly after the death of J. S. Bach, in the rococo period. Mozart matured as a creative artist at the apogee of the classical era, in 1776; while Beethoven reached adulthood in 1790. Beethoven's productive days paralleled the final ripening of Classicism, as well as its transition into the romantic century.

The content of their music reflects all of this quite faithfully. Though Haydn's music is sometimes quite passionate and stormy, it is conditioned somewhat by the pleasantries and mannerisms of the Rococo. It is likely to be level headed and good humored rather than hotly personal. The gallant style permeates much of his earlier work.

Mozart quite often is intensely subjective. It often seems that he deliberately plans for a special mood, for a certain melancholy atmosphere. A feeling of unrest, of spiritual travail and personal outpouring, saturates a great number of his mature works—especially the ones in the minor mode. What happens, of course, is that the composer cannot keep from exposing his deepest self. Mozart is very close to Romanticism here.

It is not surprising that Mozart's mature years, 1776–1791, encompassed almost exactly both the American and French revolutions. It was at precisely these portentous years that the new world—built around the new premise of assertion of the self—was wrenching itself from the old. Mozart, the artist and professional, stood in the vortex of vast social dislocations. Small wonder that we feel a curious blend of poignant regret and new adventure in his most personal music.

Beethoven lived to epitomize the very thing that had been passionately sought and finally won—the dignity and unique value of all men. Though there is great tragedy and melancholy throughout Beethoven, there is, even more, exultation and victory. Beethoven, as an artist, symbolizes totally the spiritual charter newly won at the turn of the nineteenth century.

Curiously, little things in the daily lives of these masters corroborate the above. For example, Haydn, who as a young man had brushed the clothes and cleaned the shoes of the composer Nicola Porpora (1686–1766), and who was in the employ of the aristocracy most of his life, seldom, if ever, appeared publicly without donning the formal wig. Mozart often was wigged, but an unfinished portrait of the composer by his brother-in-law, Lange, done in 1791, and others earlier, show him unwigged. Of course, Beethoven, whose shaggy mane is well known, was wigged only in his youth.

Mozart, though he had some dependence on the nobility, chafed constantly under them, and was quite capable of speaking his mind. Once, when the Emperor Joseph spoke of his music being overly refined and containing too many notes, Mozart said, "Just as many notes as are necessary, your Majesty." This, Haydn would never have dared to utter.

Beethoven, himself, had many relationships with the aristocracy—but mostly on his own terms. They were allowed to patronize his work. He came to them as an equal.

One does not study the lives of these great men in isolation. They knew each other. Beethoven studied with Haydn and played for Mozart. Haydn and Mozart were quite close.

In a sense, they were like spiritual father, son, and grandson. Between Haydn and Mozart, there certainly was a kind of familial affection. Haydn considered the young composer to be the greatest that he knew of. Mozart dedicated six of his greatest string quartets to the older man.

Mozart, after hearing the *improvisations* of the boy Beethoven, recognized his genius and fully prophesied the greatness that was to come.

Haydn, however, thought little of Beethoven's talent and never established close relations with the younger man. The very fact that they were somewhat alien temperamentally and artistically points to Haydn's belonging essentially to the older order of things; to the glittering dignity of a previous age. Beethoven was a child of rebellion, of newness, and of a new century.

Haydn

Joseph Haydn lived a long, fruitful, methodical life. From humble beginnings in a peasant's hut in Austria, he became choir boy at St. Stephen's in Vienna and came under the influence of the poet, Metastasio, and the composer, Porpora. For 30 years he served as Kapellmeister for the noble house of Esterhazy in Hungary. Late in his life there were two trips to London, where he was acclaimed as composer and conductor. His last years were spent in the outskirts of Vienna, where he wrote the great oratorios, the *Creation* and the *Seasons*.

His temperament was benign. When the girl that he loved, the daughter of a wig-maker called Keller, took the veil and entered a convent, Haydn consented to marry the elder sister due to the entreaties of her father. Though she turned out to be a shrew, it did not sour his temperament, for he had an extremely even, productive life which was marked by a steady growth of power and technique.

Haydn's output was truly voluminous, numbering many hundreds of compositions. He worked with all the major idioms of the day: opera, oratorio, mass, concerto, sonata, symphony, chamber music, song. But his major contribution was in the symphony and the string quartet. There were well over 100 symphonies and 83 quartets. He did not invent these forms, but he gave them the structure and scope that was to challenge most of the major composers after him for upwards of 100 years.

With Haydn, the symphony and its performance medium, the full orchestra, became truly modern, capable of expressing a wide gamut of emotion. The forms of the inner movements—sonata-allegro, theme and variation, rondo, song form, minuet with trio—became marvels of studied poise and balance. His development sections—intricate, coherent, logical all at once—were the models for Mozart and Beethoven. Anybody studying the brief development section from the rondo in Score Profile (p. 334) will find an uncanny tightness and aptness of individual ideas wedded with an almost blithe naturalness.

Lest we believe that all of this sophistication of form was intuitively grasped by Haydn, one needs to remember his words that his constant concern was "to observe what was good and what was weak in effect, and was consequently in a position to better, to change, to amplify, to curtail."

There is not much doubt that much of the solace in his life came from his work. In his later, honored years he often said that the early years spent in a leaky, freezing garret studying, practicing, and sleeping with his *Gradus ad Parnassum* under his pillow were the happiest of his life.

Perhaps nowhere can the vivacity and sparkle of Haydn's music be better seen than in the string quartets—especially the late ones. The finale of the *Quartet in G Minor,* Op. 74, No. 3, shows perfectly his wit and lyric power.

This movement is typical of the many "gypsy" pieces from his pen. It begins with delightful syncopations. The whole is cast in a mock-serious minor. It is not long, however, before a folk-song like tune bubbles out from the texture. On perceiving the real charm of this lyric moment we understand what he meant when he told the singer, Michael Kelly, "It is the tune which is the charm of music . . ."

Later, in the development section, three times the music seems to stumble and hesitate. But then it plunges on with incredible zest and brightness. Surely Beethoven admired these pages so full of the unexpected and of high good spirits.

Mozart

Mozart's life contrasts to that of Haydn in several important ways. For one, his background and education were completely different. Mozart's father, Leopold, was a respected and talented composer, the author of a well known method for the violin. His older sister, Nannerl, was a prodigy as was he, and together they toured Europe astounding the musical world with their digital gymnastics and aural feats.

Whereas Haydn worked hard and long for whatever he achieved in composition, Mozart possessed an astonishing facility. At the age of five, he dictated to his father impeccable little minuets.

As a keyboardist, he was supreme, and his improvisations left an indelible impression on his pupils and audiences. He played the violin almost as well. In addition to his native tongue, he understood English, French, and Italian and Latin. He excelled at dancing, horseback riding, drawing and billiards. In short, he was supremely gifted.

Whereas Haydn progressed through life ever gaining reputation and material fortune, Mozart quite often suffered agonies of want and deprivation, and died at the age of 35. He died engrossed in the writing of his great Requiem, fully realizing that it was as much for himself as for the noble who commissioned it.

In some ways, Mozart was not prepared well in his childhood for the trials of adult life. Closely supervised by his father, whom he adored ("next to God is Papa"), adulated by the most brilliant society, he remained ever the child.

He was an easy prey for unscrupulous friends like Stadler the clarinetist, lending money which he did not have, while at the same time depriving his family of the bare necessities. The stories of his procrastination and last minute flurries of work are charming but typical of the naive disorder that afflicted him always. It was not unusual for him to delay writing out orchestral parts to the overtures of his operas almost up to the moment of performance.

At the première of *Don Giovanni*, the orchestra is supposed to have played the overture from music sheets still wet with ink. Mozart's wife, Constanze, plied him with punch and exotic tales the whole night before the day of performance in a desperate attempt to keep him awake and working.

The catalogue of his works is very extensive. Köchel, who catalogued his music, gives over 600 works. In all major forms that he used, the music is unrivaled for purity, intellectual scope, and passion. Besides succeeding in Haydn's favorite forms, the symphony and quartet, he was the complete master of the concerto. There exist superb concertos for bassoon, horn, clarinet, flute, and violin, the whole collection crowned by upwards of two dozen for the keyboard. The analysis of the *C-Minor Piano Concerto* at the end of this section shows what unquestionable mastery he ultimately attained over the form. In it is represented the very essence of passion and tragedy tempered by nobility of design and purpose.

The operas of Mozart—*The Marriage of Figaro, Idomeneo, The Magic Flute, Don Giovanni*—are superb representations of his best work. *Don Giovanni*, to choose one example, was as fraught with implications for the music of the romantic century as was Beethoven's *"Eroica" Symphony*.

Tchaikovsky was smitten by *Don Giovanni*, and Chopin's first important success came with his variations for piano and orchestra on the duet "La ci darem la mano." George Bernard Shaw could not keep his piano score of the *Don* on its shelf; he was forever playing it over and singing the parts as well as he could. And small wonder. There is a complete world of expression and mood in the opera.

The opera abounds in exquisite melody. There are moments of great pathos, as at the death of the commendatore in Act I. The comedy, of course, is superb, as when Leporello reads from the list of the Don's amorous adventures in the "Catalogue Aria." The flute clearly volunteers a kind of "wolf whistle."

Example 6-5   *Don Giovanni*, Act I, Mozart

When the frightened servant in Act II tells his master of the ghostly statue at the door, the music imitates the knocking in a delightful way.

Example 6-6   *Don Giovanni*, Act II, Mozart

Analysis and Commentary: Mozart, Concerto for Piano and Orchestra in C Minor, K.491, Movement 3

This 24th piano concerto by Mozart is one of only two written by him in the minor mode. (The other is the 20th, in D minor.)

It was greatly admired by Beethoven, who patterned much of his own C-Minor Concerto, Op. 37, for piano after it. The Mozart concerto is replete with pathos and drama. It is a marvel of musical integration, the keyboard part blending naturally with the orchestra at all times. The virtuosity of the solo part never intrudes in the homogeneity and oneness of the whole.

All of this Beethoven surely admired and emulated; his work in the concerto form constantly emphasized these virtues.

Opening themes in both works are similar.

Example 6-7 *Piano Concerto*, K.491, Movt. I, Mozart

Example 6-8 *Piano Concerto No. 3*, Op. 37, Movt. I, Beethoven

The final movement, an Allegretto in C minor, is cast by Mozart as a set of eight variations on an original theme. The theme itself is one of rare beauty. In a miraculous way Mozart managed to capture within an impec-

Example 6-9 *Piano Concerto*, K.491, Movt. III, Mozart

cably patterned 16-measure frame a personal piognancy, perhaps tinged with regret. Its form is regular binary, both parts beginning with the same motive.

Example 6-10

Part A begins:

Example 6-11

The orchestra states it complete, without commentary by the piano. It is as if Mozart had wished his theme to be presented in all of its purity, without filigree or embroidery of any sort. The piano, however, quickly comes into its own. Variation 1 is entirely given over to embellishing material in the solo part with sparse chordal background in the orchestra. Two important

Example 6-12

motives arise. The second, an ascending, tripping figure, will be used as the

Example 6-13

basis of Variation 6. The second variation is evenly divided between orchestra and soloist. The orchestra plays part A of the theme through once, after which the piano joins with brilliant scales for its repetition. Part B is treated

Example 6-14

in the same manner. In Variation 3, things are reversed. The piano sallies forth with quite a stormy idea. The *sturm und drang* character of this music surely must have thrilled Beethoven. The orchestra answers with fiery

Example 6-15

material of its own, and then they do it all over again. And then, a complete change of mood in Variation 4. The winds carry this idea, *p,* a crisp little

Example 6-16

march in A-flat major, complete with saucy accents at unexpected places. The piano joins in later, featuring a bouncy rhythmic pattern of its own.

Variation 5 carries the music back to the original key—C minor. The piano is mostly in charge. It starts in a rather dense, contrapuntal manner.

Example 6-17

Shortly afterwards, ascending scales in the left hand underline the motive heard at the beginning of Variation 3.

Example 6-18

The tumult of this variation ends with a solid cadence in the tonic minor.

Example 6-19

Variation 6 enters, this time in the orchestra. Suddenly, it is in the warmth and geniality of the parallel key—C major.

Example 6-20

Prominently featured is the tiny figure first encountered in Variation 1.

Example 6-21

Variation 7 reverts back to the tonic minor key. It is shorter than previous ones and is distinguished by flashing rising scales and glittering arpeggios. All of this leads to a cadenza that ushers in the last section, Variation 8.

A very important change occurs in this variation. The meter, instead of

Example 6-22

continuing in four beats, now is in two, in six-eight. At first the music shows a tripping, hesitant mien, but then skyrocketing scales lead to a brilliant, trenchant close.

Example 6-23

Beethoven

Beethoven's early years and education form a kind of composite of those of Haydn and Mozart. His father was a musician, as was Mozart's, but he had little musical distinction. Beethoven, too, was a prodigy, but did not bud into greatness as easily or as early as had Mozart. Like Haydn, he worked very hard to achieve his style. Every new creative advance was marked by enormous labor and spiritual travail—the *Skizzenbuchen* (sketch books) attest to this.

Among his teachers were Albertsberger, Neefe, Salieri and Haydn. It was Neefe who brought him as a young man to Mozart, who is said to have uttered, "Pay attention to this lad; he will make a noise in the world one of these days."

The forms that challenged Beethoven were precisely those brought to such perfection by Haydn and Mozart: symphony, sonata, concerto, string

Ludwig van Beethoven (*Courtesy of Brown Brothers, New York*).

quartet and chamber music, the mass, opera, song. From them, he gained a rigorous sense of the principles of classic form. Indeed, a great body of his early works point in essence and form back to earlier times.

Like Haydn and Mozart, Beethoven possessed a sense of humor that saturates much of his music. The scherzo from the *"Spring" Sonata,* Op. 24, for violin and piano, illustrates this perfectly. The piano begins with a saucy little tune, which is full of bounce and snap. Then the violin joins in, sup-

Example 6-24   *Violin Sonata* ("Spring"), Op. 24, Movt. III, Beethoven

posedly doubling the melody. But, somehow, it is always one beat late, and never does catch up. Apparently, Beethoven enjoyed musical frolic so much

Example 6-25

that he could not stop from repeating the whole "out of step" process in the Scherzo from his *"Pastorale" Symphony*—this time with the oboe out of step.

Though equanimity, grace, elegance, good humor, balanced structure, can be found throughout Beethoven, it is not in this area that he was unique. Rather, it is the energy, dramatic power, exultant majesty, and intensity of mood and passion that distinguish him from his predecessors.

Quite early in life, his sympathies had been given to the forces of democracy and freedom. He devoured Plutarch and Homer. He identified with Napoleon before the Coronation. Later, Schiller made an enormous impression as did Goethe. Goethe's play *Egmont*—a romanticized expression of the rebellions in the Netherlands of the early 16th century—fired his zeal to such an extent that he provided it with magnificent incidental music. Schiller's poem to the brotherhood of man, the *Ode to Joy,* became the propelling agent and ultimate essence of the *Ninth* ("Choral") *Symphony.*

Throughout his life, there were battles with the world and with himself. In his early thirties he found that he was doomed to deafness. The Heiligenstadt Testament, written in a moment of utter despair, shows the inner struggle that he underwent:

> Yes, the cherished hope—which I brought with me when I came here, of being healed at least to a certain degree, must now abandon me entirely. As the

leaves of autumn fall and are withered, so, too—my hope has dried up. Almost as I was when I came here, I leave again—even the courage—which inspired me on lovely summer days—is vanished. O Providence—let a single day of untroubled joy be granted to me! For so long already the resonance of true joy be granted to me! O when—O when, Divine one—may I feel it once more in the temple of Nature and of mankind? Never?—no—that would be too hard! *

But despite constant physical afflictions, disappointments in love, gross misunderstanding by the public, his indomitable will and great faith in the dignity and greatness of the human spirit drove him on to achieve more with his music.

His work is generally divided into three periods. Roughly, the first period covers everything up to 1800, or the music up to the late Op. 40's. This music, though suffused by his unique dynamism, yet looks back to Haydn and Mozart. The early works, though often charged with passion and subjective power as in the *"Pathetique"* and *"Moonlight" Sonatas,* or the *Quartet in C Minor,* Op. 18, did not really surpass certain items from Haydn or Mozart.

Example 6-26 *Sonata,* K.457, Movt. II, Mozart

---

* Michael Hamburger, trans. and ed., *Beethoven, Letters, Journals and Conversations* (Garden City, N.Y.: Doubleday Anchor Book), p. 34.

Example 6-27   *Sonata ("Pathetique")* Op. 13, Movt. II, Beethoven

With the coming of the second period, inaugurated by works such as the *Kreutzer Sonata,* Op. 47, for violin and piano and the *"Eroica" Symphony,* Op. 55, Beethoven found his true artistic character. His apprenticeship had ended. The music of this period pulses with power and energy. In it can be heard everything from the agonized moans of the Funeral March of the Eroica to the philosophical detachment and serenity of the Scene at the Brook from the *"Pastorale"* Symphony, to the almost frenetic fury of the *"Appassionata"* Sonata.

The last period, beginning in the Op. 90's, also contains some marvelously exciting music: in the Gloria from the *Missa Solemnis,* for example, or the Scherzo and the Finale from the *Ninth Symphony.* But another dimension is present. There is withdrawal, a searching within. Forms become much freer, more fantasy-like, though solid principles of structure are always present. There is a decided tendency to play down effect and dazzle. Harmony becomes much more refined, and a deep, searching polyphony often reigns. The *Quartet in C-Sharp Minor* illustrates this final renunciation and inner exploration perhaps better than any other late work. Its overall structure, and its content, are revolutionary. There are seven movements, forming a loose but highly cohesive fantasy-like structure.

It is as if Beethoven remembered the words of his favorite poet Homer as he wrote the poignant music:

"But Fate now conquers; I am hers; and yet not she shall share in my renown."

Gluck

Christopher Willibald Gluck (1714–1787) was an important transitional figure. As early as 1742, he was in London writing operas in opposition to Handel. Later, in Paris, he produced great masterworks in the field, including *Iphigénie en Aulide* and *Orphée*. There was a fierce polemic with the followers of Piccini (1728–1800) and the Italian School of opera, including a bitter war of pamphlets. His operatic technique emphasized dramatic consistency and psychological true setting of music to text. This was in stark contrast to the Italian style, featuring rigid expected sequences of arias, duets, choruses, cadenzas, etc. The effect of his operatic reforms on Mozart, Weber, and later Romantics was profound and lasting.

Other composers

Other important figures of the period are Muzio Clementi (1752–1832), fashionable concert pianist, composer and manufacturer of pianos; Luigi Boccherini (1743–1805), cellist and composer of elegant, sparkling music including 20 symphonies; Antonio Salieri (1750–1825), the rival of Mozart and sometime teacher of Beethoven, who was known primarily as a composer of opera.

CHAPTER 7

Romanticism

"**I** UNDERSTAND THAT** you are fond of music that does not distract your mind from affairs of state." This comment is said to have occurred during a conversation between the composer Luigi Cherubini and the first Napoleon. This obviously did not enamor the Corsican to the composer. But the veiled sarcasm of the remark helps us to understand the import and impact of romantic composers and their music. One cannot imagine Haydn, a few years before, addressing the nobility with anything but profound respect. The written terms to his appointment at Esterhazy attests to the menial position of composers and musicians in the centuries before the nineteenth. Haydn must ". . . be temperate; must abstain from vulgarity in eating and drinking and conversation; must take care of all the music and the musical instruments, and be answerable for any injury they may suffer from carelessness or neglect; . . . that when summoned to perform before company he shall take care that he and all members of his orchestra do follow the instructions given and appear in white stockings, white linen, powder, and with either a pig-tail or a tie-wig." *

Beethoven, giving lessons, rapped the knuckles of his aristocratic pupils. The nineteenth-century composer assumed a quite different role from his counterpart of the seventeenth and eighteenth centuries. The talents of Beethoven and those who followed were for hire—but now mostly on their own terms.

The great Romantics, Cherubini, Beethoven, Rossini, Berlioz, Mendels-

---

* Thomas Paine and Klauser, eds., *Famous Composers and Their Works*, Vol. II (Boston: J. B. Millet Co., 1891) , p. 252.

sohn, and Wagner, all had attained social position. Each man was independent in a way that his predecessors could only have envied, as can be plainly seen from Wagner's comments:

> . . . The world owes me what I require! I cannot live on a miserable post of organist like your master Bach! Is it such an unheard of demand when I ask that the little bit of luxury that I enjoy be given to me? I, who hold a thousand enjoyments in store for the world! *

Whereas the majority of the baroque and classical masters were directly dependent on either the church or aristocracy for their very bread, the Romantics frequently dealt with the public directly. They realized income from concerts and from the publications of their works. Now they were professionals with dignity and a clear, independent social position.

Though he was often materially sustained by interested nobles such as Prince Lichnowsky or the Archduke Rudolf, Beethoven realized substantial income from his compositions. At his death, the equivalent of 15,000 dollars was found in a drawer of his desk. In fact, Beethoven acquired considerable expertise in his business dealings.

Cherubini, mentioned earlier, ultimately rose to the directorship of the Paris Conservatoire. Mendelssohn, the son of a wealthy banker and born as it were with a silver tuning fork in his mouth, early achieved fame to match his fortune. Berlioz attained partial independence through his compositions and conducting, but more especially through his position as a music critic for the Parisian journals. Rossini, after assailing and conquering the musical world with upwards of three dozen operas, ceased altogether to write opera although there are some charming trifles later in his life. For the remaining 39 years of his life he retired with his laurels and profits.

Paganini, the "Devil of the Violin," became affluent enough to present Berlioz with a gift of 20,000 francs after hearing *Harold in Italy*.

We do not mean to suggest that the path to material security for composers had become easy in the early 1800's. For many, it was still a very cruel fight for bare existence. But, despite this, the composer now had a voice. He was heard; the world noticed, took him into account, and was moved. Thus Cherubini could speak to Napoleon on somewhat equal terms. Napoleon had conquered his world, Cherubini his.

With the composer's new-found independence and dignity his music took on a new cast. It now became loosened, freer, expansive. Above all, it expressed deeply and tellingly the subjective state of the composer himself. The music unashamedly expressed *him* directly, and without reserve.

---

* Reprinted from *Darwin, Marx, Wagner* by Jacques Barzun (1941), Atlantic-Little, Brown and Company.

Niccolo Paganini—photograph made in 1839 (*Courtesy of Brown Brothers, New York*).

There were musical explorations into areas of human experience never before attempted. Berlioz produced a dazzling first symphony, the *Symphonie fantastique,* in 1830; its intense passions and reveries we are told are those resulting from a young hero taking an overdose of opium. The symphony displays a great scenic panorama. In its five movements Berlioz joyfully leaps about from the yearnings of a young man in love, to an elegant ball, to a rustic scene in the country, to the guillotine, and finally, to a sulphuric scene somewhere near hell, replete with witches and the death bell.

In his *Damnation of Faust* the hero literally falls screaming into hell, and is greeted by a chorus of demons for which Berlioz invents a barbaric, hideous language.

All of this tonal agony, represented by groaning dissonances and macabre orchestration is directly followed by a seraphic chorus telling of Marguerite's salvation. Berlioz constantly exulted in the violent juxtaposition of opposites, as did many of the Romantics.

But in the piano works of his contemporary, Chopin, we hear a refined, sensitive musical language depicting in minute detail the composer's many fine shades of sentiment.

Brahms collected and arranged German folksongs for voices. Folk songs cropped up everywhere: in symphony, opera, sonata, and other major forms.

Mendelssohn traveled much and gave to the world musical "souvenirs" of great charm and polish: The *Hebrides Overture,* and the *"Italian"* and *"Scotch" Symphonies.*

Nationalism became very important. Many composers occupied themselves primarily with trying to capture the spirit of their native lands. Smetana wrote the first Czech nationalistic opera, *The Bartered Bride.* His compatriot Dvorak not only produced a great many Czech-oriented works, but during his stay in America in the 1890's was instrumental in making Americans aware of their native music. Later, Sibelius became a strong spiritual voice for Finland through his music.

Program music—a major concern with the Romantics—not only represented various scenes and situations but led to the depiction of the character of different countries and peoples.

Late in the century musical realism took hold—especially in opera where it was known as verismo. Richard Strauss boasted that he could represent anything with tones—even the shine of a silver teaspoon.

Thus, the Romantics constantly searched within and without themselves for new things to express. Because of this, new technical means had to be created in order to arrive at the desired musical ends. New forms evolved, and old ones were transformed. Melody, rhythm, harmony, orchestration, dynamics, performance: all were profoundly affected.

Of course, as we have seen before, changes of attitude and of expression from period to period do not occur in an environmental vacuum. A composer and his work reflect and complement the total web and texture of his time. The Age of Romanticism saw unique developments in many areas.

Jacques Barzun, in *Darwin, Marx, Wagner* defines Romanticism as ". . . a constructive effort after a great revolution which had leveled off old institutions and old nations—including the mechanical materialism of the eighteenth century. Romanticism . . . valued individual freedom, subjective feelings, human reason, social purpose, and above all, Art." *

Individual freedom was indeed a leading motive in the nineteenth century. The French and American Revolutions had occurred in its name.

The everyday worker, who had been little more than a drudge for many centuries, now began to be valued as a human being. Enlightened industrialists such as Robert Owen in England began to ease the load of their employees. Trade Unions, arising first in Britain and America, spread slowly

---

* *Darwin, Marx, Wagner* by Jacques Barzun, Doubleday Anchor Books, N.Y., p. 17.

to other westernized countries. Engels and Marx began to rally the "proletariat" against their "capitalist oppressors." Communism crystallized.

And along with a new-found freedom, man's control over his environment increased tremendously.

Watt had already adapted the steam engine to the driving of machinery. This helped to relieve man's burden in industry. The steam engine also led to the railroad. From the time of the Greek civilization 2000 years before, the maximum average travelling speed was approximately five miles per hour. In Napoleon's headlong retreat from Russia to Paris, a distance of approximately 1,400 miles, he travelled for 312 hours. After the first railroad opened from Stockton to Darlington in Britain, man could cover the same distance in less than 48 hours. Traveling time had been reduced by nine tenths.

The steam boat achieved comparable results on water, and in 1835, the telegraph was developed through the efforts of Volta, Galvani, Faraday, and Morse.

Besides this the blast furnace came into being resulting in ". . . tons of incandescent steel swirling about like boiling milk in a saucepan."

The electric light was invented; man's life span increased; his general health improved; the stethoscope and anesthesia came into use; Pasteur established the relationship between bacteria and disease; Lister showed how to kill bacteria.

Man in the 19th century thus found himself freer, healthier, with more leisure than his predecessors, and in better control over his environment. He now had dominion over material things as never before and he could communicate with a large segment of the world with increasing speed. His horizons were expanding at an increasing rate, on all levels.

Romanticism as an era was a time of expansion. For music it was a time of heightened intensity and expression. In order to express and communicate more of himself the 19th century composer looked to his musical materials and changed them. What had served admirably for Haydn, Mozart, Clementi, would not do.

GENERAL CHARACTERISTICS

Melody

Throughout the baroque and classical periods melodic elements were deemed worthy primarily for their potential in compositional development. Fugue subjects tended to be graphic, clear, and plain. They usually became

Example 7-1   Ariadne Musica, *Fugue No. 10*, J. K. F. Fischer

charged with emotional or intellectual meaning after they were expanded, combined with other melodic elements. In short, they became interesting after they had undergone musical growth.

In the romantic period, melodies also were created for their utility. But more commonly, they were shaped for immediate, memorable tunefulness, for innate beauty. In other words, melody as such and for itself established a kind of structural hegemony over other elements such as rhythm and harmony.

Romantic melody is striking and immediate, often extremely lyric and song-like. It tends also to span larger segments in composition than in previous periods. Because of the attention given to folk and dance music in general, romantic melody frequently takes on a nationalistic or regional tinge.

Rhythm

Flexibility is a major characteristic of romantic rhythm. This shows itself strongly in tempo. In previous periods tempos tended to be uniform, the beat steady and unflagging. Restraint in tempo—as in nearly everything else —was primary. But the personal expressions of the Romanticists could not be stated within strict tempos. Rubato was used for emphasis and to intensify the emotional impact. Individual movements often exhibited major tempo changes. Tchaikovsky, in the finale of the *Symphony No. 5*, utilizes no fewer than nine tempos. They are: Andante maestoso, Allegro vivace, Poco piu animato, Tempo I, Poco meno mosso, Molto vivace, Moderato assai e molto maestoso, Presto, Molto meno mosso.

In contrast, baroque masters often gave absolutely no written terms for tempo, not even at the beginning. Tempo was deduced by the performer from the configuration of the notes on the page, from the time signature and by the style of the music in general.

Harmony

Vertical sonority particularly challenged and fascinated the romantic composer. It provided color and depth. He explored new sounds, vibrant

The Champions of the Mississippi: "A Race for the Buckhorns," by Currier and Ives (*Reproduced from the collections of the Library of Congress*).

chords, and striking instrumental textures—sounds that would touch and impress the listener and sounds that would delight the ear. Extended chords, their rich quality arresting the attention, were explored and consistently used from the time of Beethoven on.

Dissonance, which in the past resolved to consonance as a matter of rule, now often was suspended in air only to move to another dissonance. Any *key* could lead to any other; and the transition from one key to another was looser, fluid, unexpected, and colorful.

The net emotional result of this loosening of harmonic fiber for the listener was a feeling of questing and probing. This searching is expressed by the words of the seventeenth century mystic poet, Henry Vaughan, "I cannot reach it; and my straining eye Dazzles at it, as at eternity."

Dynamics and register

Expansion is the keynote in both of these areas. Extreme louds and softs and sudden shifts from one to the other were common. The sudden explosion from a quintuple piano to a double forte in this example is typical.

Example 7-2   *Symphony No. 6*, Op. 74, Movt. I, Tchaikovsky

In Tchaikovsky's *Symphony No. 5*, Movt. II, the spectrum of dynamic color is very wide indeed, from *pppp* to *ffff*, with a great many levels in between. Berlioz, in his *Symphonie fantastique*, Movt. III, asks the strings to play *ppp*, the slightest musical whisper, and adds the words *"quasi niente"* (almost nothing).

In range, romantic music shows many extreme highs and lows. Each register is fully explored for its potential in sound. Leading melodic elements might be located in the lower reaches of the bass, then suddenly heard at the top of the soprano register.

In this connection, it is interesting to note that a favorite register is the tenor. Both cello and French horn are entrusted with some of the loveliest lyric moments of the period.

Instruments and performance

The nineteenth-century concert artist, lionized by an adoring public, was a symbol of everything that is uniquely personal in romantic music. Through their magnetic presence on stage, Paganini and Liszt represented to the masses the quintessence of imagination and creative power.

As in previous centuries, many performing artists were also famous composers, including Paganini, Weber, Mendelssohn, Chopin, Brahms, and Liszt. Weber, Mendelssohn, and Wagner were famous as conductors. Sometimes, when native genius was immense, as with Mendelssohn or Liszt, the composer matched the performer. Other virtuosos on the piano such as Herz, Kalkbrenner, and Dreyschock spewed forth garish and tasteless compositions in the form of potpourris, variations on popular themes, and salon pieces.

Harold Schonberg in his book, *The Great Pianists,* tells about the herculean virtuosity of Dreyschock:

> "Dreyschock would practice sixteen hours a day with the left hand alone, and got to the point where he could play octaves as fast and as smoothly as single-note passages. Heine once said that 'when Dreyschock played in Munich and the wind was right, you could hear him in Paris'." *

Many instruments in use developed in quality, power, and flexibility. New ones, such as the saxophone, tuba, and celeste were invented. The orchestra expanded, both in size and in variety of instruments. English horn, bass clarinet, cornet, trombone, bass drum, and cymbals became increasingly common.

The concert artist and conductor became important members of society. Their skills were often prodigious, and the instruments that they played developed accordingly. Romantic music found adequate media for its expression.

Forms

It would be an error to think that romantic forms were entirely new and unique. Though the fugue was a major compositional vehicle in the Ba-

---

* From *The Great Pianists* by Harold C. Schonberg. Copyright © by Harold C. Schonberg. Published by Simon and Schuster, Inc. and Littauer and Wilkinson.

roque, it continued to interest nineteenth-century masters. The symphony, concerto, opera, and sonata, magnificently developed in the Classical period, continued to occupy a commanding position.

The solo concerto which stemmed from those of Mozart, Haydn, and Beethoven, continued in the 19th century. Cadenzas in the concerto remained as important structural units.

But though basic structural principles from the 18th century concerto remained, refinements abounded. The soloist's part became vastly more demanding. The dramatic power at his command now very nearly matched that of the collective orchestra.

Because of this, a dramatic juxtaposition often occurred between soloist and orchestra. Here again, the soloist symbolized the new-found romantic subjectivity.

Among the many smaller forms that were particularly associated with the romantic century, the *lied* and the character piece for piano were prominent. The *lied* appealed especially to the romantic composer because of the opportunity to set to music poetry of the highest order. Since the time of Beethoven the romantic composer had considered himself a tone poet *(tondichter)*. He felt that, like the poet, he could express definite things and feelings. The poems of Schiller, Goethe, Heine, Eichendorf, and Müller, accordingly, were matched by the superlative music of Schubert, Mendelssohn, Schumann, Brahms, Wolf, Mahler, and others. One need only listen to *lieder* cycles such as Schumann's *Dichterliebe* on poems of Heine to witness the very pinnacle of excellence in word-with-tone.

Nocturnes, intermezzi, ballads, novelettes, album leaves, etc., because of the possibility they held for intimate mood and atmosphere, were popular throughout the century. These occasionally appear alone but are more often grouped into suites like Schumann's *Carnaval,* Op. 9, or *Papillons,* Op. 2, for piano.

Of particular note among the larger forms was the tone poem, or symphonic poem. In these the composer attempted to depict poetic scenes or pictures with tone only. Typical of these are: *Battle of the Huns, Mazeppa,* and *Les Préludes,* by Liszt; *Manfred* and *Francesca da Rimini,* by Tchaikovsky; and *Don Juan,* by Richard Strauss.

Permeating a great many of these forms, are two important developments: program music, and musical nationalism.

The nineteenth-century composer, ever interested in expressing a broader spectrum of human experience, was very much taken with the idea of imagery. Frequently he converted typically classical forms into vehicles for tone painting. The *Harold in Italy Symphony* by Berlioz is typical. So are the *Dante* and *Faust Symphonies* by Liszt. The *Mephisto Waltz* by Liszt, the *Invitation to the Waltz* by Weber, and the waltz, "Chiarina," from Schu-

mann's *Carnaval* all show an abstract dance transformed into a fanciful vehicle for description.

Subjects for musical imagery were nearly unlimited, even to the description of split personalities. Schumann, one of the earliest to explore program music for piano, interpreted in tone different facets of his own personality. "Eusebius" and "Florestan," in the *Carnaval*, represent the opposed
sides of his psyche. "Eusebius," a limpid, dreamy piece, depicts the gentle,
sensitive tone poet, Schumann. "Florestan," volcanic and fiery, suggests
the nature of the tempestuous Schumann.

The romantic composer was also strongly attracted to ethnic elements
found in folk song and folk dance. Here was an opportunity to capture and
perhaps to elevate to highest art the musical traces of the sorrows and exultations of generations.

Sometimes composers would quote briefly from actual folk sources, as in
the Tchaikovsky symphonies; other times they would polish them to a high
gloss, as in the 26 Brahms arrangements of German folk songs for unaccompanied chorus.

More often, though, only the spirit of folk literature permeated these
works. For example, the symphonies of the Czech, Dvorak, and the Finn, Sibelius, give strong ethnic impressions without quoting at all from actual
songs or dances of the people. Other composers who particularly emphasized Nationalism in their works were Smetana, Grieg, Glinka, Liszt, Chopin, Mussorgsky, and Rimsky-Korsakov.

The influence of Beethoven

Beethoven, really a composer of the Classical period, anticipated nearly
every major musical innovation of the Romantics.

The *Pastoral Symphony* pointed the way for innumerable romantic program pieces of a bucolic nature including the excellent "Scenes in the Country" portion of the *Symphonie fantastique* by Berlioz.

The parts for chorus in the *Ninth Symphony* influenced Berlioz in his
Romeo et Juliette Symphonie and *Symphonie funebre et triomphale,* both
of which use voices. Beethoven's only opera, *Fidelio,* significantly influenced
Wagner.

The remarkable integration of soloist with orchestra in both the *Fourth
Piano Concerto* and in the *Violin Concerto* pointed to similar efforts in the
same form by Mendelssohn, Schumann, and Brahms.

Incredible harmonic progressions such as those in the 20th variation
from the *Diabelli Variations,* though perhaps used as daringly in late Wagner or Liszt, were seldom surpassed.

Many times a portion of a Beethoven work can easily pass for the work of Schumann, Chopin, or even Brahms.

Beethoven, through the rhythms and harmonies, the rhapsodic forms, and the clear emphasis on the passionate and grand, was the catalyst that made all of Romanticism possible.

The Romantics themselves were very conscious of the great master; some, like Brahms, painfully so. Brahms' *Symphony No. 1* was immediately dubbed the "Tenth." But when an admirer mentioned the similarity of themes in the finale of Beethoven's *Ninth* and his own, Brahms is reported to have said "Any ass can see that."

To realize Schubert's musical debt to Beethoven one need only listen to the *Symphony No. 9* (The Great C Major). It is cast in typical massive Beethoven style, with considerable eruptive power and sweep.

THE COMPOSERS

Weber and Schubert

Two important composers living and writing during Beethoven's life-time were Carl Maria Weber (1786–1826) and Franz Schubert (1797–1828). Both can be thought of as pre-Romantics.

Weber and Schubert were composing music at a time when Classicism was still quite strong. Weber, writing as critic as late as 1809, severely casti-gated Beethoven's *Third* and *Fourth Symphonies*. Weber's ideal was still Mozart. Though Weber was a prolific composer of sonatas, concertos, occa-sional pieces, and the fine *Konzertstück* for the piano, his major contribu-tion was in opera. He is considered to be the founder of German romantic opera. *Der Freischütz, Euryanthe,* and *Oberon,* through their beauty of char-acterization, great dramatic power, and superb orchestration, laid the foun-dation for Wagner and other operatic composers.

Franz Schubert is called by Alfred Einstein the "Romantic-Classicist." Listening to his *Fifth Symphony,* we feel that the music indeed is as lucid and as symmetrical as that of Haydn or Mozart. In the short 31 years of his life Schubert wrote an astonishing number of compositions, including nearly 600 songs. The songs, as well as the chamber works, piano pieces, and larger works, all show one supreme quality—spontaneous lyricism.

Most of Schubert's works are saturated with memorable melody. It is as if the music's center of gravity were in the melody itself, with other musical elements—rhythm, harmony, and form—revolving around and existing for it. It was Felix Mendelssohn who invented the title "song without words" for some of his smaller piano pieces, but the term can apply to many of Schubert's instrumental compositions. With Schubert, the concept of song was never distant. Several of his instrumental works were based on his own *lieder:* the *"Trout" Quintet;* the quartet, *Death of a Maiden,* the *Wanderer Fantasy* for piano.

But though lyricism is the major characteristic in his music, Schubert cannot simply be considered a purveyor of astonishingly good tunes. Some of his works possess such dramatic force and piercing intensity of feeling that they truly would do justice to Beethoven. For example, the song, *Der Doppelgänger* ("The Double"), establishes an eerie mood; one that is so psychologically true that it is almost frightening. The poem by Heine tells of the lover standing in a square gazing at the house of his loved one. Before it, in the murk of the night, stands a lonely figure of a man. The mood is perfectly established by barren chords in the piano and by the hypnotic stillness in the voice part.

He peers intently to see who the man is. The expression becomes more taut. Finally, a startling chord *fff* on a high note for the voice communicates his horror as he recognizes the face in the gloom is his own.

The tremendous harmonic power heard throughout the song is typical of Schubert's work. There almost always exists kaleidoscopic chordal color underlying simple, yet vital melody.

Weber lived to be 40, Schubert 31. It astonishes us to consider what they accomplished with so few years. We ask what could they have done if granted an average lifetime? Perhaps not much more. Perhaps the eruptive, flooding, creative power that was theirs, simply burned out their lives. Perhaps it had all been said, quickly and beautifully. Schubert is known to have dashed off six songs at one sitting. Schumann wrote the piano version of his first symphony, the *Spring* in four brief, but ecstatic days. These are incredible feats, only to be explained by the compulsive creative drive that was present in the early Romantics.

Mendelssohn, Chopin, Schumann

Felix Mendelssohn (1809–1847) is a fascinating figure of early Romanticism, both for his music and for the influence of his personality. His life was completely opposite to the romantic image of the harried, starving composer in a garret, scratching out noble compositions with numb fingers by a flickering penny-candle. His family was as cultured and honored as it was affluent. The grandfather, Moses Mendelssohn, a German-Jewish philosopher, was called "the German Socrates." His father Abraham was a wealthy banker. From his mother he took his first music lessons and imbibed his early love of music.

His natural gifts were immense. Along with a fine appearance and evenness of temper was a natural aptitude for nearly everything he took interest in. He spoke several languages and was a brilliant conversationalist. His wit was remarkable. He was a classical scholar, could draw very well, and was attracted to chess. Swimming, riding, and dancing came naturally.

His influence in the world around him and after him was great. He revived and performed the works of J. S. Bach, including the *St. Matthew Passion,* which had lain fallow for many years. He helped to found the *Bach Gesellschaft,* a society for the publication of the entire works in authentic editions.

He not only inaugurated the famous Gewandhaus Concerts but in the same year founded and directed the Leipzig Conservatory. The Conservatory had on its first faculty Robert Schumann and the violin virtuoso, Ferdinand David.

His influence as a conductor and pianist was great, and he helped a large number of composers, including Schumann, Berlioz, and Chopin.

Mendelssohn's gifts matched his material fortune and superior environment. But all of this was surpassed by his industry, good will, and modesty.

What, then, about his creative work: the concertos, sonatas, oratorios, and symphonies? As can be expected, the music is refined and polished. Orchestration is superb, with a transparency of texture reminiscent of Mozart's. The sunny, bright pieces, such as the *Italian Symphony* and the last movement of the *Violin Concerto,* or the *G minor Piano Concerto,* have rarely been surpassed for sparkle and luminosity.

Mendelssohn was always careful when it came to writing parts for others to play or sing. Ferdinand David was consulted about the *Violin Concerto* to ensure that the writing for violin was idiomatic and playable.

The vocal parts in his oratorio *Elijah,* always are well within the capability of the average community chorister. Mendelssohn never would have written the larynx-tearing choruses found in Beethoven's *Ninth Symphony* or in the *Missa Solemnis.*

"Everything in good measure, nothing in excess," well describes Mendelssohn's music. Everything is clear, rational, and well mannered.

Mendelssohn's music makes good listening. The sounds are always pleasant. But one is seldom if ever shaken and stirred, as by Bach or Beethoven. Perhaps with Mendelssohn music came so easily that it could not become sublime. Perhaps Mendelssohn revered the great masters too much:

> "Don't you agree with me, that the first condition for an artist is, that he have respect for the great ones, and do not try to blow out the great flames, in order that the petty tallow candle may shine a little brighter"? *

---

* Thomas Paine and Klauser, eds., *Famous Composers and Their Works,* Vol II (Boston: J. B. Millet Co., 1891) , p. 422.

Frederic Chopin (1810–1849) did not possess the breadth of culture and universal interest of Mendelssohn. He wrote almost exclusively for the piano, on which he excelled. His father was a French tutor who had settled in Poland and married a Polish girl. Frederick Chopin himself was educated in Poland, but spent his mature life in Paris and other important cultural centers.

His music as a whole is a compelling composite of Slavic passion and French sophistication. Pieces such as the *"Minute" Waltz* or the *"Black Key" Etude* show the utmost in refined grace and gentility. They are salon pieces pure and simple, glib but impeccably crafted, and very sensitive.

Chopin contributed enormously to the development of piano idioms and of piano technique. In fact, the new role that he established for the piano set a precedent that was to remain until Debussy completely refashioned piano technique in the early twentieth century.

The 24 *Etudes* of Chopin are amazing in that they provide the utmost challenges technically for the pianist; they are in fact a complete school of pianism. But while they serve as admirable instructional material, the music always transcends any utilitarian value it has.

Robert Schumann (1810–1856), in a sense, exemplified traits seen in both Mendelssohn and Chopin.

Like Mendelssohn, he was a positive force in musical society. His writing and crusading for better music and performance, his championing of composers with promise such as Brahms and Chopin, and his wit and eloquence remind us very much of Mendelssohn. Like Mendelssohn, he also tried his hand at a wide gamut of compositions: chamber music for many combinations, concerto, opera, symphony, sonata, program music, lieder.

He married the most famous female concert pianist of her century, Clara Wieck. With her and on his own he traveled and brushed elbows with the most important people of his time.

Schumann was extremely emotional and passionate, and his music, like Chopin's, is always pervaded by his personality. The Apollonian reserve of Mendelssohn is seldom apparent with Schumann. The prevailing characteristics of his music are intense subjectivity and great diversity of mood. His harmonic vocabulary is much more original and daring than Mendelssohn's. The best work is in the smaller pieces, the short character pieces such as those in the *Carnaval*, Op. 9, the *Kinderscenen*, Op. 15, for piano, or the individual lieder of the cycles *Liederkreis* and *Dichterliebe*. It was in these shorter pieces that the sudden flooding inspiration that seized Schumann could best be captured. The large musical canvases, such as the four symphonies, the concertos, and the choral works, suffer somewhat from a certain lack of proportion and sustained intellectual interest. Unlike Mendelssohn, who was at his best in marshalling the components of large works into co-

Clara Schumann (née Wieck)—from a painting by E. Fechner (*Courtesy of Historical Pictures Service, Chicago*).

hesive, balanced structures, Schumann frequently foundered in large works. Success in large works, where what is done to an idea is more important than the idea itself, requires detachment. This Schumann lacked. For him the ecstasy of the creative moment was supreme.

In this connection it is fruitful to compare Schumann and Brahms relative to their symphonies. We mentioned earlier that Schumann wrote the piano score of the *First Symphony* in four days. Brahms worked on his *Symphony in C Minor* upwards of 10 years.

Berlioz

The comment about Delacroix, that he was "passionately in love with passion" applies as well to Hector Berlioz (1803–1869). He was a man who could burst into tears at the beauty of a page of his own music, just finished. Here was a man who felt, felt, and felt some more, always with an ardor and vehemence that was controlled only by his superior intellectual gifts.

No effect was too sensational, no combination of instruments too unusual, if it served to express the volcanic musical ideas that were his. For his *Requiem* he required not only a large symphony orchestra, and a full chorus with soloists, but four extra brass bands placed at the four points of the compass. Obvious in any of his music is the predominance of passion and color.

As did Schumann, he married a renowned personality, in this case, the Shakespearian actress, Harriet Smithson. Unlike the match of Robert and Clara however, this marriage was unsuccessful.

His writings were as influential as were Schumann's and his book on orchestration *Traite de l'instrumentation* is still very important and useful.

Berlioz was one of the few romantic composers who was not a virtuoso on any instrument. But he, like Mendelssohn before and Wagner after him, was one of the century's great conductors.

Other composers

". . . William Tell is the work of an enormous talent, so much like genius that it might easily be mistaken for it." Thus did Berlioz, the critic, impale Giacomo Rossini (1792–1868) with his pen. We have already mentioned this enormously successful composer. His many operas are utterly winning, and the best of his comic operas, such as *The Barber of Seville* and *Cinderella,* have all the effervescence of champagne.

The fine *bel canto* operas of Vincenzo Bellini (1801–1835), including the perennial favorite, *Norma,* are distinguished for purity of melodic line and considerable power of characterization.

Gaetano Donizetti's (1797–1848) operas are similar to Bellini's. *Lucia di Lammermoor* is still very popular. The comic opera *Don Pasquale* is all froth, and compares very favorably with Rossini's work in a similar vein.

Before moving on to later developments in romantic music we will mention two other Italians and one French composer of considerable influence. Nicolo Paganini (1782–1849) was a concert violinist and competent composer of dazzling concertos for the violin. The high standards that he achieved as a player profoundly affected many Romantics, including Schumann, who, on hearing one of his concerts, resolved to become a virtuoso on the piano.

Luigi Cherubini (1760–1842) worked mostly in Paris, where he was much admired. Beethoven considered him the finest writer for the stage then living. Because his long life straddled rather neatly most of the classical period and nearly half of the romantic century, his music is particularly instructive. Basically, it is classical, with structure and balance primary. But there is also dramatic power and rich harmonic and orchestral color. Among his best works are the *Requiem in C Minor,* and the opera *Medea.*

Georges Bizet (1838–1875), although best known for his superb opera *Carmen,* produced in the last year of his short life, was responsible for a surprisingly large catalogue of works. The training ground for *Carmen* occurred over a period of nearly 20 years during which he made upwards of 2 dozen forays into the operatic field. *The Pearl Fishers* (1862–63) contains charming music, although in it he had not yet attained the dramatic power that was to suffuse *Carmen.*

The *Symphony in C* was written when he was seventeen. Obviously derived stylistically from Mendelssohn, Rossini, and Gounod, and cast in clear classical sonata form, his youthful fire infused it with the sparkling freshness of invention. The work stands as a masterpiece of its kind. The exotic element later to be found throughout *Carmen* was foreshadowed not only in the third movement of this symphony, but saturated much of his other music, especially the *L'Arlésienne Suite* for orchestra.

The mighty handful—"The Five"

Mikhail Glinka (1804–1857), the composer of the opera *A Life for the Tsar,* was the founder of the Russian Nationalist school that was to inspire the "Five."

The *Five* were a group of Russian composers who worked to create a National Russian School of music. They were: Alexander Borodin (1833–1887), Cesar Cui (1835–1918), Mily Balakirev (1837–1910), Modest Mussorgsky (1839–1881), and Nicolai Rimsky-Korsakov (1844–1908). Together they sought a new way in Russian music. Through their compositions, published articles, and teaching they fought the conservative academic establishment and resisted mightily all European musical influences that they deemed inappropriate. The European musical ethic was well represented by the brothers Anton and Nicholas Rubenstein, composer/pianists and educators. The music of the *Five* was saturated with Russian historical themes and myths as well as with folk song, folk dance, and Orthodox chant. The Russian peasant figured strongly in their works as in the literary works of the novelists Gogol and Tolstoy. All were intensely interested in Russian political life, especially as it pertained to reform. The liberation of the serfs in 1861 affected them profoundly. And their sympathies were not passive. For example, Rimsky-Korsakov published a letter criticizing the too stringent police supervision of his students at the St. Petersburg Conservatory and, because of this, was dismissed.

Balakirev was the group's spiritual leader and mentor; his was the catalystic personality around which the others gathered. Balakirev had known Glinka, and was intimately acquainted with his music, spending several years editing the older master's works. Through his travels to the Caucasus, Tiflis, and Baku, he collected many folk songs and later built colorful compositions around them. Many of these, for example the piano piece titled *Islamey* and the symphonic poem *Tamar,* show a decided oriental cast, a characteristic which often appeared in the music of other members of the Mighty Handful.

Balakirev's personality was very strong, perhaps even overbearing. He not only encouraged his nationalistic disciples in their new directions but involved himself in their actual compositions—rewriting, correcting, approving, disapproving. Though this inevitably led to friction, the artistic autocracy of Balakirev was beneficial. This was especially so in the early stages of the group's association when he was the only one with something like professional credentials. For Cui, Borodin, Mussorgsky, and Rimsky-Korsakov music at that time was little more than a passionate avocation. Cui, Rimsky-Korsakov, and Mussorgsky were in the military, while Borodin was a scientist. These gentlemen-composers, involved professionally in the non-musical social fabric of their day, gifted musically but unrefined technically, drew their inspiration from the mind and hand of the better trained Balakirev. Two of them, Cui and Borodin, attained eminence in the non-musical world. Borodin became a professor of chemistry and did important research in this field including a treatise called *Researches on the Fluoride of Benzol.* When away from the lectern or laboratory, or when on summer vacation, he developed a rich lyric style of composition. In the larger works such as the *Symphony No. 2 in B Minor,* and the opera *Prince Igor,* he attained considerable dramatic power. *Prince Igor,* along with Glinka's *A Life for the Tsar* and Mussorgsky's *Boris Godounov,* form a great tryptich of Russian nationalistic opera, each based on early Russian historical themes. In scope, and in their illumination of Russian character, they are comparable to the novels *Dead Souls* by Gogol, *War and Peace* by Tolstoy, and *The Brothers Karamazov* by Dostoevsky. Cui was an army officer, and became an authority on military fortifications, lecturing on the subject at the Artillery School and the Staff College. (One of his charges was the Emperor Nicholas II.) Cui is generally considered to have been the least gifted, musically, of the *Five*. His articles for periodicals both in Russia and in Western Europe brought attention to the work of the Nationalists. Thus both Borodin and Cui led polarized professional lives, attaining considerable influence in artistic as well as in the academic sciences. In the following chapter, the life and work of the pioneer American composer Charles Ives will offer an interesting parallel. Of the *Five*, the name most familiar to the layman is that of Rimsky-Korsakov. Of aristocratic birth, he spent 7 years at the Naval College in St. Petersburg and became an officer. In 1861 he met Balakirev and resolved to improve his talents in composition. His first symphony was written during a three-year naval cruise (with the constant supervision by mail of Balakirev) and was performed to considerable public acclaim in St. Petersburg in 1865. On his return, Rimsky-Korsakov resumed his musical studies and, several years later was appointed professor of composition and instrumentation at the St. Petersburg Conservatory.

Though he was a late starter, Rimsky-Korsakov ultimately became the finest craftsman among the Nationalists, excelling particularly in the art of orchestration. The canvas of his orchestra abounds in a riot of exotic colora-

Nikolai Rimsky-Korsakov on the clipper "Almaz" (first row, right), during its visit to New York in 1863 (*Courtesy of Sovfoto, New York*).

tion. His *Principles of Orchestration* (1896–98) is still valuable for students of that art.

The *Russian Easter Overture, Scheherazade* and the *Spanish Capriccio* are familiar and well applauded by concert audiences. In them is found an artful and exotic mixture of melodic, rhythmic and harmonic elements ensconced in a lush instrumental setting. Less well known, but deserving of attention are his several operas. Certain portions of these, such as "Hymn to the Sun" from *The Golden Cockerel* or the "Flight of the Bumblebee" from *Tsar Saltan,* are well known. But *The Golden Cockerel,* based on a fairy tale by Pushkin, and the little known opera *Mozart and Salieri* are seldom heard in the West. Without question, the composer among the *Five* with the most impressive gifts was Modest Mussorgsky. He must rank as a major figure in romantic music, especially in the areas of musical irony and realism.

His life was often in disarray, his personality disordered and unbalanced. As a young man he was a member of the Regiment of the Guards, and later entered the Civil Service, progressing fitfully through its ranks. As were the other disciples of Balakirev, he was largely self-taught. His music is thoroughly original, often twentieth century in its use of fresh sounds. Because his harmony, rhythm, and melody are often deliberately inelegant and primitivistic—strongly anti-Western—many believed his work to be uncouth and crude. In fact, it was Rimsky-Korsakov who "refinished" Mussorgsky's powerful opera *Boris Godounov* and it was in that revised version that most of the western world heard it. But his music is not crude. Rough hewn, realistic, but not crude. In 1863 he and several young intellectuals shared a "commune" apartment in St. Petersburg where they ardently discussed artistic, political, and religious ideas. Mussorgsky's later artistic credo, formed in part through his years in the "commune," contained within it a disdain for surface polish and formal beauty in musical forms; a total repudiation of art for art's sake. He said, ". . . art is a means of communicating with people, not an aim in itself." With some peasant blood in his veins, he identified strongly with their aspirations. The massed peasant scenes in *Boris Godounov* form a powerful generic undercurrent to the drama, symbolizing the composer's awareness of the incipient power and drama to be found in the mass. Among his popular works is a programmatic suite for piano titled *Pictures at an Exhibition,* often heard in the orchestral transcription by Ravel. Suggested to the composer by a posthumous exhibition of the drawings and water colors of his friend, the architect Victor Hartmann, the individual items of the suite typify Mussorgsky's artistic stance. They communicate easily; they are vividly ironic, and very naturalistic. Several of the "pictures" are introduced by little transition pieces called "Promenades," representing the composer in his tour of the exhibition. Subject matter of the pictures varies considerably: there is the sinister "The Hut of Baba

Yaga," a sentimental love ballad, "The Old Castle," a tender scene of French children at play called "Tuilleries," and the superb finale, "The Great Gate at Kiev." The song cycles, *Songs and Dances of Death* and *The Nursery*, show Mussorgsky to have had tremendous psychological insight in areas highly diverse in mood and content. *Night on Bald Mountain* for orchestra is craggy and uncompromising in its exploration of the bizarre.

THE LATE ROMANTICS

Liszt

Franz Liszt (1811–1886) is a composer of great importance. He was present and active at the beginnings of Romanticism. At one of his concerts, when he was only 12 years old, he was kissed on the forehead by Beethoven. His first published piece was the "24th variation" from the collection of variations by eminent composers on a theme by Diabelli. This was the same theme that occasioned the masterly effort by Beethoven, *Variations on a Theme by Diabelli*, Op. 120. Liszt was also square in the middle of the exciting happenings in the time of Wagner, Brahms, and Tchaikovsky.

He was as brilliant a virtuoso on the piano as Paganini was on the violin, and as popular as Rossini.

As with Mendelssohn, his was a catholic view; he championed many composers especially Wagner, Chopin, and Berlioz. His personality was pleasant and his intellectual gifts not slight. His music could be as subjective as that of Chopin or Schumann, but it was as brilliant and successful as Mendelssohn's.

His works number into the seven hundreds and are quite uneven in quality. Pieces of matchless beauty such as the *"Faust" Symphony* and the *B–Minor Piano Sonata* are joined by dozens of glittering, depthless potpourris and transcriptions.

Liszt's music had great significance for his day and for later developments. For one thing, his grasp of harmony and form was impressive. With him we find the same richness of modulation and chordal sound as in Wagner. But this is balanced by compression and unity. His large instrumental works often combined all movements into one, as in the *Piano Concerto No. 1*. **Thematic transformation** was tremendously effective in his hands. The tone poem was developed to perfection by Liszt. Pieces such as *Les Préludes* are highly original and point to Richard Strauss.

Also of importance was his work in national idioms such as the *Hungarian Rhapsodies* and the various pieces with Spanish, Italian, Polish, and

Russian flavors. There are curious piano transcriptions of "God Save the Queen" and "La Marseillaise."

In addition to Liszt, there are four other masters of first importance in late Romanticism. They are Richard Wagner (1813–1883), Peter Tchaikovsky (1840–1893), Johannes Brahms (1833–1897), and Giuseppe Verdi (1813–1901).

In discussing the essence of late Romanticism, it is customary to contrast the work of Wagner and Brahms. And it is true that each represented an opposite point of view, the conservative Brahms espousing "Classicism," while Wagner championed the "music of the future." An imaginative juxtaposition of their lives and work is fruitful.

But even more fruitful is to compare Wagner and Verdi as composers of opera and Brahms and Tchaikovsky as symphonists.

Wagner and Verdi

Wagner was a product of the great German operatic tradition by way of Gluck, Beethoven, and Weber. The Italian Verdi followed in the footsteps of Rossini, Bellini, and Donizetti. Both summed up and brought to maturity the respective operatic traditions of their land. Each was an innovator, Wagner especially scattering significant clues to be followed by Richard Strauss, Mahler, Bruckner, Franck, and the young Schoenberg.

Wagner's career was checkered by fantastic turbulence. He considered that it was the greatest of privileges for anybody to know him—and to aid him. He ran up huge debts, seldom if ever paying them back. He was eternally out of funds. He seduced many women, including Cosima, the wife of one of his strongest supporters, Hans Von Bülow. Cosima, whom he eventually married, revered him despite his constant unfaithfulness. He was exiled from Germany because of his overt anti-monarchist revolutionary actions. These included an essay, "The Revolution," an intimate acquaintance with the Russian nihilist revolutionary, Bakunin, and a public declaration asking the king to ". . . declare Saxony to be a free state." His personal and business relationships, in short, were odious, and he got himself constantly caught up in unpopular schemes and ventures. But despite this, such was the power of his personality and genius that many of his intimates stood behind him through every outrage. Ludwig II, king of Bavaria, subsidized him and especially helped in the great venture of the opera house at Bayreuth, all with full knowledge of Wagner's deficiencies. Cosima was so under his spell that she would not leave his body for 24 hours after his death.

Besides the magnetic appeal of this narcissist, and besides the immense power of his musical ideas, his idealism must have attracted many to him.

His constant championing of better performance standards, especially in singing, his drive for the new opera house, his work with orchestras, and his constant aim to "reform" opera must have appealed greatly. For one performance of *Tannhäuser* he insisted on 164 rehearsals. Such was his perfection and idealism in performance.

Verdi's personal life contrasts vividly with Wagner's. Financial success came rather early, as did fame. There was not constant imbroglio, though his republican sympathies in Italy led him also to political action. After his first wife died, he found a lifemate in his beloved Giuseppina, whom he eventually married. She was a strong force in his life, contributing to the ever deepening current of his creative life. His whole life, though occasionally steeped in shadow, as when his first wife and two children died, was one of steady artistic growth.

What, then, about the music of these two giants, so dissimilar in personality but comparable in genius? Wagner's music clearly follows in the German tradition. The great German masters of the baroque, classical, and early romantic eras had always leaned towards "idea" music, to what could be done with a theme or a motive. With them, what happened to a melodic idea was more important than its own immediate appeal or innate beauty. In the operas of Wagner we see short, trenchant themes—*leitmotifs*— "treated" in the same way that they are in Beethoven symphonies. Tunefulness, of itself, is not the point. Harmony, both in beauty of individual chordal sounds and in scheme of modulation, is emphasized. The harmonic setting of the *leitmotifs* is of paramount importance for the development of the character of the idea. The orchestra becomes symphonic, and is often entrusted with melodic elements as important as those heard in the voices. So vital and important is the orchestral part in some of Wagner's works that in concert it is sometimes played by itself, with the voice part left entirely out, as in the "Liebestod" from *Tristan und Isolde*.

The later operas become more and more homogeneous and organic. Continuous melody supersedes the old division of recitative and aria. The music never seems to end. Cadences do not lead to terminating tonics, but the music slips on and on. In this continuous, organic aspect of the operas after 1850, such as *Tristan,* the *Ring* Cycle, and *Parsifal*, we are reminded of the "unifying" theories of Darwin and Wallace, who in the 1850's were saying that all life is biologically related and stems from common origins. Jacques Barzun in his book, *Darwin, Marx, Wagner,* says:

> . . . Wagner's pretensions as a dramatist, his friendships with Nietzsche and Gobineau, place him at the heart of the biological and sociological theorizing which sprang from the idea of Evolution.*

* Reprinted from *Darwin, Marx, Wagner* by Jacques Barzun (1941) published by Atlantic-Little, Brown and Company.

In short, Wagner's music is as passionate as it is intellectual, reflecting perfectly Wagner the thinker and Wagner the poet.

Verdi was also a thinker. He also achieved magnificent drama through the force and sweep of his music. The power and dramatic unity of *Rigoletto, La Traviata, Aida,* and especially *Otello* certainly equal those of Wagner's operas, but are arrived at from another direction, that of lyric melody. Whereas Wagner completely transformed opera into music drama, Verdi still worked within the concept of the number opera and gave it new substance and meaning. It is Wagner's music, not Verdi's, that was called the music of the future, "Zukunfts-musik."

Italian opera as Verdi found it consisted of a string of lyric numbers—arias, duets, and ensembles—connected by musically static recitatives. Emphasis was on tunefulness, and display of the bel canto voice. In the hands of masters like Rossini and Bellini, number opera was compelling despite the music's center of gravity unmistakably placed squarely in the vocal line. In the hands of lesser composers, number opera degenerated into showpieces for prominent singers of the time, full of high notes, fury, and spectacle, but signifying little. Verdi took the form as it was, and gradually enriched and ennobled it. His method was simple. Beautiful melody, display of voice, scintillating ensembles, spectacle—all were abundantly present—but the composer never used them at the expense of dramatic truth.

This can be seen quite clearly in the opera *La Traviata.* Essentially it is a number opera including the basic ingredients found in Italian opera for many years before. In the renunciation aria sung by Violetta (Act II, Scene II) is found a kind of sparse, functional accompaniment that served Italian opera well for decades. However, here its simplicity is perfectly fitted to the tragic poignancy heard in the voice part. The aria, "Dite alla giovine" begins with a melody of great purity.

When the melody becomes intense with grief, the cellos, playing but two notes below, underline the pathos of the moment. And when the voice part reaches the climactic high note, it is not solely for effect and vocal brilliance, but is a natural culmination of the music.

Verdi never abandoned his emphasis on melody, but the later operas, such as *Aida, Otello,* and *Falstaff* display a fuller use of the orchestra and an increase in dramatic power.

Tchaikovsky and Brahms

A comparison of the work of Brahms and Tchaikovsky is particularly rewarding, especially in the field of symphony. Both wrote only a few symphonies: Brahms, four (plus two "practice" symphonies, the *Serenades*) ;

Tchaikovsky, six. (The Tchaikovsky *Seventh* is only a reconstruction from very incomplete sketches and should not be used for comparison.) Both lavished their most penetrating musical thoughts on these works. Both followed standard formal procedure, with very little exception. The orchestra used is very similar, though Tchaikovsky's is more colorful and sometimes larger.

The cello and the French horn figure prominently in the symphonies of both the German and the Russian. Both were strongly influenced by classical period composers. Beethoven cast his shadow on both, of course. But with Tchaikovsky, Mozart was of equal influence. A performance of Mozart's opera *Don Giovanni,* heard by the Russian when he was a young man, profoundly influenced him.

> . . . my worship for Mozart is quite contrary to my musical nature. But perhaps it is just because . . . I feel broken and spiritually out of joint, that I find consolation and rest in Mozart's music, wherein he gives expression to that joy of life which was part of his sane and wholesome temperament . . .*

Italian music moved him strongly, too. "There are melodies of Bellini which I can never hear without the tears rushing to my eyes."

Beyond a magnetic attraction to the music of Beethoven, Brahms was also influenced by the Great Cantor, J. S. Bach. The many glorious contrapuntal portions in most of the major works attest to this. One need only listen to the finale of the *Fourth Symphony,* the last portions of both sets of variations on themes of Handel and Haydn, and magnificent fugues in the *German Requiem* to see this at once.

The importance of the influence of early masters becomes clear when we see that both symphonists were concerned with preserving the essence and spirit of absolutism in their symphonies. Tchaikovsky did inject an element of Russian nationalism in his symphonies, and there is a suggested, but very tenuous program in No. 4. But all 10 symphonies—Russian and German—use strong classical forms. Occasionally, cyclic technique was used (Tchaikovsky, Nos. 4 and 5; Brahms, No. 3), but this was not entirely original; Beethoven had experimented with cyclic form in Nos. 5 and 9.

The basic problem that both masters faced was in keeping to the classical principles of form while taking advantage of new developments in harmony, instrumentation, rhythm, etc. They had to find new ways to breathe life into the old forms.

The Brahms symphonic style is really leagues away from that of Tchaikovsky, who preferred to dazzle his audience with an impressive array of in-

---

* Catherine Drinker Bowen and Barbara Von Meck, *Beloved Friend* (Boston, Toronto: Little, Brown and Co., 1937), p. 233.

strumental color and orchestral gymnastics. Lyric melody, as such, often at the expense of other musical factors, is greatly emphasized. This last factor undoubtedly explains Tchaikovsky's great popularity with concert audiences and the ease with which his music wins new friends among the uninitiated. As mentioned above, Tchaikovsky took full advantage of the rising tide of Russian nationalism that occurred in the latter half of the nineteenth century and wrote into his symphonies either real folk songs and dances or simulated ones.

Brahms occasionally dazzles, but only incidentally. Whereas Tchaikovsky arouses emotions rather easily through the means mentioned above, Brahms seems to invite thought first, which then leads to emotional response. He therefore concerns himself very little with sheer sound for its own sake or with striking instrumental combinations. What he is interested in is musical idea, beauty of form, evolution of idea, depth and richness of textures. On first hearing a Brahms symphony, the neophyte often is puzzled; there is so much to hear all at once that he tends to hear little. Overall pattern is so masterfully woven on such a titanic scale that the beginning listener is lost. Brahms is the greatest master of musical understatement; Tchaikovsky appeals directly to the listener with either high rhetorical flourish or hypersensitive lyricism.

Brahms' music makes friends slowly but surely. His style is oblique, reserved, and thoughtful. The style of Brahms is like the discourse of a great philosopher-orator who rises to the heights of passion through the accumulating force of his ideas and the fervor of his idealism. Tchaikovsky's music wins rapport immediately. His symphonic style is brilliant, hotly emotional, passionate in the immediate sense. The sounds pour out of a Tchaikovsky symphony like lava spurting from a crater.

CHAPTER 8

Early Twentieth Century

I. IN TRANSITION: POST–ROMANTICS, IMPRESSIONISTS, PRE–MODERNS

THE MUSIC PRODUCED in the waning years of the nineteenth century until the close of World War I is marked by diversity and flux. These few years linked two periods strongly contrasted in essence and manner—the Romantic and the Contemporary. In this time can be seen the dying yet still glowing embers of true Romanticism itself. Post-Romantics such as Mahler, Richard Strauss, the young Schoenberg, Sibelius, and Rachmaninoff gazed fondly back to an ebbing age and refused to let it die. Much of their music is possessed with a ripeness very near decay.

During these years Impressionism arrived on the musical scene. Its prime mover was a genuine master, Claude Debussy. But Impressionism as a movement was short lived. Its concern with and constant search for fresh sound was soon trampled under by the strident, urgent sounds of contemporary music.

All the while that the fruit of Romanticism was rotting on the bough and Impressionism was briefly flowering, contemporary music had actually germinated and new music growth could plainly be seen.

Very early, even before Impressionism, the Connecticut iconoclast Charles Ives, with works such as the *Variations on America for Organ* (1891), anticipated by 30 years important techniques of composition. In this particular piece Ives writes a perfect example of polytonality. Here the composer foreshadowed a technique that was to be explored by Milhaud and others much later.

Schoenberg's *String Quartet No. 2,* (1907–08) featured a Finale almost completely atonal. Tonality, the bed rock of all music for hundreds of years, was here all but banished.

Stravinsky, in the years 1910, –11, –13 electrified the world with three ballets; *Firebird, Petrouchka,* and *The Rite of Spring.* The tortured dissonances and nervous rhythmic patterns were in stark contrast to the "new sounds" of Debussy and Ravel.

The whole period is remarkable because of this overlap of styles.

Late romantics such as R. Strauss, Puccini, and Rachmaninoff, lived through the whole decade of Impressionism and far into the contemporary period while retaining the essential musical elements of a perished Romantic age. Simultaneously, as early as the 1890's, the seeds for contemporary music were slowly taking root.

Post-romanticism

Four post-romantic composers must be discussed when considering the transitional period from romantic music to contemporary music. They are Giacomo Puccini (1859–1924), Richard Strauss (1864–1949), Gustav Mahler (1860–1911), and Jan Sibelius (1865–1957). Each wrote important works in the late nineteenth century, yet lived well into the twentieth century. And though certain aspects in their music are contemporary, for example, the realism in the operas of Puccini and Straus, their basic outlook is that of the nineteenth century. We find again the emphasis on beauty of melody and sound. We find also the grand, sometimes bombastic, gesture. We find the same concern for the subjective, personal, passionate, and intimate. Strauss and Puccini achieved notable success with opera; Mahler and Sibelius concerned themselves chiefly with symphony.

RICHARD STRAUSS. It was perfectly natural that Richard Strauss, the son of a leading horn player in the Munich opera, should have taken to opera. His father had known and worked with Wagner. It was inevitable that the creator of *Tristan und Isolde* and *Die Meistersinger* would cast his shadow over the young man. At any rate, his three best known operas, *Salome, Elektra,* and *Der Rosenkavalier,* carry on the Wagnerian tradition through the dramatic use of voices, the large symphonic orchestra, and the use of the continuous style of melody.

An added element in these works, not usually found in Wagner, is the hyper-realism of the score. *Salome,* for example, originally a play by Oscar Wilde, is set with every detail of its gory plot minutely described by the music. When Salome offers the "Dance of the Seven Veils" for Herod, the music, while building in orgiastic frenzy, gives us a clue to what she is thinking. A theme associated with John the Baptist suddenly is heard. After the dance she asks for his head on a silver platter. The orchestra suddenly shimmers and shines with a macabre silvery sheen.

Besides opera, Strauss also wrote stunning, extravagantly detailed tone poems. *Till Eulenspiegel* is a humorous musical tale based on an early German fable. *Don Juan* and *Don Quixote,* though less uproarious, are similar in concept, while *Death and Transfiguration* and *Also sprach Zarathustra* are deeply philosophical.

PUCCINI.   While Strauss followed in the steps of Wagner, Puccini carried on in the tradition of Verdi. Unlike Wagner, who stressed the role of the orchestra in his operas, Verdi took the typically Italian view that voice and melody are primary. All of Verdi, then, is a glorious manifestation of how well the human voice can sound and how beautiful melody can be. Puccini, like his great predecessor, revered melody and the voice. His highly effective operas, including *La Bohème, Tosca,* and *Madama Butterfly,* are redolent with the melodic fragrance that has always permeated musical Italy. As in Strauss, there is great realism, a tremendous feeling for effective dramatic theater.

The Puccini orchestra is always colorful, full, luxuriant; though never impinging on the primacy of the voice parts. Puccini's harmony is highly refined, often suggesting French coloring and sensitivity.

MAHLER.   In the nine titanic symphonies of Mahler can be seen the last fruit of the German symphonic tradition. This tradition began in the later 1700's and displayed such supreme masters of the form as Haydn, Mozart, Beethoven, Schubert, Mendelssohn, Schumann, Bruckner, and Brahms. Throughout this long development the symphony can be seen as a blending of profound musical thought with the utmost in refined expression.

A deep, soul-searing musical sentiment organized through grand, cohesive structural design permeates the Mahler symphony. The tonal canvas is almost always massive. Not only are these works very long, but the forces used are sometimes enormous. For example, the *Symphony No. 8,* the "Symphony of a Thousand," employed at its first performance a chorus of 850 voices, 8 soloists, and an orchestra of 146.

Mahler, like Berlioz, was enchanted with the sound of the human voice in the symphony. In the words of Salazar, "Mahler moved from song to symphony, just as the acorn engenders the oak. In a simple melody, in a children's popular song, Mahler heard the musical murmurings of the cosmos." * The *Symphony No. 1* contains folk-like melodies taken from his earlier song cycle *Songs of a Wayfarer* while the 2nd, 3rd, 4th, and 8th symphonies all contain vocal music. There was precedent for this: we have already mentioned the voices in Beethoven's *Ninth.* Even Mendelssohn had contributed a sort of hybrid symphony-cantata, the *Hymn of Praise;* and Berlioz has chorus and soloists in his *Romeo and Juliet Symphony.* But there is a significant difference between Mahler's use of the human voice within the vast panorama of his symphonic thought and its use by his predecessors. Beethoven in the *Ninth* saw the voice as the necessary intensifying medium for the achievement of the ultimate statement of his philosophy. The human quality of the voice was a perfect tool to express the sentiments of brotherhood, love, and universality found in the Schiller text. Berlioz' use of chorus and soloists in the *Romeo and Juliet Symphony* stems from his concern with the programmatic idea. The French composer desired to make the dramatic idea very explicit. What better plan than to use important sections of Shakespeare's play in a thoroughgoing integration with symphonic style?

With Mahler, however, it is the microcosmic lied itself that provides spiritual motivation. Unlike these masters, Mahler came on the scene after a large body of lieder had developed. Schubert, Schumann, and Brahms had evolved the lieder cycle to the point where it had become one of the major forms of the romantic century. These songs represent the very quintessence of the personal, and subjective. They directly embody the intimate, poetic, and lyric; traits of basic importance to romanticism as a whole. Mahler, whose primary characteristic in his music is that of intense subjective statement—the total expression of the self—grasped the importance of the folk and art song as the agent for "humanizing" the symphony. His extraordinarily agonized personal involvement in the very web of the music can best be understood by his own words written on the score of the unfinished *Tenth Symphony,* "Madness seizes me, accursed that I am—annihilates me, so that I forget that I exist, so that I cease to be. . . ." As one listens to the symphonies, shot through with tortured, spasmodic passages, searing climaxes, frenetic exultations, and mystic murmurings, these words come true. And always, song is very near, not only actual quotations, but in the very heart of all of his lyric moments. The first melody from the Adagietto movement of the *Fifth Symphony* is a perfect example of the pervading lyricism in the symphonies. It throbs with the bittersweet poignancy of old Vienna and the travail of a troubled soul.

---

* *Music In Our Time* by Adolfo Salazar, W. W. Norton and Company, Inc. N.Y., 1946, p. 55.

SIBELIUS. Jean Sibelius, another post-Romantic whose major contribution has been in the symphony, is quite different. Whereas Mahler is ultra-passionate, super-emotional, Sibelius is spare, incisive, granitic, frequently sober.

The prevailing spirit comes about through a blend of Finnish nationalism with powerful classical structures, the whole tempered by a romantic sensitivity to sound and texture. Though Sibelius denied using actual folk songs in his symphonies, melodies such as the one below strongly suggest the hardiness and sturdiness of north European folk song and dance.

Example 8-1   *Symphony No. 2*, Movt. I, Sibelius

One does not find modernity in the basic structural elements of the music of Sibelius; melodic, harmonic, and rhythmic materials are within the romantic idiom already explored. Certainly Berlioz and Mussorgsky had handled rhythm much more freely. Wagner's modulations are vastly more adventuresome than those of Sibelius; and the fresh vertical sonorities of his contemporaries, Debussy, Ravel, Mahler, R. Strauss, far outstrip anything from his pen. As noted above, his forms were those from the past: symphony, symphonic poem, concerto, chamber music, song, and the genre piano piece. But, despite Sibelius' non-innovative approach to both inner materials and overall form, there is a very special originality in his work. It is the unique Sibelius mix of musical elements that results in high originality: the way in which the forms are handled. No matter what the overall structure at hand, sonata-allegro, ternary part form, rondo, etc., he manages to achieve something different, something entirely viable and logical.

The manner in which the composer manages motives and themes within developmental structures will illustrate this. Like Beethoven and Brahms, Sibelius does the most with the least. His melodic materials within the sonata pattern tend to be incisive, and sparse. It is in what they ultimately become that makes them interesting. Through a rigorous logical procedure Sibelius has these ideas grow, burgeon, catch fire. But his musical logic is not "classical." Rather than present an ordered sequence of themes, separated by fluid transitional passages followed by a development section as in the symphonies of Haydn, Mozart, Schubert, and Mendelssohn, Sibelius follows the lead of Beethoven in the first movement of the *"Eroica" Symphony*. Transitions are vitalized and become much more melodic so that the distinction between transition and theme is blurred. One is hard put to segmentize these forms into themes, transitions, expositions, codas, etc. Relations are totally organic; all elements are vital. There is no padding. In the process of achieving this logical mix of organically related structural materials, Sibelius often reversed the traditional developmental procedure. His method is deductive rather than inductive. Rather than present a well ordered succession of full blown themes, then proceed to explore their inner motivic structure, Sibelius first exposes plain, concise thematic ideas which ultimately are transformed into themes of high lyric intensity. The emotional climate established at the outset is one of expectancy: something is being groped after, something will unquestionably be grasped, stated and understood in proper time. The structural method of Sibelius does suggest Beethoven and Brahms, but the sound and texture is utterly different from that of any previous composer. It is unique.

Perhaps in no other way is it more unique than in orchestral timbre. The instruments used, both in kind and number are not different from what came before, in the romantic period. Sibelius' instrumentation is standard, but his orchestration is not. Orchestral coloring is of a somewhat dark, somber cast, yet it is clear and bold. The low winds in choir are much in evidence giving the texture an organ-like solidity. And it is not only the bass and tenor winds that heavily anchor the total sound; soprano instruments such as the oboe and clarinet often are made to plunge to the lower limits of their range. In these lower registers they give out a plaintive, nostalgic sound suggestive of the dark forests and somber landscape of Finland. Thus the structural materials of Sibelius' craft are traditional while the resulting sound and sense of the music is fresh and unique. What were the forces in the composer's life that helped to shape his powerful, introspective musical personality?

Sibelius was born at Tavastehus, Finland, in 1865. Born to a well-to-do family, he was given a classical education. He studied law at Helsingfors University, but like Schumann and Tchaikovsky who had also studied law, the magnetism of music soon drew him away from a career in the safe professions. He studied music with Wegelius in Finland, and with Carl Goldmark, the Viennese composer of the well-known *Rustic Wedding Symphony*. In 1897, Finland, at that time under the domination of Russia, keenly aspired for national independence, and, recognizing in the young artist a strong voice for cultural selfhood, gave him a life grant. Except for sortees abroad and to other parts of Finland, Sibelius with his family spent many of his creative years at his country home in Jarvenpaa. His was an intense veneration for the Finnish national epic, the *Kalevala*. Within the seclusion of the hardy but idyllic countryside, it was natural that the twilight moods of this immense saga should permeate his music. Among his works directly suggested by the *Kalevala* are: *The Kullervo Symphony*, the *Swan of Tuonela, Pohjola's Daughter*, and *Lemminkainen's Journey*.

In the cold my song was resting,
Long remained in darkness hidden.
I must draw the songs from Coldness,
From the Frost must I withdraw them.*
                    —from the *Kalevala,* the Land of the Heroes

OTHER POST-ROMANTICS. Of perhaps less stature, but nevertheless of considerable value are the works of several other post-Romantics: Elgar (1857–1934) in Victorian England; Fauré, d'Indy and Saint-Saëns in France; Wolf in Germany; MacDowell in America; and Rachmaninoff in Russia and the United States. Sir Edward Elgar, in the *"Enigma" Variations* and the fine oratorio, *The Dream of Gerontius,* is usually content to repeat harmonic and melodic formulas from the early eighteen-hundreds, though these are invested with great refinement and a certain elegant dignity.

The music of Fauré (1845–1924) and d'Indy (1851–1931) has overtones of Impressionism. It has little of the robust quality found in German and Italian Romanticism, but displays very subtle harmonic shading and effective orchestration. The Suite, *Pelléas et Mélisande,* by Fauré is well known.

Saint-Saëns (1835–1931) wrote polished, elegant works, often in classical forms. The five piano concertos reflect his own immense virtuosity at the keyboard. In this respect he resembles Liszt, whom he knew and admired. His four symphonic poems, including the well-known *Danse Macabre,* also point to Liszt. Among his best work is the massive *Organ Symphony,* Op. 78, and the slight but charming *Carnival of the Animals: Zoological Fantasy.*

Hugo Wolf (1860–1903) is best known for his lieder, many of which are equal in quality to the songs of Schubert, Schumann, and Brahms. Throughout the evolution of the nineteenth century lied, the piano part became more and more important. With Schumann and Brahms it frequently carries as much melodic interest as the voice part, in addition to setting the mood and atmosphere in general. With the lieder of Wolf, such as those in the *Goethe Lieder* and the *Michelangelo Lieder,* the piano part is not only equivalent to the voice but sometimes predominates. As in the operas of Wagner, where all substance and energy seem to swell up from within the orchestra, the piano part in many of the songs of Wolf is central.

The American composer Edward MacDowell (1861–1908) at one time was considered by many in the United States as a kind of musical Messiah, one who would kindle the flame of adventure and originality in young American composers while showing the way to a true school of American music. However, the effect of his music on our time has not been deep or lasting. Gilbert Chase, in *America's Music,* says:

---

* From the book *Kalevala or Land of Heroes.* Translated by W. F. Kirby. Everyman's Library Edition. Published by E. P. Dutton & Co. Inc., and reprinted with their permission.

. . . MacDowell was not a great composer. At his best he was a gifted minia-
turist with an individual manner. Creatively, he looked toward the past, not
toward the future.*

But despite the modest position that he holds among post-romantics,
there is much charm among his smaller compositions, especially those for
piano. Among these engaging pieces are *To a Wild Rose, From Uncle
Remus, From a Wandering Iceberg* and *To an Old White Pine.* The large
works, such as the *Keltic Sonata* for the piano and the *Piano Concertos* are
completely Europe-oriented, and lack originality, but seldom fail to make
their effect in concert.

Serge Rachmaninoff's (1873–1943) work has had enormous success ever
since the writing of his *Second Piano Concerto* in 1901. The public has always responded strongly to this composer's way with melody and to the
smouldering, cresting passion of the music. Rachmaninoff was one of the
world's great pianists, and his playing of his own compositions on the stages
of many continents contributed to the enormous popularity of his music.
Looked at objectively, the music is very solid; obvious Russian nationalistic
elements are subtly blended with formal and melodic characteristics seen
previously in Chopin, Schumann, and Liszt. The harmony is especially luxuriant and there is no little polyphonic ingenuity, especially in certain of
the piano preludes.

Other important post-Romantics include Mascagni, Dukas, Glazounov,
Pfitzner, Glière, Dohnányi, and Reger.

In our discussion of the post-Romantics we have emphasized their *fin
de siècle* orientation: each extended, stretched out, and ended an era that
had run its course.

Because most of these masters lived well into the twentieth century,
they must be considered as transitional. Though their musical aesthetics
were derived from a past century, they continued to write and were themselves physically active and influential while newer musical styles were
developing.

They affected a necessary overlap, stabilizing in effect, while newer
musical attitudes were in the shaping.

Impressionism

Impressionism owed much to the romantic century. For one, it is in
direct descent from nineteenth-century program music. But it emphasizes

---

* Gilbert Chase, *America's Music* (New York: McGraw-Hill Book Company, Inc.,
1955), p. 364.

imagery of nature rather than the tonal representation of plot, drama, or personal characterization as in the typically romantic *Ein Heldenleben* by Richard Strauss, or *The Huns* by Liszt.

Second, Impressionism is firmly based on tonality, in spite of the new use of principles of key, relationships of consonance-dissonance, and modulation.

In a similar way, representation is present in the impressionistic painters Manet, Monet, and Renoir as it was in the romantic school of painters. We can plainly recognize the subject—a pretty girl, a field of flowers, a cathedral —in its everyday context with the Impressionists as we do with romantic painters, but there is no doubt that their treatment of the subject differs. So tonality, like representation in painting, is always present but subtly transformed. While Impressionism is clearly rooted in Romanticism, it also points to contemporary music. Its primary concern and search for unique, original sound as such is quite modern. Debussy always looked for *le ton juste*, the precise sound, that would make an original effect. This foreshadows the experimental approach of contemporary composers.

In their search for a fresh, unique sound, the Impressionists developed new instrumental techniques. Their orchestra became a highly flexible instrument, pregnant with coloristic potential. It still is the basis for much orchestral writing today.

Also strongly suggestive of contemporary music is the objective semi-detachment of Impressionism. In its shift away from the Romantic's tonal depiction of states of subjectivity, in its moving away from psychically generated emotion, it concerned itself almost exclusively with the world outside of man, the world of nature—of things. This very de-emphasis of the emotional, personal, subjective contributed greatly to the geometrical, cerebral element in contemporary music.

A particularly curious facet of Impressionism is its brief span: from about 1892 to perhaps 1918, a little over 25 years. After that there were no significant Impressionists, though impressionist techniques were often used in combination with others. This, of course, points to its transitory role; it unquestionably bridged the gap from the idealistic, subjective, powerfully humanistic music of Romanticism to the detached, "cooler," experimental realism of our time.

If, then, Impressionism contained within itself the seed and promise of the music of our day while resting solidly on the musical ground gained in the century before, the question may be asked: what gives it its unique character? Despite its dealing with objects and things in nature—rain drenched gardens, exotic temples in the light of the moon, footsteps in the snow, the sea in its myriad moods, girls with hair like silk, rag dolls, toy elephants, regal peacocks—it decidedly does not attempt to represent these objects directly in any way. Rather, the impressionist composer simply presents to us in musical terms sensations, moods, and emotional reactions that external objects in nature have evoked from him. "Nuages," for example, is the musical response in the heart and soul of Debussy to his impressions of the particular phenomenon in nature called a cloud. A different impressionist composer would undoubtedly produce a cloud piece with a completely different sound.

Descriptive titles, of course, do head most impressionistic music. But enjoyment of the music is not at all dependent on a pre-knowledge of the title. Debussy, who insisted that his music was solid enough to be enjoyed without knowing what it was about, inserted titles only at the end of each of his *24 Preludes for Piano,* and discreetly in parentheses.

Impressionism, in a way, is also a very simple kind of music. In technical structure it is ultra-sophisticated, but in effect and in what it tries to do for the listener it is plain and simple. Debussy said, "Music should seek humbly to please . . . extreme complication is contrary to art." A piece such as Ravel's *Rhapsodie espagnole,* or Delius' *On Hearing the First Cuckoo in Spring,* appeals directly to our senses. It aims to please, to entertain. It does not preach or try to stir us up.

The artist/hero, or the artist/prophet, or the artist/teacher is foreign to the impressionist. Frankly autobiographical and sensational pieces such as R. Strauss's *Ein Heldenleben* or Berlioz' *Symphonie fantastique* were totally foreign to Debussy and Ravel who both lived rather retired, secluded lives.

And because Impressionism aims directly and unabashedly to titillate our ears, to gratify our aural sense, it is permeated and saturated with the most sensuous combinations of sounds, presented to our ears with the subtlest use of instruments and voices. Of paramount concern is the immediate beauty and effect of the sound. Thus does the Impressionist combine his instrumental colors, with a view to the utmost voluptuous quality.

Harmony is the area where this sensuous quality becomes most obvious. In fact it can be said that much of the interest in impressionistic music is generated through novel chords, and especially in the novel juxtaposition of chords. Sam Hunter, in his book, *Modern French Painting,* says of the work of the impressionistic painter Monet ". . . he had discovered that the most intense optical sensations were obtained when colors were mixed by the eye." * In similar fashion, the novel effect produced in musical Impressionism comes about when the ear mixes adjacent chordal colors that in past periods did not "go well" together.

---

* Sam Hunter, *Modern French Painting, Fifty Artists From Manet to Picasso* (New York: Dell Publishing Co., Inc., 1956), p. 91.

Example 8-2   *Preludes*, Book I, No. 1, Debussy

Another characteristic of impressionistic music is its scant use of brio sound. Rather than overwhelm, the Impressionist insinuates and suggests. Much of his music begins with a whisper and ends with the tiniest tremor of sound.

Marked, biting accents are also scantily used, though they will occasionally come, as in the "Dialogue of the wind and sea" portion of Debussy's *La Mer,* or in the "General Dance" in Ravel's *Daphnis and Chloé,* Suite No. 2. Because of the lack of both rhythmic bite and obvious melody, the music seems to some at first like an amorphous mixture of musical tremors, trills, and gurgles. With the master Impressionists, however, repeated listening reveals magnificent design and direction.

DEVICES OF IMPRESSIONISM

1) *Parallel chords* as the thickening of a melodic contour.

2) *Pedal point.* This is not new, but Debussy uses it extensively to serve as an anchor for "wandering" harmonies.

3) *Ostinato.* This is not new either, but like pedal point it serves as an anchor, and as well acts as an "intensifier." An example occurs in the piano prelude, *Footsteps in the Snow* in which the ostinato occurs throughout the entire work, with the exception of the three measures which include the climax. Debussy's comment about the rhythm of the ostinato stresses its expression of a "mournful, icy sound."

4) *Added notes.* To a chord built in 3rds, added notes lessen its original clarity, giving it a denser texture and a more diffuse color.

5) Harmonic intervals of a 2nd. The stressing of these lends "bite" to a passage. They are not treated as dissonances, but rather as "color."

6) *Tone clusters.* Any vertical structure which consists of two or more adjacent intervals of a 2nd.

7) *Cross relation.* This refers to a semi-tone change which normally had occurred in the same voice, but now crosses over into another voice.

8) *Pan-diatonicism.* The use of several tones of a scale or mode melodically and/or harmonically "as if" the use were indiscriminate. Actually, great care is taken in the choice of tones.

9) *Whole tone scale.* In the piano prelude, *Voiles,* we find Debussy's most extensive use of the whole tone scale as the basis for a work.

10) *Pentatonic scale.* The usage of a 5-note pattern such as CDEGA.

11) *Modal scale.* The main melody of the piano prelude, *The Sunken Cathedral* uses the tones of the mixolydian mode on C.

12) *Tritone switch.* Alternation of chordal structures with roots a tritone apart.

13) *Evaporation.* The piano prelude, *Voiles,* uses a B-flat pedal point throughout nearly the entire prelude, as an anchor. However, it is not present in the opening four measures, and in the 4th measure from the end it is allowed to vanish or "evaporate," the final sound being a major 3rd on C.

DEBUSSY. Without question, the two composers most successful in Impressionism are Claude Debussy (1862–1918) and Maurice Ravel (1875–1937). Though Debussy is credited with the first truly impressionist work, *Prelude to the Afternoon of a Faun,* (1894), it should be remembered that Ravel composed the piano version of the *Rhapsodie espagnole* only one year later. It is true, however, that Debussy from 1894 wrote almost exclusively in the impressionistic manner, while Ravel frequently concerned himself with other styles and compositional techniques. Of the two, Debussy is the typically impressionistic composer and Ravel, the occasional one.

Debussy was born early enough (1862) to have been strongly influenced by Romanticism, and wrote several early works in the late romantic idiom. Music such as the *Deux Arabesques* and the *Rêverie* for piano are suave, elegant, melodious, sentimental almost to excess—clearly in the romantic tradition. "Clair de Lune," from the *Suite Bergamasque,* is typical.

Despite the obvious eclecticism of these early pieces, they are immaculate in design while seldom failing to please. The superior workmanship points to the finesse and the incredible sophistication heard in the mature Debussy.

The later works of Debussy are typified by such works as the *Nocturnes, La Mer,* and *Iberia* for orchestra; *Chansons de Bilitis* for voice and piano; the *Images* and *24 Préludes* for piano; and the opera *Pelléas et Mélisande.* They are completely original and magnificent in conception. Their subject matter is far-ranging, geographically and pictorially.

The color and character of many lands is fair game for Debussy's Impressionism. There is the suggestion of an early American dance in the "Golliwog's Cake-walk," and a Frenchman's view of British pomposity in the piano prelude, *Hommage à S. Pickwick Esq., P.P.M.P.C.* An ancient Egyptian burial urn, Greek Delphic dancers and the hills of Anacapri in Italy are all in the piano preludes. *Iberia* is a smouldering portrait of Spain. *Poisson d'or* represents the brilliant sheen of goldfish on a Japanese vase, while *Pagodas* perhaps reflects the composer's interest in Javanese music which he heard at the Paris Exhibition in 1889.

Subject matter itself varies greatly: anything from *Footsteps in the Snow* to *Sounds and Perfume Turning in the Evening Air.*

The tendency of Debussy to communicate his aesthetic responses to outside scenes of nature is remarkably similar to the "plein air" school of painting typified by Manet. Here the painter strapped his easel to his shoulder, went out into the fields and woods to work, and captured an immediate impression. But, in addition to Debussy's obvious power to evoke atmosphere and mood, the music is saturated with mellow melancholy. In the phrase of Andre Suarès, it is "la douleur qui parle" (sorrow speaking) . The music frequently is as warm as it is sensuous and colorful.

Analysis and commentary: Debussy: "Fêtes"

"Fêtes" ("Holidays") is the second of three *Nocturnes* for orchestra written by Debussy in the late 1890's. The translation given here, "Holidays" rather than the usual "Festivals," is given because of Debussy's own description of the piece as given in *Achille-Claude Debussy* by Vallas. " 'Fêtes' had been inspired by a recollection of old-time public rejoicings in the Boise de Boulogne attended by happy, thronging crowds; the trio with its fanfare of muted trumpets suggests the former drum and bugle band of the Garde Nationale, beating the tattoo as it approached from afar and passed out of sight."

Swirling, sweeping music illustrates that Debussy was not all vapour and mist. Indeed, some of his more rhythmic pieces are as springy as the luminous ballerinas in the paintings of Degas. Besides the rhythmic vitality and drive in "Fêtes," there is a stunning use of climax. The fantastic, almost orgiastic climax achieved by the fanfare-march in the middle section shows that Debussy sometimes loved the great splashes of sound as well as the delicate nuances.

The orchestra is large: 3 flutes, 2 oboes, English horn, 2 clarinets, 3 bassoons, 4 horns, 3 trumpets, 3 trombones, tuba, 2 harps, timpani, cymbals, snare drum, and strings.

The piece's form is very simple: Ternary, ABA. The first section, A, is characterized primarily by the swirling figure,

Example 8-3   "Fêtes," Debussy

with a dancing background figure consisting of repeated notes.

Example 8-4

The B section is procession-like in its steady, repeated accents with a fanfare

Example 8-5

theme first heard in the trumpets, and a gradual, massive buildup to a soaring climax just before the return of the A section. The A section returns but considerably modified with occasional flashes of the fanfare theme from the previous section.

The piece begins with a brusque figure, in open intervals for the divided violins played *ff*. This serves to introduce a first theme (Example 8-3) played by the clarinets and English horn. All of this is *ff*. Suddenly the dynamic level drops to a hushed *pp* and the accompaniment figure now appears fleshed out in parallel ninth chords.

Example 8-6

Above this, the first theme

Example 8-7

is handed down from treble to bass in crescendo leading to a brilliant, but brief heraldic statement in the brass, *ff*.

Example 8-8

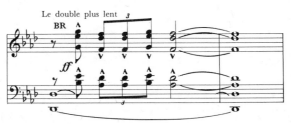

Note the 3rd measure in Example 8-9, which is now quite different from Ex-

Example 8-9

ample 8-3. This comes twice. Then, a rough figure in the horns backed by bassoons

Example 8-10

is answered by a blithe idea, *piano* and staccato, in the clarinets and English

Example 8-11

horn. Both Examples 8-9 and 8-10 are heard again. Then the first truly lyric theme of the piece occurs, in the solo oboe:

Example 8-12

Example 8-4 is always heard in a background that is electric, and rhythmically vital. Example 8-12 soon is heard again, but this time with flutes added, the whole higher in the soprano, and again crescendo. Ultimately, the oboe and flutes joined by the clarinet give out a new idea,

Example 8-13

which is accompanied by the strings playing a figure derived from earlier materials.

Example 8-14

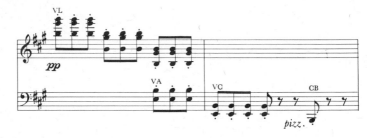

A portion of Example 8-12 re-enters in the clarinet and horns, surrounded by echoes of Example 8-4 fluttering about in the divided strings. For the remainder of the A section, Examples 8-12 and 8-13 alternate, the whole finally building to a crashing climax which, just before cresting,

Example 8-15

drops suddenly to the hypnotic, eerie march rhythm, ultra-soft:

Example 8-16

This signals the beginning of the B section. Above the shuffling march rhythm and above an A-flat in the bass that remains throughout the section, as if out of nowhere, three muted trumpets give out a fanfare theme, *pp*.

Example 8-17

Later the woodwinds take up the fanfare. The horns sally forth with the basic motive of the fanfare rising,

Example 8-18

to be answered by the falling winds.

Example 8-19

When the trumpets, buttressed by trombones, reiterate the complete fanfare theme (Example 8-17), the strings play a version of the first theme (Example 8-3). Thus the leading melodic idea from A joins with the theme of B to provide unity and homogeneity. The A section returns, with most of the melodic materials also returning but with many changes of orchestration.

Instead of the original heraldic statement of Example 8-8 followed closely by the harp glissandi, the composer writes a broad figure in the strings,

Example 8-20

followed immediately by this passage in the trumpets.

Example 8-21

The other themes—except for Example 8-13—come back in order and the music gradually becomes more and more quiet, terminating in the pianissimo tremors of the last measure. But before the music fades away, echoes of the fanfare theme of the B section

Example 8-22

and a strange, new melodic fragment

Example 8-23

glow quietly through the gathering stillness.

RAVEL. Ravel also possessed a gift for musical imagery. But he did not use it as often as Debussy. Nor is his Impressionism as sweet and warm. Stravinsky called Ravel the "Swiss watchmaker." Indeed, his music is fastidiously put together, as neat and ordered as a French formal garden.

To know the essential difference between the two Impressionists one need only compare Ravel's *Pavane pour une infante défunte*

Example 8-24   *Pavane pour une infante défunte*, Ravel

with Debussy's "Sarabande" from *Pour le piano,*

Example 8-25   *Pour le piano*, "Sarabande," Debussy

"El Jaleo," by John Singer Sargent (*Courtesy of Isabella Stewart Gardner Museum, Boston*).

both written in the late 1890's and both re-creations of early court dances. The Ravel is tender, yet somehow cool and reserved. Its harmonies are sometimes frosty. The Debussy, on the other hand, pulses every moment with a warm, romantic glow. It is more relaxed, freer, less formal.

On listening to the music of Ravel, the listener is much more conscious of structure and a clear beat. His tempos generally are firmer. Typical are the *Valses nobles et sentimentales, Daphnis and Chloé,* and *La Valse.* The *Bolero,* of course, is well known. *Le Tombeau de Couperin* includes three dances from the Baroque, a "forlane," a "menuet," and a "rigaudon."

Ravel's feeling for Spanish music, is perhaps superior to that of Debussy. The *Rapsodie espagnole* and the one-act comic opera *L'heure espagnole* capture every nuance and all of the excitement of Spanish music. The composer's mother was descended from a Basque family. His later compositions, particularly those after World War I, show little of the impressionistic style. The *Piano Concerto in G* shows the influence of American jazz, as does the *Violin Sonata.*

The opera *L'Enfant et les sortilèges* is remarkable. The "Duet of the Cats," for example, and the "Insect Music" are fantastically realistic. There is a clear use of polytonality near the beginning of the piece.

Example 8-26   *L'Enfant et les sortilèges*, Ravel

Durand & Cie, Editeurs-propriétaire Paris.

OTHER IMPRESSIONISTS. Among several others writing with impressionistic techniques is the Russian Alexander Scriabin (1872–1915), whose exotic, almost mystic music is a curious blend of late romantic expressivity and French color. Among his best work is the *Poem of Ecstasy* for orchestra and the sonatas for piano—especially the *Sonata No. 5 in F-Sharp Major.*

Works such as *Nights in the Garden of Spain* for piano and orchestra by Manuel de Falla (1876–1949) show an interesting blend of Impressionism with indigenous Spanish musical elements. Falla was acquainted with Debussy in Paris. In fact, it was a postcard sent from Spain by Falla to Debussy picturing a gate of the Alhambra that inspired the piano prelude, *La puerta del Vino* by the Frenchman.

Frederick Delius (1862–1934), wrote many compositions in the impressionistic style. They are lusciously vaporous, sometimes overripe; but pieces such as *Brigg Fair* and *Walk to the Paradise Garden* are nevertheless charming.

Charles Griffes (1884–1920) was an American Impressionist whose untimely death at the age of 36 cut off a very promising career. His *Poem for Flute and Orchestra* is quite effective.

The pre-moderns/satire and the experimental attitude

As mentioned earlier the period we are now examining produced a tremendous overlap of styles. We have seen that post-romantics such as Sibelius and Rachmaninoff continued to write many years after the establishment of the contemporary style. Rachmaninoff wrote the frankly romantic *Rhapsody on a Theme of Paganini* fully 21 years after the riot-shot premiere of Stravinsky's *Le Sacre du printemps*. Two important figures were anticipating contemporary musical idioms and attitudes by at least 20 years. They are the French iconoclast, Erik Satie (1866–1925), and the American iconoclast, Charles Ives (1874–1954). Satie was perhaps the first to revolt against romantic "expressivity" and bombast. His music is rather ascetic, often mordantly witty. The *Gymnopédies* are chaste, objective, and detached. Titles of many of his works are highly ironic, meant to arrest the attention and to pique the curiosity; for example, *Desiccated Embryos,* and *Cold Pieces,* both for piano. Satie's playing directions are outrageously humorous: "Play like a nightingale with a toothache," or, for the "Tango" in his *Sports and Diversions for Piano,* "Play in moderate tempo and very bored."

Satie's attitude affected Debussy, who himself had a rather caustic sense of humor. It also influenced later French composers such as Poulenc, Milhaud, and Auric. His non-sentimental approach is similar to that of Stravinsky, who in the twenties and thirties ruthlessly resisted all "expression" in music. "For I consider that music is, by its very nature, essentially powerless to express anything at all. . . ." These words by Stravinsky could well have been uttered by Satie, who resisted all expressionistic or impressionistic suggestions in his own music. *Socrate,* a symphonic drama based on Plato for soprano with chamber orchestra, is considered to be Satie's most impor-

Poster by Toulouse-Lautrec (*Courtesy Musée Toulouse-Lautrec, Albi, France*).

tant work. In its pale simplicity and homely, non-coloristic mien, it symbolizes the anti-romantic outlook of many twentieth-century composers.

In many ways, Satie's ballet *Parade* exemplifies his position as precursor of the experimental attitude in composition. This playfully sardonic work, conceived in part in the spirit of Dadaism, was the result of the touching of the minds of five of the most fecund, adventuresome figures of this century. Produced by Diaghilev for the Ballets Russes, its scenario was written by Cocteau and it was choreographed by Massine. Sets and costumes were done by Picasso. The score itself anticipates certain important trends to be seen several years later. Satie's use in the music of foreign "instruments" such as the typewriter and the siren suggests the organized sound of Varèse in the 30's. Its use of elements from ragtime was earlier than that of Stravinsky in his *L'Histoire du soldat* and was one of the first pieces of art music to come to terms with the indigenous popular music of the USA.

In contrast to Satie, who was at the center of the fluid, exciting developments in Paris at the turn of the century, Charles Ives was a musically isolated figure whose originality is now well recognized. He was little touched by European artistic currents, but was saturated with folk, popular, and church music of his own land. The New England Transcendentalists, especially Emerson, influenced him. These, added to a natural inclination for experiment in tone, strongly encouraged by his bandmaster father, led to some incredibly prophetic work.

One of the masterpieces of Ives is the orchestral work *Three Places in New England*. This is the work of an ecstatic visionary with musical roots deep in his land, who perhaps set the stage for many of the younger men of contemporary music.

Debussy was the first important composer in the 20th century to point the way to the detached experimental attitude. In his way of synthesizing and combining, in his use of the whole-tone scale and of chords as color rather than function, he set the stage for all future experiments in music. We have already seen the structural devices of Impressionism which include new uses of harmony pointing away from Romanticism. But Debussy's roots lay very deeply in the music of Romanticism and before. Though he did point to new directions he did not subvert the romantic style, at least not intentionally. It is with Satie and with Ives that we see an overt effort to reject the aesthetics of the immediate past. Their method was that of satire and irony.

The titles of many of Satie's works are obviously satirical, while the music is primitive as well as sophisticated and fresh. An iconoclasm similar to Satie's may be seen in the social satire of the playwright G. B. Shaw, in the barbed shafts of the critic H. L. Mencken, in the flamboyant posters of Toulouse-Lautrec. A like raucousness was found in the impudence of the

brash Dixieland style. In items such as the *Livery Stable Blues* can be seen an intention parallel to that of Satie in his *Three Flabby Preludes for a Dog*.

Ives, under the influence of his father, and with his own fresh approach was afraid of neither tradition nor dissonance. The final blurting chord of his *Symphony No. 2*, containing all of the tones of the chromatic scale but one, is as irreverent as the W. C. Fields remark, "A man who hates dogs and children can't be all bad."

When Duchamp, the French cubist, painted a mustache on the Mona Lisa in 1920, or when Picabia in the same year put a toy monkey in a frame and called it a portrait of Cézanne, they, with Satie and Ives, were serving notice that the old ways would no longer do.

II. AFTER DEBUSSY

The contemporary composer has complete freedom of choice. As a result of this freedom, however, he is much more responsible for his choice. The independence of the individual in his thought and in his action is predominant in the world today as in no other time.

This has been reflected in the arts as well. Andy Warhol's painting of a can of soup—whatever it is of itself—is a statement *against* all preconceived ideas of what art should be. Experiments in music that deny the use of regular vibrations of sound and emphasize noise are statements against all former concepts of music. The emphasis on the random expression, the interest in a "happening," is exactly opposed to the conception that a work of art is a *selection* of materials in an ordered form. All of these experiments are a symbol of the search for new stimuli that is prevalent in our society today.

These rejections of previous concepts raise an important point that has been stated very clearly in the writings of Jean-Paul Sartre. Rejection of authority and tradition is not enough. Something must take their place. The establishment of meaning now rests with each individual.

"The existentialist . . . finds it extremely embarrassing that God does not exist, for their disappears with Him all possibility of finding values in an intelligible heaven." * Sartre also says ". . . the first effect of existentialism is that it puts every man in possession of himself as he is, and places the

---

* Jean-Paul Sartre, *Existentialism and Humanism*, translation and introduction by Philip Mairet (London: Methuen & Co., Ltd., 1946, 1948, reprinted 1960) , p. 33.

"The Sonata," by Marcel Duchamp (*Courtesy of Philadelphia Museum of Art*).

entire responsibility for his existence squarely upon his own shoulders." *
And this is the dilemma of the twentieth-century composer. The entire responsibility for a new composition is his. And since every door is open to
him, his decision is the more difficult.

There are no rules of composition, but there are principles of organization. Each composer must find these for himself. We have seen, in the evolution of music, in each period, constant searching and constant change. What
was accepted at one time is no longer true in a later time. What was true in
a later time became superseded itself by a new expression. Each age must
find its own expression. This expression—when it is true—does not result
from formulas that already exist, but from an inner need to express, and
from a seeking of the way to make this expression meaningful.

Major influences

STRAVINSKY. The work of the twentieth century that had perhaps the
most far-reaching, as well as the most immediate effect, was *Le Sacre du
Printemps* (*The Rite of Spring*). Igor Stravinsky, born in Russia in 1882,
was brought up in musical surroundings, began piano lessons at the age of
nine, and thereafter began to compose. He was self-taught with the exception
of two years of study in orchestration with Rimsky-Korsakov.

Before *Le Sacre,* however, Stravinsky already had two large works to his
credit, which had achieved success. He had already written *The Firebird,*
and *Petrouchka* for Diaghilev's Ballets Russes in Paris. But where "*Petrouchka* had shaken the musical art of the period," according to Alexandre
Tansman, "*The Rite of Spring* delivered a blow from which it was never
again to recover. . . ." Stravinsky's concept of rhythm seemed to the audience barbaric and relentless, after the "lovelinesses" of most romantic and
impressionistic music. Stravinsky's tonal concepts were basically those of the
impressionist school. But whereas Debussy had been criticized for the vagueness in his melody, Stravinsky was attacked for its absence. It was even said
by some musical reactionaries that Stravinsky was incapable of writing a
melody. Where Debussy had alternated chord structures to blur the tonality,
Stravinsky combined them. What the critics could not comprehend in the
music of Stravinsky was only what they had not comprehended in the music
of Debussy: originality. They constantly tried to assess the new by what they
were familiar with in the old.

Stravinsky was to influence two generations of composers with his
harmonic procedure and his exposure of the "raw nerve" of rhythm.

---

* *Ibid.,* p. 29.

Petrouchka. In the opening measures of the *Petrouchka,* "Shrove-Tide Fair" (1947 revision), there is a 41 measure ostinato begun by the clarinets. The peculiar repetitive treatment of the melody is, however, uniquely Stravinsky's. This technique may be seen in many places throughout his works. In this instance, it consists of repeating a short fragment of melodic material but, in the repetition, changing the accent or adding or subtracting a note. This gives the melody a rhythmic force which propels it forward. This might almost be described as a "darting" melody; short thrusts forward, differing slightly in length and in direction, but constantly moving ahead, while at the same time imparting a nervous, kinetic energy to the texture.

The opening of the next section of *Petrouchka,* the "Danse Russe," shows us, in addition to the use of parallel chords, an example of the modal influence in Stravinsky's writing.

It is of interest to note that Stravinsky disagrees with the terms "revolution" and "revolutionary" as applied to his music and the general thought of the times in the first years of this century. In his "Poetics of Music," he has this to say: "Let us not forget that *Petrouchka, The Rite of Spring,* and *The Nightingale* appeared at a time characterized by profound changes that dislocated many things and troubled many minds . . .

"I am well aware that there is a point of view that regards the period in which the *Rite of Spring* appeared as one that witnessed a revolution. A revolution whose conquests are said to be in the process of assimilation today. I deny the validity of that opinion. I hold that it was wrong to have considered me a revolutionary. When the *Rite* appeared, many opinions were advanced concerning it. In the tumult of contradictory opinions my friend Maurice Ravel intervened practically alone to set matters right. He was able to see, and he said, that the novelty of the *Rite* consisted, not in the 'writing,' not in the orchestration, not in the technical apparatus of the work, but in the musical entity." *

Now what of *Le Sacre?* Does it logically follow *Petrouchka?* Is it a development of a musical philosophy, or is it an upheaval in musical thinking?

La Sacre du Printemps. The bassoon solo which opens *Le Sacre du printemps* is an excellent example of Stravinsky's melodic style. The constantly high *tessitura* of the solo is unique, but this aspect is one of tone color which rightfully falls within the art of orchestration. (See page one of score.) More to the point, the solo is an example of Stravinsky's individual way with a melody. The limited range, the rhythmic exploration of a limited number of notes, the careful addition of new notes, the constant

---

* Igor Stravinsky, *Poetics of Music,* (transl. by Arthur Knodel and Ingolf Dahl), ©︎ by Harvard University Press, Cambridge, Mass., 1947, p. 9. Reprinted by permission.

Rudolph Nureyev as the puppet, Petrouchka, in a performance at the Royal Opera House, Covent Garden (*Photo by Authenticated News International, New York*).

repetition of melodic patterns while at the same time their rhythmic grouping or accent changes—they are all there.

We might describe this individual melodic style of Stravinsky's by the
phrase, "a constantly evolving ostinato." Paradoxical though the phrase may
seem to be it does describe the *yielding obstinacy* of this kind of a melody.

An analogy comes to mind. It is as if Stravinsky were looking at a gem,
turning it over in the palm of his hand, at first slowly, and catching only a
few of the different glints of its facets in the light; then turning it more
quickly, and at the same time seeing a new glint, and then turning it to his
first view of it again, but at a slightly different angle.

The rhythmic heart of the matter is found in the "Danses des Ado-
lescentes" which follows the "Introduction." The throbbing, elemental
rhythm with its sporadic accents takes us back to a more primitive form of
expression. The rhythm is seen in a $\frac{2}{4}$ meter, but this is of no concern to
the listener. What he hears is a steady succession of chords of even note
values. Nor is the listener aware of the bar lines. These are for the convenience of the orchestral player. The listener hears this:

Example 8-27

    1 2 3 4 5 6 7 8 9 / 1 2 / 1 2 3 4 5 6 / 1 2 3 / 1 2 3 4 / 1 2 3 4 5 / 1 2 3 /

In this example we have the core of Stravinsky's approach to rhythm. The
bar line for over two hundred years had indicated the natural accents inherent in a piece of music. Stravinsky has in essence removed the bar line. It
appears in the music, as suggested before, only as a convenience for rehearsal
purposes.

Stravinsky, having achieved international recognition, next surprised
the world by turning away from the orchestra of symphonic proportions,
and in 1918 he presented *L'Histoire du Soldat* written for seven instruments
—a work for the stage, "told, acted, and danced." The sparse and ascerbic
writing confounded many listeners, but this change of direction was but the
first of many that Stravinsky would take. He has often been likened to
Picasso; each of these two artists never let himself be put in a special category, but constantly sought for unique ways of expression.

With his ballet *Pulcinella* (1920) Stravinsky entered a phase designated
as **neo-classicism.** In this work and later works such as the austere *Octet*
(1923) and the *Capriccio* for piano and orchestra (1929) he went back to
earlier times to draw on music or style as the source for a new inspiration.
With the *Symphony of Psalms* (1930), for chorus and orchestra, Stravinsky
turned again to large forces. This work with Latin text shows Stravinsky's
interest in the words not for their meaning so much as for their particular

Model of sculpture for Chicago Civic Center by Pablo Picasso, 1965 (*Courtesy of The Art Institute of Chicago*).

sound. A later work, the *Cantata* for soprano and tenor and a small chorus (1952) illustrates the same interest.

Perhaps the most striking thing about Stravinsky is his diversity of styles. He differs from many composers who evolve slowly into what is often considered their mature style. Aside from what has already been mentioned, Stravinsky's output has included *Ragtime* for 11 instruments (1918), an arrangement of the *Star-Spangled Banner* in 1941 (which was banned), *Ebony Concerto* for the clarinetist Woody Herman and his orchestra, and a ballet for elephants and ballerinas of the Ringling Brothers, Barnum and Bailey Circus (1942).

Stravinsky has remained a dominant and constant force throughout his life, not only in his music, but also in his many appearances as conductor and through writings such as *The Poetics of Music* and *Conversations with Stravinsky.* At several points in his career it was thought by many that the well-spring had dried up, but Stravinsky continued to produce music, undaunted and uninfluenced by opinion, picking his own path in his constant search for expression, *his expression.* Although he said that "Music has no meaning," his music has had meaning—growing ever clearer—for a constantly growing audience. In the early 50's he astonished the world by turning to the 12-tone method of composition. The opera *The Rake's Progress* (1951) shows Stravinsky in complete possession of his full powers, and he still continues as of this writing (in his late 80's) composing, conducting, writing, and appearing in television documentaries. However, since about 1945—with World War II coming to a close, and the year in which Webern died—the strongest new influence on the younger composer has been the Schoenberg-Webern method of 12-tone writing.

Stravinsky was heir to the musical legacy of Debussy. Romanticism was dying, and the new Expressionism was beginning to manifest itself in the arts.

THE VIENNESE SCHOOL. One definition of *Expressionism* * speaks of it as a "revolution from the 'superficial' . . . to a style directly expressive of the artist's soul in all its hidden depth and with as little interference as possible from formal and compositional elements." In further explanation, "The artist paints the expressive character of the object. Instead of painting a tree, he paints its convulsiveness or its strength."

The term "Expressionism" did not come into use until 1911, but we see convulsiveness in the late paintings of Van Gogh, who was a forerunner of both the expressionist and Fauvist movements. In 1900 Sigmund Freud published *Interpretation of Dreams,* the first public statement of his theories. Met at first by incredulity and scorn, during the first decade of the twentieth century his doctrine gained wider and wider acceptance. The theories of Freud were not without their effect in contributing to the dominant thought

---

* Runes and Schrickel (eds.), *Encyclopedia of the Arts* (New York: Philosophical Library, 1946), p. 340.

of the time. The exploration of the subconscious helped to lay bare man's inner nature. The probing into the innermost thoughts was equated with the removal of a mask. The original shock that met the exposures of the inner self in Freud's writings was not too different from the shock that the audience felt at the first performance of *Le Sacre*.

SCHOENBERG.   Arnold Schoenberg, even more than Stravinsky, shows the influence of the expressionist movement. An early work, *Pierrot Lunaire,* reflects this in its choice of subject and the treatment of that subject.

Sprechstimme is notated so that it indicates a pitch which is not maintained by the singer but is barely suggested and immediately moved away from. It is ideally suited to express Pierrot in the moon-struck night, to depict his mind-wanderings, and his sense of futility. For voice and only five performers using seven instruments, *Pierrot Lunaire* pictures convulsiveness that can lie under the innocent mask. Although the impact of his music was less immediate than that of Stravinsky's, his ultimate rejection of the old was even more complete than that of Stravinsky. His search for a new means of expression finally turned him completely away from tonality.

Schoenberg (1874–1951) was born in Vienna. In addition to his studies, which included violin, cello, and counterpoint, he gained some practical experience in orchestration through the commercial avenue of arranging music for popular consumption.

In view of his later rejection of nineteenth-century Romanticism and its tonal system, it is somewhat ironic that his first successful work, written in 1899, is probably one of his best known, and certainly the most played of his entire output. This is *Verklärte Nacht (Transfigured Night)* , written originally as a string sextet. Its later arrangement for string orchestra is the version that is usually heard, and it is this arrangement also that provided the music for the ballet, *The Pillar of Fire.* The work is in the full romantic tradition.

This romanticism was carried to its extreme in his work, *Gurre-Lieder,* which was begun in 1900. In addition to five solo voices and a speaker, the score calls for four separate choruses, and a very large orchestra. It is a massive work in the tradition of Mahler.

Debussy had pointed the way to the use of dissonance for color rather than tension; the natural extension of this concept led Schoenberg to the place where no dissonance needed to be resolved. His *Three Piano Pieces,* Op. 11, written in 1908, are important pivotal works in his progress towards the "emancipation of dissonance." They also illustrate the angularity of melodic design which is to characterize many of his later works.

The Twelve-Tone Method. Schoenberg's constant search for new methods of expression gradually turned him away from all previous methods of composition, and in 1924 he initiated the serial technique of composing with 12 tones. In this system the tones represented by the 7 white notes and the 5 black notes of the piano keyboard are completely equal. The *Five Piano Pieces,* Op. 23, of 1923 show Schoenberg arriving at the system of writing with 12-tones. Important works that are completely 12-tone are the *Third Quartet* (1926), *Variations for Orchestra* (1928) and the *Violin Concerto* (1936).

The idea of diatonic scales with "coloring" chromatic tones, the concept of tonal center and keys, the idea of tendencies of tones inherent in all preceding scale patterns, and the idea of tonality affirmed by the root progressions of chords are all abandoned. The basic concept of twelve-tone writing is the establishment of a "row." This row is the placement of all of the 12 different tones in an order that uses each and all of them in series as set up by the composer. Both the melody and the chords arise out of the order of the tones. When the tones are used melodically, the approach is in a way similar to the statement of a subject in contrapuntal writing, and thus it is natural to the system to use the devices of counterpoint: imitation, transposition, retrograde motion, inversion, and so on. When the row is used chordally, dissonance and spacing are completely at the discretion of the composer. Writing in the system of 12 tones does not *necessarily* abrogate the use of tonality, but Schoenberg's use of it was a rejection of tonality in the traditional sense. Although Schoenberg disliked the use of the term *atonal,* it has been consistently applied to his twelve-tone method of composition.

The possibilities inherent in **serial writing** attracted wide attention and influenced composers throughout most of the Western world. The system of writing with 12 tones can be at once the most abstract and yet the most personal. That it yet leaves the rhythmic aspect, chordal spacing, orchestral color, and all the other aspects of composition to the composer still puts the burden of choice on the shoulders of the composer. This is as it should be.

It was at one and the same time hailed as the solution of all compositional problems and condemned as an artificial strait-jacket which allowed for no imagination; it was also described as an easy way out for composers with no talent, and by others as the only way in which to achieve a new freedom. It is but a system of organization. Like all systems it is only a means to an end. As the contrapuntal style could be—and was for some—an exercise in the mathematics of relations of tones, so can be twelve-tone writing.

Schoenberg's influence through his compositions and his teaching was world-wide, and there have been many who adopted the system of writing with 12 tones. Some composers adopted it completely, others used its techniques as part of a larger, over-all system. Two outstanding composers who used the system were Anton Webern and Alban Berg.

BERG.   Alban Berg (1885–1935) was born in Vienna. After some untutored music study he began the study of composition with Schoenberg, who became not only teacher but friend. Berg aligned himself with the private performances of new music that had been organized by Schoenberg and supervised by Webern. He taught, lectured, and wrote articles on new music for magazines.

His adoption of Schoenberg's twelve-tone method, in contrast to that of Webern's, allowed for a freer use of the disciplines of serial technique. Whereas the writing of both Schoenberg and Webern has been considered pointillistic, or dry and acerbic, Berg did not deny himself a lyricism that many listeners readily identify with. This lyricism, as well as the use of tonality when he chooses, have allowed for a readier acceptance of his music than is true in the case of both Schoenberg and Webern.

Two important works that illustrate these qualities are the *Lyric Suite* for string quartet (1926), and the *Violin Concerto* (1935) which is discussed in some detail below. Berg also contributed two operas, *Wozzeck* (1921) and *Lulu* (1935). *Lulu* was not quite completed but is performed nonetheless. Both of those works are highly expressionistic.

Analysis and commentary: Berg, Violin Concerto

One of the most felicitous works written in the twelve-tone system is the *Violin Concerto* of Alban Berg. It is this work that we shall look at in some detail. We shall examine Berg's use of the twelve-tone system, and concurrently it will become evident that Berg was not willing to abandon all implications of tonality.

Dem Andenken eines Engels—thus is the *Violin Concerto* of Alban Berg dedicated: "In remembrance of one of the angels." Berg had been approached in 1934 by the American violinist Louis Krasner to write a violin concerto. The project of the concerto lay dormant in Berg's mind until, in the spring of 1935, a close friend, an *intime* in Berg's circle, died. This was Manon Gropius, the 18-year-old daughter of the widow of Gustav Mahler. Berg decided that the concerto would be a memorial to her memory. It was his last work.

Although a memorial, the *Violin Concerto* is not a brooding work, nor does it depict an attitude of resignation. It has rather an aura of quiet reflection, an intellectual contemplation, as it were, on the mystery of life and death. Though we shall discuss the work with this in mind, the listener should seek his own personal relation to the work.

The *Violin Concerto* is in two movements. The movements are further divided as shown in the table below.

In the *Violin Concerto* there are tonal implications both within and without the twelve-tone row. In the opening measure of the work (Example 8-28) we hear pyramiding perfect fifths over a pedal B-flat sustained by the

1st Movement

TIME SIGNATURE		MEASURES
$\frac{4}{4}$	Introduction: Andante	1–10
$\frac{2}{4}$	Section I	11–103
	Improvisatory style (ruminative)	
$\frac{6}{8}$	Section II	
	Scherzando: Allegretto	104–136
	Trio I	137–154
	Trio II	155–175
$\frac{3}{8}$	Scherzando (like a waltz)	176–213
	Folksong	213

2nd Movement

TIME SIGNATURE		MEASURES
	Section I	
$\frac{3}{4}$	Allegro (like a cadenza)	1–62
$\frac{4}{4}$	Written cadenza	63–96
	Pedal point on F	97–135
	Section II	
$\frac{4}{4}$	Adagio (chorale)	136–200
$\frac{3}{4}$	Folksong	201–213
$\frac{4}{4}$	Coda (chorale)	214–230

Example 8-28   *Violin Concerto*, Berg

Used by permission of the Theodore Presser Company and Universal Edition A. G. Vienna.

bass clarinet, which is an implication of a tonality that is later clarified in the setting of the chorale in the final pages of the work. The solo violin enters in the second measure, imitating the bare fifths of the first measure, and establishing *G* as a second important tonal "root." The bass clarinet B-flat continues during this measure.

Example 8-29

Used by permission of the Theodore Presser Company and Universal Edition A. G. Vienna.

We first see the tone row that is basic to the work dispersed throughout the harmony in measures 11 to 15.

Example 8-30   *Violin Concerto*, Berg

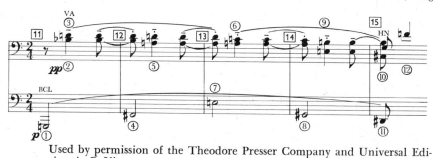

Used by permission of the Theodore Presser Company and Universal Edition A. G. Vienna.

The row is then clearly seen in melodic order in the solo violin entrance which begins in measure 15.

Example 8-31   *Violin Concerto*, Berg

Used by permission of the Theodore Presser Company and Universal Edition A. G. Vienna.

While the row is being played *en toto* by the solo violin the row is also being played simultaneously by the accompanying instruments but scattered through the harmony to form chordal structures. You can see from measures 11–14, shown above, that the composer has considerable freedom—even within the row—in choosing the notes to form a chord and in choosing their specific position within a chord.

Let us "step aside" for a moment to emphasize that the twelve-tone row is only a method of organization of sound. Whether the basis of a piece of music is pentatonic, modal, tonal, twelve-tone, or otherwise, the basis and the resulting consonance or dissonance possible within the system is but the means to the end. What is important is the composer's ability to handle his materials within the all-encompassing concept of music as existing in time. It is the rhythmic movement of the work that is the deciding factor. The rhythmic movement—in all its diversity of tension and release, climax and calm, ebb and the flow—is the essential, the *sine qua non*. The melody and the harmony may seem more interesting at times, and they are easier to discuss; the orchestration adds the piquancy of color; but these are, and can only be, a part of the time concept.

There are several ways in which this row may be grouped. It may be thought of primarily as a series of ascending thirds from (1) through (9) and of major seconds from (9) through (12).

Example 8-32   *Violin Concerto*, Berg

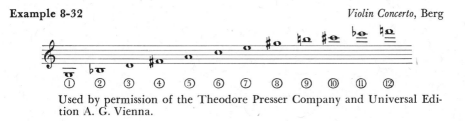

Used by permission of the Theodore Presser Company and Universal Edition A. G. Vienna.

It may also be considered for its possibilities of forming triads.

Example 8-33   —   *Violin Concerto*, Berg

Used by permission of the Theodore Presser Company and Universal Edition A. G. Vienna.

It may also be considered as three four-note groupings, in which the first two groups form identical chord structures, with the third group being the whole-tone tetrachord that is the hallmark of the Bach chorale, *Es ist Genug,* which concludes the work.

Example 8-34

But note that the Bach chorale, *Es ist Genug,* is not only the goal of the entire work. It is at the very heart of it. The twelve-tone row that is the basis of the work is so designed that the end of the row and the opening of the chorale will "mesh."

Example 8-35   *Es ist Genug,* J. S. Bach

Before continuing with Berg's concerto, it is wise to become familiar with Bach's chorale. The chorale is given in Example 8-35 in the key of Berg's presentation. The particular sections that he uses to alternate with the solo violin are bracketed.

The folk song near the end of the first movement

Example 8-36   *Violin Concerto*, Movt. I, Folk Song, Berg

Used by permission of the Theodore Presser Company and Universal Edition A. G. Vienna.

may be thought of as representing the simple joys of everyday life.

WEBERN. Anton Webern (1883–1945), born in Vienna, studied at the University of Vienna. He conducted theater orchestras, taught composition and became actively involved in a series of performances organized by Schoenberg for the purpose of presenting new musical works without the "benefits" of press coverage. In his adoption of the twelve-tone method he extended the idea of non-repetition of tones into the area of tone color, so that there is a constantly changing "wheel of color," as it were. His output was not large and, at first, acceptance of his work was tentative, but since his death the circle of appreciation has been growing larger and larger. It was Webern, finally, more than Schoenberg and Berg, who was to be the strong influence on many composers of today. This influence has been international.

Webern was strongly impressed with the compact brevity of Schoenberg's *Three Piano Pieces,* Op. 11. They became for him an ideal, and in following this ideal Webern went even further in the concentration of materials. Webern's music is not exploratory or developmental: his method is not to be thought of as an essay or a journey. It is epigrammatic: the music's statement is the final statement. The conciseness of Webern's musical thought—adhering to the belief that something need be said only once—demands great concentration on the part of the listener. Webern's *Five Pieces for Orchestra* (1911–1913) are but one example of his concise style of writing. The five pieces take a total of about 10 minutes to play. The shortest, the fourth piece, is 7 measures long and takes under 20 seconds to play. Webern had already abandoned tonality, and we see in these pieces the looking forward to the 12-tone method which came about in 1924 with his *Three Songs,* Op. 17. Webern's innate sense of rhythmic flow is not readily apparent to the listener, but it is there, nevertheless, as a unifying factor in the music. His attitude of meticulous concern for the placement of every tone with respect to rhythm and pitch make it easy to understand why he did not employ the use of *Sprechstimme.* His total output is contained on four discs. Other important works are: *Symphony for Chamber Orchestra,* Op. 21

(1928) ; *Concerto,* Op. 4 (1934) ; *Das Augenlicht* for mixed chorus and orchestra (1935) ; *Variations for Orchestra,* Op. 30 (1940) ; and *Cantata No. 2,* for soprano and bass soloists, chorus and orchestra.

It has been stated that "his music often seems to be on the verge of silence," and it is in this as well that the way was prepared for later and bolder experiments.

HINDEMITH AND BARTÓK.   Paul Hindemith (1895–1963), born in Germany, attained proficiency early on several musical instruments. His main instrument was the violin, and his ability was such that he became concertmaster of the Frankfort Opera. His interest then turned to the viola, and it is this instrument that he played in quartet tours of Europe. He later maintained that a composer should be able to play, at least a little, any instrument that he wrote for. This is an interesting ideal, and there is certainly nothing that can be said against it. But it has not, by any means, been effectively demonstrated in practice.

Paul Hindemith (*Photo by Ellsworth Ford, New York*).

Hindemith began in Berlin what was to be a long career in teaching, in addition to his composing some of the most important works of our day. His differences with the new political regime resulted in his leaving Germany in 1935. He toured as violist in the United States in 1937 and at later times, but it was through his teaching in this country after 1940 that he influenced a considerable number of composers. It was in the summer of that year that he taught at the Berkshire Music Center, and in the same year he was appointed to the faculty of Yale University.

Hindemith, along with Stravinsky, Schoenberg, and Bartók, was one of the dominant forces in musical thought in the United States until at least the middle of the twentieth century. Hindemith contributed to this influence further through several books that he wrote. *The Craft of Musical Composition* is a standard work used in many colleges across the country, in addition to his *Elementary Training for Musicians*. *A Composer's World* is a collection of essays delivered at Harvard University in 1949.

The amount of music he wrote was not only prodigious but much of it gained immediate acceptance and was performed regularly in the leading musical centers. He wrote for all instruments and in every genre. And he conducted performances of his own works along with those of other composers in the major capitals of the world.

His style was his own. His technique, as expounded in *The Craft of Musical Composition,* was a careful construction that included a contemporary way of approaching music, which, nevertheless, had its roots in tradition. His melodies, which often seem both to evade and to suggest tonality, are sometimes modal in flavor but spiked with jagged contours that temporarily disguise the mode. His harmonies are based upon a system of comparative tension of vertical structures.

An early short opera, *Hin und Zurück,* showed the use of a basic contrapuntal retrograde device applied to a total work. The story and the music having proceeded about half way, each thereupon goes backward until the end, which was the beginning. Hindemith also believed, contrary to most contemporary composers, in practical music, *Gebrauchsmusik*—music that may be performed by amateur groups. A concert of his music at Harvard University in 1949 was an example of this. The concert was on the occasion of the birthday of Mrs. Coolidge, sponsor of the Coolidge Quartet. For the occasion Hindemith had written a round, which he taught to the audience so that they could sing it to Mrs. Coolidge.

Also in line with the practical approach was his setting for himself the task of writing a sonata for each orchestral instrument.

Among his outstanding works are the opera, *Mathis der Maler,* from which he later extracted a symphony; *Nobilissima Visione,* originally a ballet; *Symphonic Metamorphosis of Themes by Weber* for orchestra; *Der*

Schwanendreher for viola and small orchestra; and *Das Marienleben,* a cycle of songs.

Of all the outstanding composers active in the first half of the 20th century, Béla Bartók (1881–1945) received the least general recognition while alive. The financial rewards as well as the plaudits were minimal and performances were few. His death in New York City in 1945 released the floodgates, however, and his music began to be played, published, recorded, and discussed in a surge of belated recognition.

Béla Bartók was born in Hungary in 1881. His father died when he was seven, and there developed between mother and son a close bond. It was she who gave him his first piano lessons when he was five, and it was she who discovered that he not only had perfect pitch, but a Mozartean faculty for remembering a tune he had composed, not needing to write it down until some time later. At the age of 11, Bartók made his first public appearance as both pianist and composer, a dual role he was to maintain throughout his life. Perhaps the most important phase of his career was entered when he notated a Hungarian peasant song, taking it down from the singing of a young peasant girl. This brought him to the realization that there was a vast native music of which he was unaware. He began a study of peasant music, and with Zoltán Kodály he spent about two years recording the native music not only of Hungary, but also of the Rumanians, Slovakians, Walachians, Turks, and Arabs. The peasant folk song became central to Bartók's compositional style, and examples of this influence may be found on many pages of his work. To it, however, Bartók applied a constantly fresh, imaginative, highly original technique.

Whereas Hindemith had a system that encompassed all of his writings, Bartók had no general system, but rather approached each work anew. The system for that work would arise out of the composition itself. Thus, if Bartók is harmonizing a Hungarian folk song, he may find the harmony from the melody itself, by "verticalizing" the melody.

Bartók's manner of approaching each work may be seen most conveniently in his six volumes for piano, *Mikrokosmos.* The title is indicative of his intent. Within a specific small world of a certain number of tones Bartók will explore and probe every corner. This small world is sufficient unto itself. It desires no other world, nor does it need one. What this technique does require, however, is a certain kind of composer, because this kind of writing can lead the composer into the trap of monotony. For each piece Bartók sets the problem, and he finds the solution. But the solution is unique for each piece. This approach may be seen in Bartók's last large work, the *Concerto for Orchestra,* written for a commission by Serge Koussevitzky. The entire first movement has as its seed and its defining feature the interval of a perfect fourth.

PROKOFIEV AND SHOSTAKOVICH. Sergei Prokofiev (1891–1953) began composing at the age of nine, and before he graduated from the St. Petersburg Conservatory he had become an excellent pianist and was performing his own works. He later traveled extensively as a concert pianist, including trips to America. His biting, ironic style of writing produced *Diabolical Suggestion* and *Sarcasms* for piano and earned him a reputation as a "futurist." *Scythian Suite* was his first important orchestral composition, and is an example of his barbaric, primitive style. Its approach is somewhat similar to that of Stravinsky in the *Rite of Spring*.

He also wrote music that is simple, charming, and naive. *Peter and the Wolf* was written for a children's theater and has since attained great popularity. Although Prokofiev's music contains sudden juxtapositions of keys, polytonality, and other contemporary practices, it is rooted in the tonal system. In his music may be found a mixture of Russian nationalism, neo-Classicism and French colorism. He was a prolific composer and wrote in all idioms, including music for a film, *Alexander Nevsky*. His *"Classical" Symphony* is a superb example of sophisticated wit, concise form, and clear, sparkling orchestration.

Dimitri Shostakovich, who was born in 1906, is best known in this country for his symphonies. His *First Symphony,* composed when he was 18, is still one of the most popular. The *Fifth Symphony* is also often performed. His "Polka" from *The Golden Age,* a ballet, is exceedingly well-known. After World War II he was in great favor in both his own country and the United States, and the completion of his new symphony in 1942, the *Seventh,* set off a flurry in the world press. Known popularly as the *"Leningrad" Symphony,* it was widely hailed. As the representative composer of Russia, Shostakovich often found himself in a precarious position. He was often denounced by the Russian government as learning towards the "decadence" of capitalism and would as often admit his "fault." During a visit to New York in 1949 he tried to expound—somewhat unsuccessfully—to the press why a composer must be guided by his political and national ties.

His symphonies are large in scope, somewhat bombastic and militaristic, but well-knit and appealing.

GUSTAV HOLST. Gustav Holst (1874–1934), although not as dominant a force in the resurgence of English music as Vaughan Williams, his contemporary and friend, was nevertheless an important part of the musical scene in England in the early twentieth century. Holst wrote in all forms, with choral works forming the largest part of his catalogue, but an interest in Eastern literature and in astrology produced a number of works of unique appeal. One of the most important works was a result of this interest. *The Planets,* a suite for orchestra in seven movements, was first presented in a semi-private concert in 1919. Holst's interest in text in his choral writings led him to the use of uneven time-signatures and changing time-signatures in order to produce a freedom and elasticity of rhythm that would enhance the text.

RALPH VAUGHAN WILLIAMS. Vaughan Williams (1872–1958), the elder statesman of twentieth-century English composers, may be understood most immediately by making reference to two of his most familiar works, *Fantasia on a Theme of Tallis* (1910) for orchestra: and his arrangement of the rugged church tune *Old Hundredth*. In each, in his choice of materials and in his choice of harmonic setting which springs out of traditionalism, we see the mark of the Englishman. We also find influences of the earlier English polyphonic style.

His texts show a very strong preference for English writers, from Chaucer to Hardy, with the Bible being a pervading influence. Vaughan Williams wrote in all forms. His output included operas, many choral works, chamber works and nine symphonies.

WILLIAM WALTON. Walton (1902–   ) a generation later than Vaughan Williams, and a child of the twentieth century, nevertheless retains in his work some elements of Romanticism. In a time which brought forth Bartok's *Allegro Barbaro* (1911), Schoenberg's *Pierrot Lunaire* (1912), Stravinsky's *Le Sacre du Printemps* (1913), and Berg's *Wozzeck* (1914–21), Walton retained the restraint typical of the English. His *Belshazzar's Feast* of 1931 is representative. A large choral work, it is colorful and theatrical, although based on the book of Psalms and the book of Daniel. The orchestra is large and the score also calls for two extra brass bands. A charmingly ironic setting for small chamber orchestra of Dame Edith Sitwell's set of poems, *Façade*, written when he was 20, was the first work to bring him considerable attention.

BENJAMIN BRITTEN. Britten (1913–   ) a prolific composer who has assayed music in all forms is perhaps best known for his operas, of which he has written ten. For a while—from the year 1945 on—Britten turned out a new opera each year. *Peter Grimes*, in 1945, was followed by the *Rape of Lucretia, Albert Herring,* a new version of John Gay's *The Beggar's Opera,* and in 1949, *Let's Make an Opera*. This last is a chamber opera that begins as a play and shortly involves the audience in the performance.

Britten's first opera, *Peter Grimes,* was such a success that it soon was being produced on the stages of famous opera houses throughout the world. Britten had, prior to this, written the scores to over a dozen films, and had also written an operetta, *Paul Bunyan,* produced in New York at Columbia University in 1941. His first important work was *Variations on a Theme of*

Frank Bridge (1937) for string orchestra. Britten's compass is large, evidenced not only by the variety of his works, but by the scope of his musical thought within a work. He is also an accomplished pianist. Most recently he has been the fountainhead for an opera house at Aldeburgh where he keeps fresh the stream of live performance, often including his own works. He is producer, manager, money-raiser, and conductor. The works best known in America are the operas *Peter Grimes, Albert Herring, Billy Budd,* and the more recent *Turn of the Screw* which effectively adapts Henry James' chilling psychological novel for the operatic stage. His *Serenade* for tenor, horn, and strings, identified with the superb artistry of the late eminent French horn player, Dennis Brain, shows Britten's felicitous use of smaller forces. His *Young Person's Guide to the Orchestra: Variations and Fugue on a Theme of Purcell,* was written in 1945 as the score to an educational film. Both witty and robust in its presentation of the instruments, it is a uniquely refreshing work, and has become Britten's most recorded work in America. Grandiose and well-wrought, the *War Requiem,* written in 1962 to commemorate the rebuilding of Coventry Cathedral, is a dramatic composition based on the English poems of Wilfred Owen and the liturgical requiem mass.

HEITOR VILLA-LOBOS. The leading Brazilian composer, Villa-Lobos (1887–1959), is one of the most prolific of twentieth-century composers. Filled with boundless energy he has not only written hundreds of works in every genre, but also has been internationally active as a conductor, and in addition found time to become one of the leading educationists in his native country. His efforts in this last area resulted in the establishment of his own National Conservatory in 1942. He had already been appointed Superintendent of Musical Education in Rio de Janeiro. His musical life was influenced by two opposing factors. As a youth he made several forays into various interior parts of Brazil, usually as an itinerant musician, and in this way became well-acquainted with the various kinds of folk music and popular music that was his heritage. In later years he spent some time in Europe, much of it in Paris where the influence of Ravel was important. His music displays these two seemingly opposing factors. It is both nationalist and international. One of his most endearing and well-known works, *Bachianas Brasileiras No. 5* for voice and cellos, exhibits both his national and personal emotional expression combined with his love for the objectivity of the music of a composer removed from him in distance and time.

CARL NIELSEN. The strongest voice in the music of Denmark has been that of Carl Nielsen (1865–1931). Somewhat overshadowed for many years by Sibelius, he began to be noticed in America about mid-century, and now a good body of his works are available on recordings, including several concertos, much chamber music, and his six symphonies. Nielsen writes in a broad, expansive style that combines uses of modality and chromaticism, and often he uses conflicting tonalities in a unique way to achieve a tension which is resolved sometimes with the simplest of harmonies. His work is easily assimilated and his audience is growing ever larger.

Other important composers

LES SIX. In the Paris of post-World War I, the names of six composers were grouped together by Henri Collet in a newspaper article as representative of the new expression in French music. Known as Les Six, and with Satie as their "spiritual" leader, they made a strong impact. Only three of these six composers moved forward in the twentieth century to take their places in the main stream of music.

Arthur Honegger (1892–1955) symbolized the machine age with *Pacific 231,* a musical "imitation" of a locomotive. This attracted much attention, but Honegger moved away from this "representational tone-painting." A prolific composer, he wrote five symphonies, as well as operas, choral works, ballets, chamber music, piano music, and songs. He also composed for film and radio. His large choral work *King David,* is representative. His chamber work, *Sonatine,* shows the influence of jazz. Although he used devices such as polytonality and suggestions of atonality, his music was tonally based and lyrically melodic.

Darius Milhaud (1892–   ) has written a steady stream of music from his student days in Paris. One of the first to exploit polytonality, a pianist, conductor, and teacher, an experimenter in forms as well as means, he has written in every important genre in interesting styles that encompassed the lyrical and the rhythmical, the dramatic and the playful. He has exerted a great influence on young American composers through his teaching in the United States. One of his earliest works is still the best known: the ballet *La Création du Monde.* Written for a small orchestra, the musical idiom suggests not so much jazz, as is often stated, as the music of the night-club of the 1920's.

Francis Poulenc (1899–1963), of the three composers discussed here, is the most representative in his music of a certain delightful kind of Gallic wit and charm. His style is eclectic, but a certain tongue-in-cheek approach often adds a distinct individuality to his scores. His work covers satirical chamber works, concertos and ballets, large choral works both secular and sacred, and opera. The opera *La Voix Humaine,* is a splendid example of his ability to impart an immediacy to his work that is compelling in its portrayal of a woman at the telephone.

The other three of Les Six—Georges Auric, Louis Durey, and Germaine

Tailleferre—did not go on to fulfill the promise that seemed to be theirs as members of an elite group. In addition to works in traditional forms, Auric is the composer of scores for several successful films, among them: "Caesar and Cleopatra" (1945) , "The Queen of Spades" (1948) , and "Lavender Hill Mob" (1951) .

COPLAND.   Aaron Copland, born in 1900 in Brooklyn, New York, was one of the first American composers to study in Paris with Nadia Boulanger. The "trek" had begun, and many young American composers after Copland were to come under her wing. Growing up in an America that was seeking to find itself musically, Copland was influenced in Paris by the frenzied search for expression. He was energized by the cosmopolitan exchange of ideas of the artists there. He purposely sought to become an "American composer," and in so doing we find for awhile the influence of jazz in some of his works. His *Piano Concerto* (1927) reflects this. He then turned to the music of an earlier America, and the barn dance and the hoe down became prominent parts of his style. In *Rodeo, Billy the Kid, Appalachian Spring,* all ballets, we find the "prairie" style in the homely dance rhythms.

Copland has sometimes been referred to as the dean of American composers, not so much for an Americanism that is found in his music as for his constantly active life as a composer, conductor, author, lecturer, and teacher. In addition, he has constantly proselytized for the young American composer.

He wrote several books, which have had wide dissemination, one of these being *Our New Music.* He has always pleaded the work of the American composer—calling attention to it, discussing it, analyzing it, performing it, conducting it. For many years his influence was strong in his position as head of the Composition Department at Tanglewood.

OTHER AMERICANS.   Roger Sessions, born in 1896 in Brooklyn, New York, was influenced early by Ernst Bloch, with whom he studied, and later to some extent by Stravinsky. His writing is highly individual, with emphasis on a tight contrapuntal style and uncompromising dissonance, with the result that his work has not gained wide acceptance by the public. His thoughtful, probing approach has not produced a large number of works, but there are four symphonies, a variety of chamber works, some concertos and choral works, and an opera among his output. As a teacher at Smith College, Princeton University and other institutions, he has had widespread influence. This influence was extended by a text on harmony, as well as other writings.

Walter Piston, born in 1894, was handily served during 36 years of teaching at Harvard University by the proximity of the Boston Symphony Orches-

Aaron Copland at Tanglewood, Lenox, Mass. (*Photo by Egone Camera Artist, Boston*).

tra, for which he wrote many commissioned works. In his personality are still discerned traces of his Maine heritage. We find a workmanlike approach, a sense of craftsmanship, and a careful concern for design. There are six symphonies to his credit, and much delightful chamber music, but his most played work has been the ballet *The Incredible Flutist,* introduced by Arthur Fiedler and the Boston Pops Orchestra in 1938. His teaching resulted in three important texts, each of which is widely known and widely used: *Harmony, Counterpoint,* and *Orchestration.*

Samuel Barber has been the recipient of many commissions and many honors. Born in 1910, and considered to be American to the core by some, his work nevertheless has its roots in Europe. His diatonic style is easy to listen to. His *Essay for Orchestra* is one of his most played works, and his *Overture to the School for Scandal* is also well known.

Elliott Carter studied with Piston and Nadia Boulanger. He was born in 1908 into a well-to-do family in New York, and acquired a leisurely, thorough education. Some of his early works show influences of Stravinsky and Copland, but his style was constantly developing towards a rhythmic concept that was to be unique. His Piano Sonata of 1945–46 is considered his first outstanding work. Others are the *Sonata for Cello,* the *String Quartet,* and the *Variations for Orchestra.* Although his work was largely unknown before 1950, it has been gaining much notice and far wider acceptance in the last few years. Perhaps Carter's most important achievement has been what he calls "metrical modulation," in which the speed is carefully adjusted by special metronomic designations for successive note values.

Underlining the strong Americanism of William Schuman (born 1910) is his *Chester Overture* for band, based upon the hymn tune by William Billings, a composer of American Revolutionary times. Among others writing in this pleasing, colloquial style are Douglas Moore (1893–1969), Howard Hanson (1896–   ), Virgil Thomson (1896–   ), Roy Harris (1898–   ), Paul Creston (1906–   ), and Randall Thompson (1899–   ).

Gunther Schuller (1925–   ), another New York composer, is one of the recent leading lights on the musical scene in America. His activities are many and varied, and in this respect he may be considered a latter-day Aaron Copland. He has written much for small groups; and also has to his credit a *Symphony for Brass and Percussion,* which is an exceedingly well wrought piece. It is one of the few works written for brass by a composer who knows how to handle these instruments well, from practical experience. His best-known work is *Seven Studies of Paul Klee,* and it takes its place beside a work written well over a half-century before—Mussorgsky's *Pictures at an Exhibition*—as a composer's reaction to a graphic expression. Schuller has not only been active in the music of the concert hall, but has concerned himself with the most serious personal expression of the times—jazz. Originator of the phrase, "Third Stream," which refers to the blending of jazz and art music, he has been intimately involved as composer, conductor, and promulgator of these apparently opposite expressions in an attempt to find a new expression of our times; to explore the fusion of these two opposed forms of expression which combine the emotional and cerebral.

MUSIC FOR THE THEATER.   Two composers, some distance apart, and of rather opposite backgrounds, met, as it were, in midstream to produce two of the most important works in musical theater. They were George Gershwin and Leonard Bernstein. They had been preceded by Kurt Weill, who in 1933 brought over from Germany *The Threepenny Opera,* a modern adaptation of *The Beggar's Opera.* In its social satire the popular song style is purposely used to illustrate social decadence. It is used so well that one of the songs, "Mack the Knife," has *become* an American popular song. Weill settled in America in 1935 and thereafter produced several successful musical

plays, among them *Knickerbocker Holiday, Lost in the Stars,* and a folk opera, *Down in the Valley.*

Gershwin grew up in the world of popular music. Born in Brooklyn in
1898, he began playing piano in music stores at the age of 16 to demonstrate
the current songs for buyers of sheet music. Gershwin was not a jazz musician, as has been so often claimed. This confusion on the part of many writers was caused by the fact that the twenties were referred to as "The Jazz
Age," since the popular music and all orchestras of the time that played for
dancing were referred to as "jazz" orchestras. He was, however, a highly
gifted composer of popular songs, and in turning his talents to works in
larger forms successfully synthesized the popular music element with the
aims of these large dramatic forms. This is apparent in his *Rhapsody in
Blue,* the *Piano Concerto,* and *An American in Paris.* His supreme achievement, however, was his folk opera *Porgy and Bess.*

Gershwin had already become extremely familiar with the multitudi-
nous problems of producing successful musical theater by writing many musical comedies. Gershwin brought into this field his unique approach to
writing popular music.

Popular music is, in certain ways, a folk music. It is not written for the
concert hall, and it is not usually written for instruments; it is written to be
sung. It is similar to true folk music in that it is for an individual singer
with or without accompaniment. That it is often trite or insipid is true, but
unimportant. And the fact that jazz has often used popular materials in its
art expression has no bearing except perhaps to show how much difference
there is between popular music and jazz. Gershwin's contributions to popular music were of the highest order.

Besides this, Gershwin brought his experience in writing his orchestral
works in the larger forms. In addition, *Porgy and Bess* exhibits influences of
the blues and of the Negro spiritual. The opening song, "Summertime," in
its almost totally pentatonic usage, is reminiscent of the spiritual. None of
these elements make a successful work, but in *Porgy and Bess* they are a part
of its importance.

Leonard Bernstein's musical background was the antithesis of George
Gershwin's. Born in Lawrence, Massachusetts, he studied music at Harvard
University and went on to study further at the Curtis Institute in Philadel-
phia. Here, in addition to piano, he studied orchestration and conducting.
At the Berkshire Music Center he became first a protégé of and then an as-
sistant to Serge Koussevitsky, director of the school and conductor of the
Boston Symphony Orchestra. In 1943, Bruno Walter, conductor of the New
York Philharmonic, fell ill, and on short notice Bernstein filled in. His
achievement was noted in the press, and he went on to conducting engage-
ments with major symphony orchestras throughout the world.

Leonard Bernstein and Dr. Serge Koussevitzky at Tanglewood, Lenox, Mass.
(*Photo by Orkin, New York*).

He wrote symphonies and chamber works, ballets and vocal works. More important to his ultimate contribution to the theater were *On the Town* in 1944 and *Wonderful Town* in 1952, both extremely successful musical comedies. In *Trouble in Tahiti,* a one-act opera, and *Candide,* a rather "serious" musical comedy, he received further experience in the theater, culminating in 1957 with *West Side Story,* which successfully reflected the issues of contemporary America.

Gershwin began as a composer of popular music and finally broadened the scope of his talents through constant study so that he finally embraced the larger forms. Bernstein learned the formal aspects of music first, and thoroughly, and then allowed the popular music idiom to permeate his work for the theater.

It is important to stress that in each of these composers the ultimate expression, which embraced both popular music and the larger dramatic concept, was not a forced expression. The fusion was the natural result of an honest appreciation of both types of expression. Neither had to search to *be* an "American composer." Each *was.*

Gian-Carlo Menotti (1911–   ) has been a somewhat controversial figure in this country. Commissioned to write a short opera for television in 1951, he was thrust into immediate renown and, as well, into the forum of discussion regarding his merits as a composer. This work, *Amahl and the Night Visitors,* has been a staple on television during the Christmas season for a number of years. Its commercial success, and the commercial success of his operas which followed, produced in the manner of Broadway plays and not by the Metropolitan Opera Company, were part of the reason for the criticism. The criticism included a discussion of his writing obviously for the people, his eclecticism—especially his musical style as reminiscent of Puccini—and his dramatic approach, which some thought to be too ebullient for the twentieth century. Nevertheless, in his operas—perhaps most notably in *The Saint of Bleeker Street*—he has shown that he has the capacity to do what every successful operatic composer must do: write a musico-dramatic work which not only happens in the mind of the composer but is a complete, well-wrought work on the stage which ultimately becomes a complete expression for the opera-goer. That he achieved these aims is beyond question. Whether he has written works of enduring quality is something for the future to ascertain. Nonetheless with Weill, Gershwin, and Bernstein, he has contributed importantly to the cause of American musical theater.

CHAPTER 9

The Other Side: Folk, Jazz, and Pop

FOLK MUSIC

THERE HAS ALWAYS been the other side; that side of music—sounding not in gilded court or bourgeois salon but in the field, hut, barge, and tavern. Folk music, both song and dance, not only has expressed man's deepest joys and agonies, but also has been a vital thread within the fabric of the human community. The fish-monger chanted his wares before the walled courtyards in great Chinese cities; blacks moaned their spirituals and later their blues to lessen their pain; and many a colonial maiden in 1776 sang of her absent love:

> O Johnny dear has gone away,
> He has gone far across the bay,
> O my heart is sad and weary today,
> Johnny has gone for a soldier.

Though the physical part of common man more often than not has been abused and debased, that human portion of his being, that part which is at the core of music, has never been touched. Man sings so as never to lose his human selfhood. Throughout this book we have referred to folk music, though we have not emphasized it as such. One cannot speak of the masters

---

"The Harvest Home," print by Thomas Rowlandson (*Courtesy of Roland Nadeau*).

and their times without taking into account how folk lore has touched and stimulated their creative lives. We have seen a humorous quodlibet at the hands of J. S. Bach where two German folk songs are intertwined within a most sophisticated contrapuntal texture. We saw the "Mighty Handful" in nineteenth-century Russia sparked by folk music and dance contribute a superb body of music strongly suggestive of the rich earth and the people closest to it. In the previous chapter it was shown how a folk song may crop up in a serial work, the first movement of Berg's *Violin Concerto*. Shortly, you will see in complete Score Profile a work based on four German student songs, Brahms' *Academic Festival Overture*.

Folk music research

It was in the nineteenth century that music historians and musicians first took serious account of the creative musical voice of the people. But as early as 1778, the philosopher/critic Johann Herder pointed the way to the rediscovery and utilization of folk art with literary works such as *Volkslieder*. Early in this century Bartók and Kodály scoured mideastern Europe, compiling large numbers of folk songs and dances, assimilating them into their own personal musical expressions. Vaughan Williams in England, Villa-Lobos in Brazil, and Carlos Chávez (1899–   ) in Mexico experienced a similar folk "enlightenment." Thus, not only did the music of the people enter the domain of the concert hall, but it also became the object of careful research and philosophical speculation. If folk music pervades the life of man, both in the quotidian and intellectual sense, what makes it so vital? What is its essence?

The essentials

For a music to be of the folk it must have simplicity and immediacy. It must be easily understood and savored by the mass and be simple enough technically to be played or sung by anyone with a desire to do so. It's harmony, if present, is uncomplicated and its formal structure is often quite plain. Many folk songs from the Western World can be set to elementary harmony consisting of a few chords. Much of the time its structure is *strophic:* a tune is repeated several times to changing text. Also, it must have permanence and universality; it must have been fired and toughened by the collective life experience of a people until it endures. The universality of all folk music lies in its reflection of the emotional identity common to all mankind. Just as joy, grief, love, hate, resignation, aspiration reside everywhere, so does it underlie the folk music of the world. This universal emotional pulse in all folk music persists even though the music's exterior musical shape varies from people to people, from land to land. One should not be hampered with fruitless speculations on the validity of folk music relative to its anonymity. There have been many who held that to be truly of the folk, music must spring from the anonymous mass. The French critic Tiersot thought that, "There is no such thing as a folk song whose composer is known, not only by his name but even approximately by his place of origin or the period of his life." And Carl Sandburg suggests the same thing speaking of his superb collection of folksongs: "*The American Songbag* comes from the hearts and voices of thousands of men and women. They made new songs, they changed old songs, they carried songs from place to place, they resurrected and kept alive dying and forgotten songs." What really matters is not so much its origin—individual or collective—but its acceptance, molding and transmission by the mass. Once a people is moved by what Sandburg calls, "strips, stripes, and streaks of color," over the years they gradually give it a contour and atmosphere which is uniquely theirs. The music then becomes of the folk; it has acquired a patina, a durability that transforms it into a cherished item of human culture. Once the idea is accepted that a folk music is selected, refined, and transmitted by the mass, there is little difficulty in understanding why certain popular items, no matter what their source, are a true folk music. The French tune, "Au clair de la lune" certainly must be seen as a folk expression. Yet it was written by Lully, the court composer to Louis XIV. Many of the popular songs of Stephen Foster, and songs such as Daniel Emmet's minstrel tune, *Dixie,* became folk. A broadened view of folk music to include much composed or improvised music makes it easier to see the role of jazz as lying somewhere within the purview of folk. The jazz critic Nat Hentoff calls for a broader concept in this way: ". . . if 'folk' as a term is to have any operative (rather than merely promotional) meaning, it will have to be redefined. And considerably elasticized. It will have to allow for broad heterogeneity of material and musical interests in a single performer, united by a firmly personal stamp of conception and style." * Folk music need not be anonymous, and it need not be unlettered. Some of it originated in musical notation, and much of it has been handed down this way. Actually, a notated folk song can no more lose its plasticity than a country yarn can lose its punch by appearing in a newspaper or magazine. It is the special manner in which folk music is performed each time that keeps it fresh.

---

* *The American Folk Scene: Dimensions of the Folk Song Revival*, ed. by David A. Deturk and A. Poulin, Jr., "The Future of the Folk Renascence," by Nat Hentoff, p. 328.

Folk/art music

There is however a serious question about folk songs and dances transcribed or arranged by modern composers. There are many of these: the collection, *Old American Songs* by Copland; Britten's arrangements of *Songs of the British Isles;* Falla's *Seven Popular Spanish Songs;* Bartók's *Roumanian Folk Dances* are but a few. Here, already well-formed expressions of the people have been polished, honed, and adjusted to the composer's highly personal musical language. Though tune and text are left close to the original, the sophisticated harmony in the accompaniment devised by the composer transforms the music into a kind of hybrid: a folk/art music. These settings result in valid works to the degree that the composer identifies with and sublimates the simplicity and universality of his folk material. However, to label this synthetic fusion as folk music is questionable.

Modern folk: USA

What about the resurgence of folk music in recent years? What is it? Does it contribute to the cultural climate of the world? Is it true folk? Does its unabashed commercialism reflect in any way on its validity and integrity? In the rural areas of the USA, folk music has always been a pervasive force. Through the process of acculturation a polyglot music from many corners of the world became Americanized. In the "culturally deprived" countryside and among the working class in general it waxed true and strong. In the fields of the South the black slave sang

> Bendin' knees a achin',
> Body racked wid pain.
> I wish I was a child of God,
> I'd git home bimeby.

to music that would ultimately suffuse the blues, ragtime, and then jazz. The colonial maid, singing forlornly the words

> Shule, shule, shule agrah,
> Time can only heal my woe,

from "Johnny has Gone for a Soldier," cared little that the song was of Irish import. Alan Lomax tells that this soldier tune was used as well for a lumberman's complaint, and a sea chantey. And although America's truly indigenous Indian music had little impact on the broad current of folk music, various folk expressions reflecting immigrant ethnic sub-cultures did. The two most powerful influences on the development of folk music USA were those musical elements coming from black Africa and from Anglo-Saxon Europe. In the early twentieth century, folk scholars such as John A. Lomax (the father of Alan Lomax), and the Englishman, Cecil Sharp combed the land, collecting large numbers of authentic songs. In the 30's and 40's these found their way into many printed collections. In the 30's John and Alan Lomax, using primitive recording instruments, captured the actual sound of many native songs. But it was when they introduced the great blues singer, Leadbelly (Huddie Ledbetter) to large urban centers that the folk "arrival" really began. This was the crucial hour. Modern folk music as we know it today is essentially a big city, college campus music. Only when the hardy stock of traditional countryside music became leavened by urban intellectual curiosity and ferment did it burgeon into the pervasive force that it has become. What it has become in the last decade is of a perplexing variety and quality. Robert S. Whitman and Sheldon S. Kagan list modern folk as falling into several basic categories: traditional as practiced by Texas Gladden; interpretive—Peggy Seeger; straight—Joan Baez; pop—Kingston Trio; art—Richard Dyer-Bennet; parody—the Smothers Brothers. Today our culture is flooded with enormous activity in this field, buttressed by powerful commercial interests. Folk and rock-pop have virtually elbowed jazz out of the popular market place. There are some who abhor the commercialization of folk. G. Legman, for example, cries out, "One of the most encouraging signs in the present development of the folk song fad is the overcrowding of the field. This will inevitably result in the driving out of a sizeable group of folklore fakers, Johnny-come-latelys, city-billies, folkniks, folksongsters, and other opportunists who have been attracted by the tales of a quick buck, plenty of beer, girls, and public acclaim . . ." * But whether or not modern folk will ultimately join the body of permanent folk music, its cultural effect has been and will perhaps continue to be significant. This cultural effect may well be positive, if only for the reason that such great numbers of young people are now actively involved in *making* music, not just hearing it. In a sense this involvement, made possible by the mass production of recordings, folk instruments, and concerts may have a comparable effect to that of the mass production of Henry Ford's flivver. The flivver led to our being a highly elastic, mobile society. Today's young folk songster-player may well be led through the now sound of modern folk into a love of the superb body of traditional folk music. From this he will grasp the pulse and essence of the human identity. Perhaps he will move on to an appreciation of those "classical" masters who were steeped in the music of the people. This is not to

---

* *Ibid.*, "Folksongs, Fakelore, and Cash," by G. Legman, p. 314.

say that the desirable end is the progressive assimilation of ever finer music by young people. Rather, we suggest that a serious personal involvement in folk could lead to a significant broadening of musical perception, and could contribute to a new attitude toward musical culture: one that is catholic, discriminating, and inclusive. Alan Lomax, speaking of the recent surge of folk in his book, *The Folk Songs of North America,* puts it this way: "What is more important, however, is that a whole generation of creative young people are becoming expert practitioners of our native folk song and thus are coming to grips with the profoundest American emotional problems . . . in them the young people discover the source of their own malaise and by singing them, they begin to face these problems with increased maturity . . . So long as these keys to our past lie rusty and unused we will repeat the old stereotypes and half-truths in glossy and increasingly superficial guises—in comic books, records, films and advertisements; new legends and new art forms will not arise and we will continue to play, like children, in the sunny forecourt of creation." *

JAZZ

The seeming paradox of jazz is that it is both a personal expression and a group expression. On the one hand, it is the highly subjective, spontaneous personal expression of the jazz soloist; on the other, it is the constant group expression of the other players, which seeks to align itself with the soloist and support him. There is ever-present, in good jazz, an "electric current" connecting the soloist and the group. Each of these two expressions— that of the soloist and that of the group—is sparked by, and sparks, the other. Thus there is a constant cross-reaction. To put it another way, the soloist is part of a "performing collective."

The performance of symphonic music, to take one kind of art-music, seems to be a large group effort. But each does not so much seek to spark and be sparked by his fellow player as to play his individual part as well as possible. The playing of a symphonic composition is in reality a one-man operation in spite of all the words that have been written to the contrary. The one man is the composer. And everyone from the conductor to the single player is intent on one thing: to carry out the composer's wish. And this is as it should be. Unless the composer himself is the conductor, this kind of performance can be an exceedingly impersonal project.

* *Folk Songs of North America* by Alan Lomax, Doubleday and Company, Inc., N.Y., 1960, p. xxviii.

The important thing about jazz is its immediacy. The composing soloist, the improviser, is there, on the spot. It happens here and now. This is
the excitement of it. Whether jazz was born in New Orleans is not pertinent
to our discussion here, but New Orleans certainly nurtured it through its
first years and sent it out into the world. Jazz at various times has been described as an unhealthy, and even wicked, offspring, but it has shown an
amazing vitality through the years, and the diatribes against it have abated
to the extent that it is now invited into the church (e.g. Ellington's *A Concert of Sacred Music*). The result of a fusion of the culture of the African
Negro, European harmonies, and some American folk idioms, early jazz also
contains traces of Creole French and West Indian. It has always borrowed
and absorbed whatever seemed interesting or pertinent to its expression, but
it has never lost its own individual personality. It is recognized throughout
the world as America's unique contribution to music. But critical and academic recognition has come slowly in America.

Jazz is an Afro-American contribution. And what a contribution! When
the black man as a slave first put his feet on American soil, American music
was mostly European music. Since the time of Stephen Foster jazz has
changed the course of American popular music so that it finally is no longer
dominated by European traditions.

And less directly it changed music for the theater from operetta in the
style of European opera to the musical comedy which is America's other
unique contribution to music. But the acculturation of the black man's
African musical heritage with the European harmonies of the hymn tunes
which he learned in the churches of his masters resulted in one of the most
moving kinds of group vocal expressions. The African rhythms and the
African melodic scale fused with the European harmonies to produce the
spiritual, at once one of the most personal and the most universal expressions of the sorrow and the longing, the suffering and hope of a people. It
may be said that white America could not truly understand the expression-
through-music of the black American, but this new African-American expression was absorbed by white America, even though the black himself was
not. The early "hollers" and shouts, the work songs of the field and the
boat and the barge, the improvisation that was inherent in the call and response pattern, the rhythmic dynamism, the pentatonic basis of much African melody; somehow all of these (containing both secular and sacred elements) were refined in the crucible of the spiritual, and somehow solidified
to become the blues. Out of a music that was originally functional (in every
aspect of the term) arose an expression that was to become a traditional art
form. The blues became the heart of jazz. And certain characteristic blue
notes (resulting in the so-called "blues scale") have infused not only jazz
but practically all popular music in America. Whether the slow recognition

of jazz was due to the nature of its origin, or just the fact that it was in an America that was trying to acquire its culture from Europe cannot be argued here. But it can at least be pointed out that once again the new, the different, the strange could not be accepted by those attempting to find their social plateau in the comfortable surroundings of the traditional.

The call and response element of the work song and the slave song was still to be noted in the group songs of recent civil rights demonstrations. The spiritual changes the early American hymn-tune into a more spirited affirmation of faith, while at the same time retaining an affinity for the tribulations of the Hebrews of the Old Testament. "Swing Low, Sweet Chariot" and "Nobody Knows the Trouble I've Seen" are representative of the many spirituals which, often pentatonic in structure, are given life by the jabbing accents of *syncopation*. The use of the pentatonic scale may be seen in "Swanee River" by Stephen Foster (1826–64) who attempted to simulate the plantation songs which were the inspiration of much of Foster's writing.

The blues

The origins of the blues are not quite clear, but somehow out of the work songs, hymns, spirituals, and other sources it developed to become a basic expression in jazz. Its text, almost always secular, in its *statement, restatement,* and *conclusion* has a vernacular simplicity that is disarming, because within this text may be found plays on words, sophisticated humor, a statement of resignation tinged with hope, and very often a sexual connotation. There are other blues, but the classic form is 12 measures long, in 3 phrases of 4 measures each, to match the text.

Not only as a basic form of jazz still in use today, but as an influence on all jazz, the blues has had considerable impact. Its melody contains the contours of the pentatonic spiritual plus the *blue notes*.

Any melody which is pentatonic has two notes of the major scale missing; thus a melody which is pentatonic is a "gapped" melody. This is found in early blues. The expression, *blue notes,* refers primarily to the lowering in pitch of the 3rd and 7th scale steps of the major scale. These lowerings of pitch are superimposed onto the major scale. If we use C major as an example, the blue note E-flat of the melody sounds simultaneously with E-natural of the harmony. The same principle holds for the blue note B-flat.

The origin of the blues was in vocal expression, but the blue notes may be performed by most instruments of the jazz orchestra. The pianist tries to approximate the inconstancy of the blue note by playing the lowered 3rd and the regular 3rd of the major scale simultaneously.

The final cadence of a blues phrase often avoids melodic stepwise motion to the tonic. Thus the tonic may be approached from the 6th scale step below, or from the flatted 3rd above. Further, these lowered tones may vary in pitch through distortion. The distortion of tone has become one of the outstanding characteristics of jazz expression and has been carried further to other notes of the major scale, and in addition this distortion has been carried over to the type of sound each instrumentalist produces on his instrument. The distortion is part of the personal expression of each jazz musician; the change of the instrumental timbre also follows. The use of various mechanical devices is also a natural extension of this desire to "personalize" the sound. Whereas the brass player of the symphony orchestra rarely uses more than one mute, the jazz brass player has used a wide assortment of mutes: straight, cup, wow-wow, stem, buzz, and so on. Also derby hats, felt hats, buckets, and bathroom plungers. The variety of cymbals and other varying effects used by the drummer are part of this picture. The saxophone player has rarely resorted to mutes since he can get a unique, personal sound by his manner of playing and the various adjustments he can make to the reed.

Ragtime

The *rag* is a syncopated instrumental dance: in its classic shape mostly written for piano. Making the perfect foil to pathos-ridden blues, it was a happy music which began in the "gay nineties." Scott Joplin's "The Maple Leaf Rag" (published in 1899), one of the first ragtime "hits," came out of a honky tonk in Sedalia, Missouri, called the Maple Leaf Club. But the rag's jerky syncopations could be heard in New Orleans, St. Louis, Little Rock, Nashville, and, as far north as Chicago.

It was the white ragtime pianist, Ben R. Harney, billing himself as "author, musician, comedian, and dancer," who claimed to be the originator of ragtime. Harney's successful rag song, "Mr. Johnson, Turn Me Loose," was actually published in 1896 but it was probably appropriated from a tune already extant and popular.

But much more important than who wrote the first rag was who gave it the spirit and the impetus that caused it to race through this country and Europe. It was the black composer, Scott Joplin, who, with "Maple Leaf" and others, set the style and pace. The rag's influence was strong. It was heard not only in the clubs and bordellos but in the parlors of genteel homes. It even left its mark on "serious" composers. Stravinsky included a pseudo-rag in his *Histoire du Soldat* (1918) and in the same year, wrote a *Ragtime for Eleven Instruments*. The French impressionist, Claude Debussy was charmed by the *cakewalk*, one of the dances that led to the rag, and wrote two little piano pieces patterned after it. One he called the *Golliwog's Cakewalk,* the other, *The Little Negro.*

By the early twenties, classic ragtime had about run its course. Jazz began to take over in popularity, as is suggested by the reactionary title of a rag of 1921 by James Scott, "Don't Jazz Me—Rag (I'm Music)." Indeed, jazz took over and raced through the country at this time, but it should not be thought that it was born in the twenties. There was considerable overlap. Jelly Roll Morton claimed to have used the word jazz as early as 1902 in the pristine days of classic ragtime. He tells of his "jazzing" any type of music: quadrilles, Sousa marches, folk songs, operatic selections, and even rags. All of this can be verified by listening to the Library of Congress recordings of Jelly Roll's playing.

Jazz gradually assimilated certain characteristics from ragtime in the same manner that it absorbed the essence of the blues. The blues, ragtime, and jazz, at the beginning of the twentieth century actually coexisted for many years before jazz gained ascendancy. Of the three separate forms, only jazz and the blues continued as a major factor in American musical life. The blues continues to this day in its classic shape at the hands of singer-instrumentalists such as B. B. King and Otis Spann. And, instrumental jazz still holds within its core a strong element of the blues.

Why is it that ragtime, in its pure form fell by the wayside while the older blues and the younger jazz continued to develop? Perhaps it was because both of these forms—jazz and the blues—held the possibility for subjective involvement of the performer, and both relied heavily on improvisation.

Gunther Schuller, in his book *Early Jazz,* notes that, "At even the most superficial level of listening it is clear that [Jelly Roll] Morton has moved away from the stiff, 'classically' oriented right hand and the march-like left hand. . . . Morton accomplished this innovation by making improvisation, especially in the right hand, the keynote of his piano style, thus directly opposing it to ragtime, a music largely written down." * And later, ". . . the blues, especially at the turn of the century, was essentially improvised. . . ." †

It was out of improvisation that jazz evolved. And though its increasing sophistication ultimately necessitated its notation and a more "schooled" musician to read this notation, jazz has never to this day lost its inner core of spontaneous and irrepressible improvisation.

One needs only compare the playing of a ragtime pianist/composer on a player piano roll with the actual music page to see that very few liberties were taken. In fact, Scott Joplin in his *The School of Ragtime—Six Exer-*

---

* *Early Jazz* by Gunther Schuller, Oxford University Press, N.Y., 1968, p. 144.
† *Ibid.,* p. 145.

cises for Piano (1908) is severe in his demand for a strict realization of the printed page of music, "It is evident that, by giving each note its proper time and by scrupulously observing the ties, you will get the effect." And there is evidence of the influence of the European musical ethic in the rag too. Some rags show the direct influence of classical compositions or classical styles. Joseph Lamb tells how his "Ragtime Nightingale" was suggested by Ethelbert Nevin's "Nightingale Song." And though he may not have consciously planned it, the first few notes in its left-hand part are identical with the basic accompanimental figure in Chopin's *"Revolutionary" Etude.*

Rob Hampton's "Cataract Rag" (1914) owes as much to nineteenth-century European virtuosic figuration as to indigenous American influences. Rudi Blesh and Harriet Janis in *They All Played Ragtime* put it somewhat laconically in speaking of "Cataract": "Parts of the third theme, for example, seem to echo a Brahms chamber work of the late Bad Ischel period." Perhaps it was the excessive influence of formal European approaches to composition that led the ragtime composer astray, so that the rag perished in the early twenties. In attempting to make ragtime "respectable," he turned too far from those rich springs of musical creativity originating from black American acculturation that had made ragtime possible.

Its sources

What then were the musical sources of ragtime? A formal structure in three or four clearly articulated and contrasted parts, including a trio in the subdominant key, clearly points to the early marches of Sousa and others. But, whatever the effect of the march on ragtime, its real roots lay in the banjo dances and songs of the minstrel show and plantation life. The cakewalk, the buck and wing, the "coon" songs; all contributed to classical ragtime. In New Orleans, at Congo Square, the beating of the drums and the frenzied dancing of the black slaves to the *Bamboula* pointed to an even earlier influence, that of Africa. It was in 1847 that the young American composer Louis Moreau Gottschalk attempted to capture the spirit of this wild dance in his piano fantasie titled, *La Bamboula-Danse des Nègres.*

Its musical elements

Without question those elements at the very heart of ragtime that most clearly define it are in the area of rhythm—tempo, meter, and accentuation. Tempo was rock-solid, motoric, but never very fast. Joplin, in the *School of Ragtime,* admonishes, "Play slowly until you catch the swing, and never play

ragtime fast at any time." His tempo indication given for the rag illustra-
tions in this set of études is "Slow march tempo (Count Two) ." Thus their
tempo was moderate and their meter was duple. (Almost all published rags
have a duple time signature of two-four.) Each beat was strongly marked by
the lowest bass notes in the left-hand part. Against this march-like bass, the
right hand articulated mostly quarter, eighth, and sixteenth-notes. The triplet is not used. Favored rhythmic figures were: eighth-quarter-eighth; six-
teenth-eighth-sixteenth; 8 sixteenths beginning on the first beat but with the
fourth and fifth sixteenths tied; and several variants of these basic patterns.
These figures are arranged in a rhythmic figuration that constantly pulls
against the basic beat by providing a nervous, bouncy syncopation. Instrumental ragtime melody, energized by the above syncopated configurations,
often outlined chordal shapes, but also made use of scale patterns with
dashes of chromatics. The right hand traversed an extensive portion of the
keyboard as it traced the melody.

The rag's harmonic scheme was simple, usually incorporating one key
change—to the subdominant for the trio. Chords and chord progressions
were highly suggestive of "barber-shop" harmony: progressions of linked
dominant sevenths at cadence points, sliding diminished seventh chords, and
many triads with added sixth.

The harmonies of jazz

The harmonies of jazz are essentially composed of what we might term a
"cultivated folk music." Originally based on popular materials such as hymn-
tunes and marching tunes, the harmonies were traditional European chords
(plus the implications of the pentatonic mode) . The effect of the blues was
melodic rather than harmonic, although it did produce a new kind of dissonance. Later, jazz arrangers picked up some of the harmonic devices of the
impressionist period, and this kind of harmony became the basis for much
big band jazz until the middle of the century. There were some influences
from the music of Stravinsky (and certain other contemporary composers
as well) , but the main point is that the music of jazz maintained its traditionally tonal basis, harmonically and melodically, and a concomitant diatonic scale. Such chromaticism as was introduced—to no matter what extent
—revolved around the diatonic tones of the major scale.

The instruments

The saxophone, which to many is the representative instrument of jazz,
was not present when jazz began. After the Civil War the easiest instru-

ments to obtain were those that were Army surplus. There were many Negro marching bands which played for various public functions. The basic instruments of these early bands were the clarinet, the cornet, the trombone, the brass bass, and the drums. These became the instruments of the early New Orleans jazz bands. When the music moved indoors there was no need to worry about the portability of an instrument, and the bass fiddle began to replace the brass bass which, with the drums, supplied the rhythm. To the rhythm section was added the banjo (of African origin), which was later to be replaced by the guitar. And the piano, which had been the chief voice for the immediate progenitor of jazz, ragtime, joined forces with the other rhythm instruments.

Louis Armstrong

This is the way it was when Louis Armstrong was born in New Orleans on July 4, 1900. He learned to play bugle and cornet in a waif's home, and after that he learned by listening to the sounds around him, especially to those of King Oliver. King Oliver went up the Mississippi River to Chicago, and when he sent for Armstrong in 1922 it had already begun. Jazz had left the cradle of New Orleans and was taking its first steps in a society that would greet it alternately with enthusiasm or surprise; that would dance and drink to it but not respect it; that would embrace it or treat it with scorn; and that finally might learn to love but never really understand it.

The first recording of a jazz group was made in 1917. The Original Dixieland Band was a group of five white musicians playing clarinet, trumpet, trombone, piano and drums. With the exception of the piano, these are the instruments that came out of the marching bands. You can hear the 2-beat accent of the march, you can also hear the pattern of the blues, and you can hear the distorted tones. You can also hear, further, special effects, such as a horse whinney. And finally you discover that this is also entertainment. For years jazz retained some of its element of humor and entertainment, but when these are over-emphasized the jazz element deteriorates. We have mentioned that the blues contained elements of humor—but an ironic humor. Jazz is never funny, it is never cute; in its best moments it has always been a serious personal expression.

While the Dixieland groups were making recordings, Armstrong began to carve out a technique and a style that was to be admired by jazz musicians the country over for more than two decades. Armstrong was not a Dixieland player. Whatever kind of a band that he led or played in through different periods, his was a solo style.

The possessor of tremendous endurance, an exceptionally well-controlled high register for his day, and a phenomenal feeling for the beat—on it or between it—he set the standard for years.

Bix Beiderbecke

Bix Beiderbecke (1903–1931) may perhaps be considered the founder of the other school of trumpet playing that was to influence many a jazz musician. Whereas Armstrong had an extreme high range, a powerful, vibrant sound, and a feeling for the beat as if it were an entity all by itself, Bix played in the middle register with a cooler sound and a different feeling for the beat; not as an entity but as something to "play around." Bix's rhythmic style was likely a result of the influence of the recordings of the Dixieland Jazz Band, and therefore his style was in the tradition of what has come to be known as Dixieland. The influence of Louis Armstrong may be seen later in Bunny Berigan's high soaring lines; that of Beiderbecke first in Red Nichols and later Bobby Hackett.

The legend of Beiderbecke—as is true of most legends—has become somewhat larger than life. His short life of twenty-eight years was an immediate propellant of the legend.

Bix made his first recordings in 1924 with the Wolverines, including *Davenport Blues,* named for his home town in Iowa. His recordings became record collectors' items, and include those made with his own group,.as well as with Frankie Trumbauer, the Wolverines, Gene Goldkette, and even Paul Whiteman. In the large bands he suffered the same fate that Bobby Hackett did later in the band of Glenn Miller. He was mostly buried in the band, and only occasionally will you hear a short solo. But the brief solo would often be the only highlight of the recording.

Bix also played piano, and wrote several pieces which show definitely the influence of the impressionist school. *In a Mist* is the best known example.

Fletcher Henderson

In 1919 the Fletcher Henderson orchestra went into the Roseland Ballroom in New York for the first time and made reappearances there until the mid-thirties. Henderson was a pianist, but his greatest influence was to be as an arranger-composer. It was he who was the first to produce a big band with a drive and a sophistication that was to set the tone for big band writing to the present day. His writing shows a feeling for the effect of ensemble writing in tutti, the polyphony of brass section against sax section against rhythm section. His band was the first to exhibit a polish of performance that had previously not even been considered necessary. Among the musicians in the orchestra, the "sidemen," there were many with highly individual talent as expressive solo players. One of the chief of these was Coleman Hawkins, whose later recording of "Body and Soul" became an all-time classic.

Henderson's influence extended further when his arrangements became the basis of the "book" for the Benny Goodman orchestra which came to high notice in the mid-thirties.

Swing

In the early thirties the American public was seeking entertainment wherever it could be found. The financial disaster of 1929 was now in the past, and the only direction the economy could go was—up. The public danced as it had never danced before. Big bands—jazz bands and commercial bands, black and white—were constantly on the road touring from one end of the country to the other. And on the radio, late at night, many of them could be heard live from the ballrooms, from the hotels, from the nightclubs, on coast-to-coast hook-ups. The names of Don Redman, Fletcher Henderson, Duke Ellington, the Dorsey Brothers, Glen Gray, Isham Jones, and many more became household names. The big band era was in. In 1935 Benny Goodman came riding in on the wave with a band of polished performers that found scores of ready listeners. His theme song, "Let's Dance," was the motto for the spirit of the times.

His facile technique on the clarinet was the beginning of a new expression in jazz that had less of the heart and more of the mind in it. The precision of the tight-sounding brass, the exploitation of the "saxophone chorus"—a display of the saxophones as a section—the drum solo as an expression of its own, these all came to a peak. For some musicians it was too organized, too neat. The Fletcher Henderson arrangements seemed to have lost some of their personality. Some musicians preferred them as played originally by Henderson.

But the wave was not to be stopped. The big bands multiplied and some became permanent fixtures on sponsored radio shows.

Goodman was the first to successfully integrate white and black musicians. He brought Teddy Wilson in on piano, and Lionel Hampton on vibraphone to become part of the Benny Goodman trio or quartet.

Artie Shaw as a clarinetist opposed Goodman for awhile and was preferred by many musicians, but his more volatile temperament, which accounted for his more flexible clarinet style, also contributed to the impermanency of his organization. Goodman remained to rule the scene until World War II began the break-up of the big bands.

Lester Young

The tenor saxophone playing of Lester Young first came to national attention during his four years with Count Basie at the end of the thirties. His style established a new ideal, not only for saxophonists, but for all jazz musicians. Influenced by Frankie Trumbauer of the Bix Beiderbecke years, Lester Young set an ideal of improvisation that was dynamic but controlled. Other tenor saxophonists of the time often played the instrument more than they played the music, resorting too often to honks and squawks to the detriment of melodic line. Young was either ahead of his time, or if he was just right, then time would catch up to him. His playing was emotional, yet controlled, and had a rhythmic drive capped by a feeling for creative continuity that still stands as an ideal. Young antedated not only the entire cool school of playing that was to come after Bop, but also the life-style of the generation coming to maturity in the late fifites and characterized by Marshall McLuhan. A representative recording to listen to is "Lester Leaps In" (which also has Charlie Parker on it), in the album *The Essential Lester Young*.

Duke Ellington

Before, during, and after Goodman and the swing era there was Duke Ellington. It almost seems as if there has always been Duke Ellington. Born in Washington, D.C., he is more truly a New Yorker with all the sense of sophistication that this might imply.

His first successes were in New York, the first big one as a result of his opening at the Cotton Club. Ellington's style of writing is one of the most distinctly individual of all jazz composers. Most jazz musicians, whether in small groups or in big bands—from the 20's to the 50's—have drawn heavily upon popular music. This might consist of songs clearly current and "commercial," or of the quality products of Jerome Kern, George Gershwin, or Cole Porter. Ellington also used popular music as source material, but this is a minor part of his output. Ellington's contribution lay in his completely original writing. And in many cases, with lyrics added later by a professional lyricist, this "became" popular music.

Ellington had the feeling for orchestration which only comes from living with an orchestra and knowing each player's abilities intimately. To this, he

Duke Ellington in Zurich (*Photo by Black Star, New York; Copyright by Fred Mayer, Zurich*).

added his talent, and some of the freshest sounds in jazz were originated. Ellington's music often included the inspirations and the suggestions of the individual musician during rehearsal, and thus many of the works were a joint effort of Ellington and the men of the orchestra. It is impossible to list Ellington's important works here—these are too many—but they range from "Ebony Rhapsody" (from the music of Liszt) and with the voice of Ivie Anderson, through works like "Sophisticated Lady," "Mood Indigo," "Reminiscing in Tempo" and "Solitude" to his more recent album *Far East Suite*.

Ellington has always tried to reach his audience, but he has rarely followed the musical trends of the times. For many years he set the trend. He was playing with a "swing" before it became a label for an era, and his unique approach to the organization of sound will probably last for many years.

The kid from Red Bank

This is the title of one of the works played by Count Basie and his orchestra. It refers not only to his place of origin, Red Bank, New Jersey, but to the spirit of his pianism. The essential characteristic of youth is its curious mind. This characteristic remains, not changed in its essence but expanded, to become the inquiring mind of the artist. This combination of "youth and artistry" is true of Basie as of all jazz musicians, and flows over into the playing of the musicians. Not a composer-arranger like Ellington, Basie is nevertheless the guiding force. His orchestra has a vital drive and constant awareness of the beat *as a group* that is hard to match. Like Ellington, the Basie band has had many imitators, but unlike Ellington it has never been as experimental. As a result it does not reach the heights or fall to the depths as has Ellington. But it has a record for a polished presentation which, for those who seek the delights of Ellington at his best, consider "mechanized." For others it is like drinking cream from the top of the bottle.

Bop

During the years 1942–1946—the war years—the big band era came to an end. Charlie Parker, Dizzy Gillespie and a few others brought in the new era with a return to small groups. The hard, clean, jagged lines of Bop were the reaction to what had become almost a national fetish: the large well-oiled machine that the big band had become left, in many cases, small room for the jazz soloist. This reaction resulted basically in a single melodic line with supporting percussion. The percussion now became free-wheeling, doing away with the steady four beats to the bar which had been the beat for swing. The piano no longer was a rhythm instrument per se, but a soloist. The bass fiddle as well went in this direction.

Parker and Gillespie introduced a technique heretofore unheard of for its agility. Their fresh version of the tune at the beginning and the end, but more especially their individual solos, confused many listeners who asked the same old question, "Where is the melody?" The bop musicians were employing a form that goes back to Haydn, Mozart, and Beethoven: *theme and variations.* This form had been the accepted one for most jazz since its inception. But in bop often the stated theme was itself a variation. The best-known example of this is "Lullaby of Birdland," based on an old "standard," "Love Me or Leave Me."

In spite of much chromaticism in many of the melodies, with an especial emphasis on the flatted 5th, the basic harmony of bop was traditional.

The "Cool" school came on the heels of bop and with it brought jazz to an about-face. Where once "hot" was the adjective that denoted an excellent improvisational performance, "cool" was now the term, and in addition somehow implied an even closer involvement with the problem of personal expression. It connoted an intellectual reserve in contrast to the emotionalism which was the aura of hot playing. And it suggested control.

But the big bands had not died out completely, and two that attracted a large following in the forties and fifties were Woody Herman and Stan Kenton.

Woody Herman had begun in 1936 at the Roseland Ballroom in New York City with some of the musicians, and at first some of the music, of the disbanded Isham Jones orchestra. It soon became billed as "The Band That Plays the Blues." But Woody's best and best-known group has been what is called *The First Herd.* As a clarinetist Herman was never outstanding, but he knew how to pick men and how to make a band. The First Herd had an excitement in its playing that has rarely been equalled.

Stan Kenton's approach to the sound of the big band—at one point in his career—was in a sense a precursor of the idea of Third Stream music, which was to come in the late fifties. After his popular "Artistry" phase (*Artistry in Rhythm,* etc.) of the late forties, he encouraged composers to experiment with new ways of writing which extended beyond the concept of the jazz beat as the central core. For example, *City of Glass,* by Bob Graettinger, non-motoric in beat, shows a structured concept of composition which lay more in the realm of art music than in jazz.

Third stream

In the late fifties there began a more serious effort to fuse jazz and non-jazz. One definite result of this was a recording of Gunther Schuller's *Sym-*

phony for Brass, coupled with works by J. J. Johnson (*Poeme for Brass*) and others, in which jazz and non-jazz techniques formed part of a whole. And a concert at Brandeis University in 1957 presented works by jazz-oriented composers George Russell, Jimmy Guiffre, and their non-jazz contemporaries, Harold Shapero and Milton Babbitt.

Schuller later appended the term "Third Stream" to this fusion of the two musics.

To many the fusion is an impossibility. But a supposed impossibility does not stop a creator from looking for a solution. The use of the term Third Stream has faded but the search for the fusion has not. Eddie Sauter wrote a non-jazz set of backgrounds specifically as a vehicle for Stan Getz' improvisation in an album titled *Focus,* and Sauter and Getz collaborated in a similar effort for a film score, *Mickey One.*

Dizzy Gillespie

Dizzy Gillespie stands with Charlie Parker as one of the innovators of Bop. The results of their efforts changed the face of jazz to make it once again a more personal expression. The angularity of melodic line, the chromaticism, the advanced technical facility, the expansion of range, and the rhythmic loosening—all these had the most profound effect and made possible the burgeoning of a talent such as Coltrane's.

John Coltrane

The powerful voice of the New Wave of expression that occurred in the 60's was that of John Coltrane. His first influence was Lester Young, but later he was attracted by the styles of Johnny Hodges and Charlie Parker. He played at various times with the bands of Dizzy Gillespie, Johnny Hodges, Miles Davis, and Thelonious Monk. This was the best kind of training that could be had. Each of these men have been outstanding figures in the development of jazz. Coltrane began to come into his own when he formed his own quartet in 1961. Constantly searching, constantly becoming aware, he does not arrive at a certain point, but keeps searching for a new solution. The extent of the unique contribution of John Coltrane may be seen in the diverse approaches that he took in the explorations of expressions by briefly scanning some of his albums: 1961 *My Favorite Things;* 1964 *A Love Supreme;* 1965 *Ascension*—(total improvisation), preceded by Ornette Coleman's important *Free Jazz;* 1967 *Kulu Sé Mama.*

Miles Davis

Miles Davis is a very special figure in jazz. He was responsible for the reaction to Bop—in some ways it was an expansion of Bop—by making recordings in the late forties and early fifties which expanded the size of the Bop combo. His album *The Birth of the Cool* is typical. Consisting of 9–10 musicians, the size of the group necessitated more orchestration, but nevertheless more room was left for improvisation than during the big band era. Important figures associated with Miles Davis were: J. J. Johnson who was to become a leading trombonist, and as well a composer, for a number of years; Jerry Mulligan, baritone saxophonist, who was to later form a quartet without piano, and John Lewis who went on to form The Modern Jazz Quartet that was to represent the essence of cool, and make important contributions to adventures in Third Stream Music. Miles Davis has consistently searched for new ways of expression, always remaining himself but constantly synthesizing, absorbing and experimenting. His album *Sketches of Spain* is a notable example in which Davis tries to fuse the Spanish idiom and his reaction to it into a new expression. A more recent album, *Filles de Kilimanjaro,* shows him in a new place, with a deepening maturity which has resulted in a wider but more personal expression. This is evidenced, not only in his own sound, but also in that of the group. The rhythmic and harmonic concept encompasses both a new improvisatory freedom and the purposeful boundaries of repetitive ideas. The scope is ever broader.

Art Blakey

We have already spoken of roots of jazz which are in Africa, and jazzmen have always been aware of this. But in the sixties there has been a more conscious effort to connect the new expression in jazz with the African expression. Black musicians in both jazz and popular music have been consciously seeking to re-affirm their heritage. This means not only the African heritage, but includes the American experience as well. John Coltrane made the connection in his album *Africa Brass*. But let us turn to Blakey. Art Blakey and the Jazz Messengers have had many successful albums and he, as a percussionist, has had a strong influence all through the sixties.

Particularly pertinent to our discussion here is his album, made in 1962, *The African Beat,* in which the personnel consisted of Blakey and seven other percussionists on a large variety of percussion instruments (the majority African) plus a bass fiddle, and Yusef Lateef on various melodic instruments, including oboe, flute and tenor saxophone. Blakey was looking

not only for a new fusion of African music and jazz, but also to "new ways in which African and American musicians can enrich each other." This effort seems to be more successful than most of the Third Stream attempts at fusion thus far.

Jazz—in conclusion

There is a certain distinction—a dichotomy, perhaps that may be discerned between the jazzmen of the 30's–40's, and those of the 50's–60's. Jazzmen of the earlier period had a certain naiveté. Although all artists in every field begin by copying the earlier masters whom they admire, they do so with the full awareness that after they have mastered the techniques and probed the minds of those who are their idols, they must go beyond this to attain—each, in his own way—their own personal manner of expression. The earlier jazzman did not necessarily believe that he had to overthrow what he had learned, but should add to it. The later musicians, in what seems to be a more feverish search for identity, also had their masters. But it seems that from the Bop period on this search for identity could not rest in development but must be accompanied by a desire to turn off the old as completely as possible in order to find the new. We spoke of the naiveté of the earlier jazz musician. What we mean is that though he was aware of his heritage, of the influences around him, of the musicians he idolized, he did not consciously think of it, discuss it, explore it, or perhaps abandon it. He let it permeate his being, and then took it from there. Whatever would happen to him would happen. But he believed that if the talent were there it would be expressed in a new and wonderful way. The later jazz musician, especially the more consciously aware black musician, specifically looked for roots, and this is especially true of the black musician—and in seeking them he has sometimes denied his correspondence with the world about him, the world (especially the world of music) in which he grew up—that world of music that was his milieu, that formed his life-style.

Whether you are aware of the music of Schoenberg or not, its impact on the world makes ripples which affect your own existence.*

The earlier jazz musician may not have been aware of the ripples, but they were there. The later jazz musician is not only aware of the ripples, but is consciously turning these ripples into waves. In doing so they may be look-

---

* Le Roi Jones speaks to this subject very aptly in *Black Music*, William Morrow & Co., Inc., N.Y., 1967, p. 70.

Miles Davis (*Photo by George W. Martin, Corona, L.I., New York*).

ing for the wrong thing. Duke Ellington has always been aware of his heritage, and he has often spoken of his music as representing the jungle of Africa. But he didn't quite mean this. His jungle music—with brass plungers and growls and the saxophone and clarinet wails—was always filtered through the sophistication of Ellington as a conscious urbanite. Perhaps it is the wrong point of view to wed African music to the jazz of today. Perhaps it is somewhat similar to Aaron Copland searching for American roots in prairie music, although he was a Brooklyn Jew of the city, by the city, and for the city. George Gershwin was not so misled. Also a Brooklyn Jew, his roots were imbedded in the music of New York—popular and jazz. Understanding this, his greatest achievement, the folk opera *Porgy and Bess,* utilizes everything he knew as a sophisticated musician in the New York world of popular music, which had been strongly influenced by the music resulting from the black experience in America. He did not have to search for his identity. He knew what it was. He knew that he was a sophisticate, he knew that he had written scores of successful musical comedies. He knew that the strongest influence of popular music in America had been the contribution of the black man. He put them all together, and added to it the usual dedication of an artist, which in this case took him to South Carolina to study the lifestyle and the music of a black community. He came up with an opera that is not African or Jewish, or anything else alien to George Gershwin as a New York musician and composer. He came up with an extremely credible work that represented what he knew through a musical idiom that was natural to him. This is what Aaron Copland did not achieve. This is what Milhaud and others did not achieve. The jazz that Milhaud and Honegger and others tried to put into their music was more in the way of a novelty rather than a feeling for the idiom itself. Never really understanding the jazz idiom they used it for effect. Stravinsky, strangely, seemed to understand jazz better. His various works which utilize jazz effects, do not so much seem to *use* jazz as to *look* at jazz.

The leading members of the avant-garde, both in jazz and in non-jazz, more and more have been getting together in New York and other major centers—listening to each other, talking to each other, and writing. The search continues. It is not like the efforts of a Copland or others to absorb jazz into art-music; and, on the opposite side, the borrowing by jazz musicians from some European composers to become a kind of "symphonic jazz." Both efforts are equally vain.

As the search continues, many old notions will fall by the wayside. Evolution has been a part of the history of music. Whatever kind of music there has been has given way to a new expression. This must be true of any expression in which originality is constantly sought.

POP

While jazz musicians were searching out the possibilities of Third Stream music, and certain others were reacting to the diffusion and watering down of the cool approach, a new expression developed which employed a harder driving style, termed either *funky,* or hard-bop. The blues combined its vocal origins and instrumental uses to become rhythm & blues. Hard driving and insistent in its beat, it became the new popular music as jazz had once been. Jazz itself became more and more avant-garde, along with avant-garde art music, and as it lost its beat it lost its audience. Recordings now became dominated by the names of soloists or groups of singers backed by a small but loud rhythm & blues band.

Out of rhythm & blues came rock 'n' roll, a more commercial expression with the jazz-influenced patterns of rhythm & blues turned into a simpler, on-the-beat style. The syncopations were still there but the traditional feeling of jazz that rhythm & blues had maintained was essentially eliminated.

Guitars rather than saxophones became the predominant sound. Rock 'n' roll was dominated by young performers and many of the lyrics of its earliest years were expressions of youth. As a result it appealed strongly to a young group of listeners. A majority of the listeners were now teen-agers and many older people thought it would be a passing phase. But its history has been hardy, and it still exists alongside other expressions.

Elvis Presley brought to the public a kind of rock flavored with a mixture of country style and blues. The public had heard blues singers with the bands of the swing era. Jimmy Rushing, Joe Williams, and Joe Turner with the Count Basie band were accepted—perhaps because Basie was accepted. Jack Teagarden was a blues singer as well as trombonist with his own band and later with Louis Armstrong. And there had been Dinah Washington, and Billie Holiday. But Elvis Presley outraged most of the middle class. His first appearance on an Ed Sullivan TV show, even though his hip-swinging was censored, was controversial. His physical gyrations are now standard among the rock 'n' roll and Soul or Gospel singers of today.

The Beatles brought to rock 'n' roll a new inspiration. In addition to their constant evolution throughout all of their albums, they made a visual impact, and an impact on the life-style of young America that has turned it around.

Ray Charles and James Brown, as the outstanding spokesmen for the young black and the young black's new mood, have also had an impact on the total way of thinking. Ray Charles cannot be put into any special cate-

gory. He is most often called a Soul singer, but his background is broad, including jazz, rock and popular. Both Charles and Brown are primarily entertainers. But they and other musicians in the forefront today must be considered also for their effect on the social attitudes of the young people of today. Perhaps the most important thing to note is that music is now more than music; it is social and political in its effect. The orbit of popular music today is constantly enlarging. The music is absorbing influences from a variety of sources and transmuting these influences into an ever new expression.

Just as jazz was a fusion of Africa and American/European strains, and later contained within itself such divergent strains as Impressionism and Latin-American rhythms, so popular music today is reaching to the music of India, is dipping back again into jazz (as seen in the Blood, Sweat, and Tears), and is experimenting with large forms. *Hair,* the first rock-musical comedy, will certainly spawn other attempts. And now there is a rock opera, *Tommy,* by the Who. Analyze them, criticize them, dislike them, or like them. Say that rock opera is not a real opera, and you may find yourself in the position of every other traditionalist who was dismayed at any new expression or art form.

The imaginative performers and artists, young and old, never stop searching, experimenting, and synthesizing. Duke Ellington, although recognized throughout the world, has never let himself be categorized. Two of his more recent works have been as diverse as the titles of the albums suggest: *Far East Suite,* and *Concert of Sacred Music.*

John Coltrane has also searched for the spiritual essence of man and tried to express it through his *Love Supreme,* and *Meditations.* His album *Cosmic Music* and *Sun-Ra's Heliocentric Worlds* suggest an awareness of mysticism.

Henry Pleasants, in *Serious Music and All That Jazz,* has this to say: "The new younger generation, both black and white, is making its own music on its own terms—not just on the musician's terms, but on terms valid for the entire generation."

We would like to hope that this statement could prove true not only in the microcosm that is music, but also in the macrocosm that is society.

The projection of sound through amplification

During the decade beginning in 1960, the various break-throughs in electronics have opened up myriad possibilities for enhancing or changing the

---

Scene from the 1970 production of the rock-musical, "Hair" (*Photo by Martha Swope*).

sound of musical instruments and for producing musical sound. The instruments of the jazz band had been limited to those which could be heard above the noise of the crowd. This was one reason for the acceptance of the saxophone into the circles of jazz. Much has been written about what constitutes a jazz instrument. But as now can be seen the matter has been mostly a practical one. Instruments which could not compete in volume with the saxes and the trumpets and trombones—not to mention the percussion—just were not practical as jazz instruments. The only major exception to this was the guitar. However, the guitar's chief role was as a rhythm instrument for the benefit of the men in the orchestra only. It was not until the guitar was amplified that it made a breakthrough as a solo instrument. And the incidences of time and place converged to make Charlie Christian, while he was with Benny Goodman, the progenitor of the new, melodic-line solo.

In the fifties and sixties other instruments became part of the jazz expression. Even the flute, in spite of its soft tone, could be heard when played at the microphone. In the last few years various instruments have employed electronic devices. Amplifiers are attached directly to the instrument so that the volume can be controlled to any degree desired. Thus not only the guitar and flute but also the trombone and other instruments may have the advantages of electronic magnification. An even later device enables the instrument to change its register and timbre. The amplification of the guitar has, changed the whole style of popular music. This has led to the electric guitar which is itself an electronic instrument. Both the electric guitar and the amplified acoustic guitar are in common use.

It is certainly true that much of the popular music of today, with its never-changing, insistent rhythmic pattern and limited harmonic variety, provides little to intrigue the more careful listener. But we must remember that in the swing period the same criticism could be made of many so-called swing bands. The charge of monotony and ineptness could be levelled at many of the bands which, although inspired by real jazz, went on to produce a slick commercial product where the making of money became of greater import than the making of music. The "swing and sway" bands of the thirties and forties—and there were many of them—helped bring on the demise of the big band era. But good things last, and the weak imitations fall by the wayside.

Imagination and talent are permanent qualities, and the current groups that have these qualities will be remembered.

CHAPTER 10

Since Webern

IN THE EARLY twentieth century certain composers turned away from their romantic heritage and established new modes of musical thought. Debussy, Ravel, Stravinsky, Bartók, and Schoenberg are now considered masters of their time. In whatever idiom they worked, each left a definitive body of music now recognized and revered by a sizeable concert-going public throughout the world.

Through their musical legacy we see a sharp break from traditional concepts of tonality, rhythm, and form. We see a more catholic approach to the selection of materials: new harmonic combinations, new rhythmic concepts, borrowings from the related arts, inclusion of cultural elements from all parts of the globe. We also see the beginnings of a progressive alienation of the mass listening audience and, most important, the firm entrenchment of the attitude of experiment. With the *new* giants, now to be examined in this chapter, there is an intensification and acceleration of these trends. New sounds include not only traditional pitch relationships, but also sounds from nature and/or sounds produced synthetically. The alienation of the average concert goer, symbolized by the violent audience reaction to the premiere of Stravinsky's *Le Sacre* has now reached the stage where one of the more important avant garde composers, Milton Babbitt, feels that it is no longer necessary for the composer to communicate with the layman. He and others find sanctuary in the musical laboratories of the university. Whether or not Babbitt is representative is not to the point. The very fact that any composer would write off a segment of humanity as his potential audience, is evidence of the widening chasm.

The earlier twentieth-century composer's tendency towards the universal and inclusive has led to an emphasis on the integration of heterogeneous elements. Works in mixed media are now prominent. The Greek sculptor Takis, for example, has exhibited works activated by electromagnetism, some giving out a musical sound. And Earle Brown has written an aleatory composition called *Calder-Piece,* for four percussionists and "mobile"; the performers take their "chances" with the music according to the speed and position of the mobile by Alexander Calder.

And there are bold, newer departures. Since Webern, there have arisen radical tendencies fraught with both dangers and promise for the future of musical art. These tendencies lie primarily in the essentially opposed areas of pre-determinancy and of chance. The move toward total pre-determinacy and control comes out of total abstract serialism, its chief progenitor and protagonist being Webern. Ultimately this led to electronic composition where the composer's choice of each sound is pre-set by mathematical formula and each performance also totally controlled through the elimination of the interpreter/performer. The responsibility is entirely that of the composer. Uniformity of product and faithful reproduction is assured. On the other hand, anti-control is of the essence in chance music. Here the final result cannot be planned. The performer has the last say. The responsibility lies less with the composer than with the performer. The music can never be the same. The spontaneous instant is all. The audience must understand and receive the message at once and only once.

Implications arising out of both of these radical philosophies of composition are shattering. Implied is a revolution of the whole social basis of artistic communication. Added to all of this is the accelerated pace of stylistic change, and a great diversity of effort on a world-wide stage. New idioms multiply and composers leap over each other in their rush to the future.

CONSTRUCTIVIST CONCEPTS IN THE ARTS

The French painter Cézanne had said, "Deal with nature by means of the cylinder, the sphere, the cube." When the Fauvist painter, Matisse, in a moment of derision, coined the word *Cubism* when speaking of the work of Picasso and Braque, he chose an apt term. The Cubists transformed traditional elements of perspective into disciplined, mathematical fragments and facets. Through these were projected the inner essence of the object, beyond and deeper than that given by a representative reproduction. When one sees Picasso's "The Ladies of Avignon" (1906–07), or Duchamp's "Nude Descending a Staircase," (1912), the first impression might be that of overlapping images as seen through a prism. But, one ultimately sees the texture of inner life, shorn of unessentials. There is motion, and the raw nerve and heartbeat of what really is. Braque's montage and collage techniques, out of Cubism, combine assorted mounted materials which are synthesized into an expression emphasizing tactile qualities. So did the work of Constructivists, such as Tatlin and Pevsner, who also dealt with elements of cubic space.

Several composers also investigated the use of mechanical concepts in their compositions. Typical are: Honegger's *Pacific 231*, simulating the rhythmic throb of the locomotive; George Antheil's *Ballet mécanique* (decor by the Cubist Leger) with the use of airplane propellers; Prokofiev's *Leap of Steel*, and Mossolov's *Iron Foundry* (including the sound of shaken sheet metal reflecting the new industrialism of the young USSR).

THE EXPERIMENTAL ATTITUDE

In light of the above, and later developments in music, it is interesting to note that Edgard Varèse (1885–1965), acquired an engineering degree before becoming involved in the intricacies of music. This double interest prepared him for his unique contribution which led him ultimately into electronic music. Even before his involvement with electronic music his inclination towards engineering resulted in works which are partially mathematical in their basis. His *Octandre* may be thought of from at least one point of view as a continuous re-shaping of a three-note pattern. This mechanistic piece for eight instruments is in line of succession to the neo-baroque objectivity of Stravinsky's *Octet*. In 1931 came *Ionization*. Scored for 37 percussion instruments manned by 13 players, it symbolizes the new search for new sounds. Among the instruments are two sirens, two tam-tams, and two anvils, each pair in two registers, high and low. It was the engineer in Varèse who titled his work for solo flute, *Density 21.5*. The work was written for the inauguration of George Barrère's platinum flute: 21.5 is the density of platinum. The inherent musical abstraction of the total percussion of *Ionization*, points away from traditional pitch usage. It showed the way to later developments in computer music which also abandoned the usual pitch distinctions. Varèse, the first to recognize the possibilities of total percussion, stopped writing in 1937, but was drawn back to composition, perhaps by the lure of electronics, in the 50's.

Henry Cowell (1897–1965) was one of the early experimental composers. He was at first self-taught, and when 15 years of age he came upon the idea of playing upon the piano keyboard with his forearm or fist, thereby producing large clusters of sound. This technique may be used to produce percussive sounds or soft "multiple vibrations." This, and a procedure of plucking the piano strings as if it were a harp, opened the way for many younger composers into experiments with sound. Cowell also, with Leon Theremin, produced a Rhythmicon, an electronic instrument that could produce multiple rhythms concurrently. Composer of over 1,000 works, he was constantly active in championing new music. His experiments—including others not mentioned—have been perhaps his outstanding contribution to contemporary music.

Charles Koechlin (1867–1950), only rather recently coming to notice because much of his work has been seldom played and less often published, was a powerful individualist who drew on all sources to make his own unique statement. Koechlin, in the company of Ravel, Milhaud, and Honegger, had been taught by the French pedagogue and theorist, Henri Gedalge. In turn, Poulenc and Sauget were guided by Koechlin. Koechlin was also a strong influence on Milhaud; Koechlin's approach to the uses of tonality/polytonality was important in the development of Milhaud's extensive utilization of mixed tonalities.

One of the most important and individual of Koechlin's works is the massive, pictorial cycle based upon Kipling's *The Jungle Book*. One section of *Les Bandar-Log,* sub-titled "Scherzo of the Monkeys," shows the broad spectrum of Koechlin's musical thought. Here we find a melding of diverse sounds. In illuminating the imaginative Kipling text where the monkey-world is perhaps seen as the microcosm of the human situation, Koechlin weds heterogeneous musical styles and techniques: expressionistic, coloristic orchestration and harmony, a serial fantasy, a polytonal invention, and a fugue built on the subject from a French folk song "J'ai du bon tabac." Koechlin's Kipling cycle brings to mind the jungle scenes of the French primitivistic painter, Henri Rousseau. There is a like feeling in both artists for the enigma and mystery of the jungle. Koechlin's identity with, and encouragement of, the fresh and the new accounted for his ever-changing creative vistas. At the age of 80 he wrote orchestral interludes to go with an earlier work, the *Seven Stars Symphony* of 1933. The stars: Charlie Chaplin, Douglas Fairbanks, Emil Jannings, Marlene Dietrich, Clara Bow, Lillian Harvey, and Greta Garbo.

Olivier Messiaen (1908–   ), through his treatise on methods of composition, as a teacher at the Paris Conservatoire, as well as through his association with the group *La Jeune France,* has had considerable influence on younger composers. Some of his works are massive in scope and contain ele-

"Merry Jesters," by **Henri Rousseau** (*Courtesy of Philadelphia Museum of Art*).

ments of mysticism and oriental influences, using various modes. To enhance his expression he has used unusual percussion instruments, as well as the electronic instrument, the *Ondes Martenot* (named after its inventor), which produces a sound not unlike a female voice with a tremendous range. *Turangalîla,* his 10-movement work for orchestra, exhibits his full technique, and in spite of its length is a masterful expression, almost hypnotic in its profound probing. From the perspective of our time it may be seen that Messiaen in his role as composer, teacher, and writer was a pervasive influence on the younger avant-garde. He taught, among others, Boulez, Stockhausen, Nono, and Barraqué.

In his credo that "technique serves expression"; in his expression of such diverse elements as angels, birds, the genesis of life, and the mystery of the earth; in his use of Sanskrit and his own pseudo-Sanskrit; in his interest in the Ondes Martenot; we see a broad-ranging, universal approach to artistic creation. In his later works Messiaen became interested in the actual songs of birds as a basic element in his materials of composition. Here is the catholic fusion of resources—those from nature, and those from the most advanced technical developments of our time.

Turangalîla contains rhythmic innovations similar to Schoenberg's use of pitch serialism. This rhythmic serialism was later adopted by Stockhausen.

Musique concrète

The acceleration of technological evolution and discovery in the twentieth century could not be unfelt or unnoticed by twentieth-century composers. Beginning chiefly with Debussy, the idea of pre-determination before composing has become stronger and stronger.

It is to be noted that more and more composers are also mathematicians, engineers, and inventors. Austin in his *Music in the Twentieth Century,* in presenting a list of important developments, states: "Varèse made experiment the foundation of all his work, and published only his distilled achievements. The list includes, on the other hand, inventors, some of whom did not compose at all, and most of whom composed pieces that caught attention only briefly. . . ." * We have already noted Cowell's experiments with the strings of the piano. John Cage (1912–   ) followed Cowell by using a "prepared piano." The piano strings are prepared by inserting upon or between the strings various foreign objects such as pieces of metal or paper. It was Cage's attitude and vision, perhaps far more than his results, which were to have

---

* William W. Austin, *Music in the 20th Century,* © W. W. Norton & Co., Inc., New York, 1966, p. 378.

a strong and lasting effect on many composers working in new directions in mid-century and thereafter.

As early as 1937, Cage was saying that "the use of noise to make music will continue and increase until we reach a music produced through the aid of electrical instruments which will make available for musical purposes any and all sounds that can be heard. . . ." Cage's *Three Dances for Prepared Piano* were presented in Carnegie Hall in 1946.

In 1948 in Paris Pierre Schaeffer, the first exponent of *musique concrète,* furthered the attitude of experimentation by recording sounds (not necessarily pitched) and then re-recording them distorted in one way or another —changing the speed of the original recording, by repeating and mixing portions of the recording, and manipulating the original to achieve new effect.

Called *musique concrète* because it deals with a collage of sounds and concrete noises rather than with abstract emotional expression, it contained the element of chance because of the empirical method of trial and error which is diametrically opposed to predetermination. These two concepts— predetermination—and chance, separately or combined—were to invade the minds of composers to the present time. The first important work of musique concrète was that of Schaeffer and Pierre Henry, *Symphony for One Man,* produced in 1949.

Pierre Boulez (1926–   ) has become since Messiaen the dominant figure of the avant-garde, not only in France, but throughout the musical world. Having studied with Messiaen and with Renée Leibowitz, disciple of Schoenberg, he absorbed Messiaen's searching attitude and combined it with the rigorously mathematical twelve-tone system. He became a leading exponent of the new serialism which has pervaded the thought of principle avant-garde composers. This new serialism, originally suggested by the works of Webern, predicates a thorough-going serialism including not only the choice of tones but also counterpoint, durational values, and choice of instruments.

Boulez has carried the experimental attitude to a near scientific level. Here pre-determinism is almost absolute. This points the way to his later involvement with electronic music. *Grove's* describes Boulez' workshop as the "adventurous alchemist's rather than the methodical chemist's." Boulez, regardless of the system and the planning, retains the *sine qua non* of every worthwhile composer, fertility of the spirit.

The Boulez influence has been disseminated through an ever-widening range of activities, such as his appointment as Director of Music at the Jean-Louis Barrault Theatre in Paris in 1948. In recent years he has done more and more conducting throughout the world, his most recent appointment being that of Music Director of the New York Philharmonic. In addition to his instrumental works we may mention *Le Soleil des Eaux* as one of his more accessible earlier works (1948–50). This is a cantata based upon two poems of René Char, the Surrealist poet. His best-known work is *Le Marteau sans maître*, also based on the work of Char. Heterogeneous in its mixture of severe Webernesque serialism and the dream world of Surrealism, with the aroma of the Far East, the sounds and silences of discontinuity, it nevertheless forms a synthesis that is uniquely Boulez.

Chance music

The element of chance has always affected the inspiration of the composer in one way or the other. For example, the musical family gatherings of the Bachs, where they improvised quodlibets out of whatever melodic materials came to mind, is typical. A Russian folk song capturing the attention of Balikirev in his travels in the Baku, later sparking a symphonic work is to the point. A recent example occurred when the Duke Ellington orchestra was touring the East. As Duke Ellington's co-composer, Billy Strayhorn, sat in his room, through the window came the song of the Mynah bird. This song became the motive for *Bluebird of Delhi*. It has been left to the composer of the twentieth century to systematize chance as a basic thrust of composition. Its first intentional use was a part of the organized sound of musique concrète. Chance was more and more to suffuse the work of the younger composers.

Experiments in random composition have included what may be termed a "musical mobile." The mobile effect is achieved through assigning to each performer a certain number of "examples." Each example will contain a certain amount of notated music, from one note to perhaps several measures. Each performer chooses the order in which he will play these examples. In the next performance, either immediately or at some later time, the order is again chosen by the performer. In other words, the particular "viewing" depends upon the way "the wind blows," as with a mobile.

Random composition would most certainly include improvisation, and while this had once been a vital force in music, especially in the Baroque, and also during the Classical period, it waned during the nineteenth century. The spirit of improvisation has never died out in folk expression, nor in the great tradition of organ extemporization. Until the advent of jazz, however, it did not contribute again to any growing cultural body of music.

Improvisation, dead in the concert-hall, was brought to life again by jazz in the early twentieth century. Through the entire history of jazz, improvisation has been its life-blood, constantly nurturing it and revitalizing it. Im-

---

"Ghost," mobile by Alexander Calder (*Model for "Ghost," by Alexander Calder, from Calder, by H. H. Arnason and P. E. Guerrero. Copyright © 1966 by Litton Educational Publishing, Inc., by permission of Van Nostrand-Reinhold Company*).

provisation has always been understood by the jazz musician. It is seriously open to question whether the non-jazz oriented composer has known how to handle it.

Aleatory, or chance, music may include improvisation, but as this includes the possibilities of selection by the performer, there are many experiments that emphasize the aleatory aspect—that of "gambling" with the results—even more. Such experiments include the throwing of dice to decide the order of tones, or sections of music. There are those who have severe reservations about current aleatory composition. The arts critic Roy McMullen puts it this way: "The procedure yields nothing more philosophical than the effect of a solemn jam session by a very cool jazz outfit, with perhaps an ultrasophisticated rhythm section. The random elements float, as it were, inside serial or post-serial forms." * Whether or not there is philosophical yield is not as important as whether viable communication is at all possible. Within this new reality is it possible for the performer to be enough aware of compositional procedures to realize the composer's intention? Are the composer's "notational guidelines" enough?

Aleatory music cannot be created by only one man. There must be at least two: one to plan, the other to produce. In the case of aleatory music for ensemble, the composition is truly collective.

The question is not that of the validity of chance elements in music. Music as a time-art has always included the unforeseen as an element of its performance. No two performances of a single work have ever been the same. In the past composers have always known this; often they have deliberately planned for spontaneity. Time/space left by composers for improvised cadenzas in early concertos illustrate this. And the baroque composer neither expected nor desired that every one of his notes would be realized exactly as penned. Within his figured bass parts a wide latitude of options was left to the performer/improviser. But implicit in the baroque master's use of "aleatory" elements was a trust in the taste and competence of the interpreter. Besides, his musical materials were common enough to all—composer, performer, listener—so that communication of some sort was assured.

In our day, musical language is extraordinarily complex and heterogeneous. And it changes in style and direction by the decade rather than by the century. Since Webern, its basic thrust has been along mathematical, ultra-technological lines. What is required then is an entirely new breed of performer: one who is utterly dedicated, superbly trained technically, highly aware and conversant with the latest compositional materials, and willing to work out a symbiotic relationship with the composer. John Cage has been a continuing and ever-more influential force in his exploration of aleatory

* "Music, Painting, and Sculpture" by Roy McMullen, *The Great Ideas Today*, Britannica Great Books, 1967, p. 106.

music. His book, *Silence,* taken from his lectures and articles, dating from 1939 to 1961, symbolizes his constant concern with new directions. His well-known attempt to negate the very foundations of composition and performance is a piece called *4 minutes and 33 seconds.* During this length of time a pianist (although it is not necessary for him to be one) sits at the piano, but does not play. This particular work has had its influence. Discussion continues as to its merit. In the case of such a work as this, there is no need to await the verdict of posterity. There can be no verdict; there is no evidence.

Music has come out of "song and dance"—as all music must—to become an exploration in "sound and time." This is the essence of music. When the exploration leaves sound and time—i.e. when it is no longer discernible by even the most astute listener over a very decent length of time—then it may be a new experience, a new art form, but it is not music. It should then be called something else. Just as the table or the chair is no longer a table or chair when it is chopped up—it is then just wood—so then is music no longer music when it is chopped up beyond recognition as music. It is then something else, name it what you will.

One of the most important figures affected by the new wind blowing across the contemporary scene is Karlheinz Stockhausen (1928–   ). He has aligned himself with all contemporary developments including chance music, the new serialism, and electronic music. He is at the very cutting edge of further new developments. Having begun with works for conventional instruments, his first influence was Webern. Of this period is the *Kontrapunkte* for ten instruments where each note has a special placement and sound patterns have their own individuality. Of his works for piano, *Piano Piece XI* (1956) was an interesting experiment in chance. It consists of 19 fragments which may be played in any order at the whim of the pianist. The pianist also has the choice of any of 6 different tempos, dynamics, and articulations. Stockhausen specifies that when one fragment is played three times the piece must end. His *Gruppen* (1955) for three orchestras investigates spatial dimensions in the fashion of the antiphonal choirs in Venice in the early Baroque. The three orchestras, by combining, synthesize their separate strands of orchestral, chamber, and soloistic music. A work similar to *Gruppen* in attempting to capture the spatial relations of sound is *Gesang der Jünglinge* of the following year. It is composed for five loudspeaker groups and includes not only electronically produced sounds, but vocal sounds. The text, biblical in origin, is partially comprehensible and partially incomprehensible, as the sound of the vowel is more important to Stockhausen than the meaning. Again we are reminded of Stravinsky in his use of antique texts, not for their conceptual meaning, but for their abstract, "concrete" properties.

FISH:A BALLET FOR WOODWINDS

The duration may be fixed arbitrarily in minutes and seconds, etc, or it may be determined by allowing the number of cards (see below)chosen by the players to work out the length ad lib.

a. Cut along the lines dividing the page; this will produce a group of small cards, to be mixed up in any order.

b. Each performer chooses a number of cards* (previously determined); these are divided into
    1) single sustained notes.
    2) groups of 2 or 3 notes to be repeated several times.
They are read as follows:
    1. notes are at concert pitch (treble clef).
    2. tempo of groups may be ♩ = 40-80
       (average♩=60 - extremes of either tempo range are to be avoided).
    3. dynamics may be p-f (extremes: pp-ff or special effects such as sudden crescendo, fp, etc, are to be avoided).

c. After cards are chosen the performer begins reading them in this manner; 1) Sustained notes are held the length of one breath or about 20-40 seconds. 2) Repetitive groups are to be played, alternately, 6,11,14, or 20 times (that is, the performer may begin with any sequence but should use up all 4 possibilities before he returns to the first).
NB After each card is played,the performer must change his physical position, that is, move to another part of the performance area. These movements should be as expeditious and quiet as possible,and are the only time during the performance when the performer is to be silent (except, of course, rests which are part of the groups). However, they (the position relative to the performance area. Movement among, behind, to the side of, or over the audience, if any, is acceptable. "Theatrical" actions not necessary to the performance of the piece are to be avoided.

* The number of cards may be increased to any number necessary for performance;this may be done in any number of ways, obtaining additional copies, duplicating this copy, or copying out the groups by hand.

June 1961
New York City

"Fish: A Ballet for Woodwinds," a composition by Joseph Byrd using aleatory
techniques (*from "An Anthology," published by La Monte Young and Jackson Mac Low,
Bronx, N.Y., © 1963*).

THE NEW SERIALISM/ELECTRONIC MUSIC

We have seen that the influence of Webern on various major figures has resulted in an ever more inclusive serial application. We will now discuss composers who have been strongly identified with serial technique of various sorts. The original impetus and influence of the Schoenberg "idea" has been superseded by the differing and unique approaches of his students Berg and Webern. There are those within the new serialists who retain the lyricism that Berg did not deny himself. Other more radical members of the avant garde take the ascetic purity of Webern's strict serial technique as their ideal. Among those who temper the strictures of serialism by joining with it other attitudes are Luigi Dallapiccola (1904–   ), Rolf Liebermann (1910–   ), Hans Werner Henze (1926–   ), Mel Powell (1923–   ), and Ernst Krenek (1900–   ). Dallapiccola, first as a student and then as a teacher at the Conservatory in Florence, has combined the Italian love of lyricism with the exactitudes of the procedure of twelve-tone writing without losing the innate Italian flavor. In his work at Tanglewood as teacher at the Berkshire Music Center, and as a professor at Queens College of the City of New York, his influence was greatly felt by young American composers. Two of his better known works are: *Il prigioniero* (The Prisoner), an opera of 1944–1948; and *Variations for Orchestra,* 1954, commissioned by the Louisville Orchestra.

Liebermann, born in Zurich, at one time was on the musical staff of Radio-Zurich, and in more recent times he has been holding the post as Director of Music at the Hamburg State Opera. His style is eclectic, embracing a use of the twelve-tone technique which does not deny the use of sonorities more common to earlier styles. His *Concerto for Jazz Band and Symphony Orchestra* of 1954, originally performed in Germany, was recorded in this country by the Chicago Symphony with the Sauter-Finegan Orchestra.

Henze is now coming into prominence on the world stage, not only as one of the few contemporary composers who are writing in the large symphonic style, but as a conductor with broad talents. With five symphonies to his credit, all recorded and conducted by him, he has also been responsible for a revived interest in ballet in Germany with his *Ballet Variations* (1949), and *Ballet Scenes for Orchestra* (1950). Henze has also contributed to the repertoire of opera with works for the opera stage and for radio. Also he has incorporated certain jazz elements into his work, such as his ballet, *Jack Pudding. Undine,* in 1959, received the greatest acclaim from the public and brought knowledge of his work outside of Germany to England and the USA. Henze is able to imbue his work with a lyricism that is not anathematic to his controlled use of the serial idiom.

It is interesting to note that almost all writings which discuss Krenek speak foremostly of his jazz-influenced opera *Jonny Spielt Auf!* (1927). There is no doubt that this has been his most popular work. It was translated into 18 languages, it was heard in more than one hundred opera houses, and it gave him an international reputation.

He emigrated to America in 1937. He had now decided that the row technique of Schoenberg would be his new stance. He has included admirably clear explanatory notes with his scores.

Mel Powell (1923–   ) was one of the very few jazz musicians (he was pianist for Benny Goodman) to take the step into serious art music. It is likely true that it is easier for a jazz man to enter the ranks of art music than vice versa, but it has been rare for the jazz composer/arranger, to enter the "hallowed halls." Powell is an exception. Formerly professor of music at Yale, Powell's best-known work is *Filigree Setting for String Quartet.* Here he seeks to combine the improvisation of jazz with the extremities of the twelve-tone method.

In this connection mention should be made of the coming together of avant-gardists in both the jazz and art music fields. The Liebermann *Concerto for Jazz Band and Symphony Orchestra* was a forerunner of the concept of Third Stream which originated with serious jazz musicians, and this particular work points up the continuing interest among serious composers in the ever-flowing fresh stream of jazz. Stravinsky had shown a renewed interest in 1946, not in the style of jazz per se, but in the use of the jazz instruments in his *Ebony Concerto* (not of serial origin), written for the Woody Herman orchestra. And later, in 1957, we find another attempt at "fusion" at a Brandeis University concert where the program was divided equally between compositions by jazz-oriented and non-jazz-oriented composers. Among the works represented were Babbitt's *All Set* and George Russell's *All About Rosie.*

One of the more recent attempts at fusion is by Gunther Schuller. His opera, *The Visitation,* dealing with the race problem in America, continues in this trend. There is a jazz band in the pit along with an opera orchestra.

There are four important names which are clearly associated with the severe serialist approach. They are: Bruno Maderna (1920–   ), Luigi Nono (1924–   ), Luciano Berio (1925–   ), and Iannis Xenakis (1922–   ).

In Italy, the home of *bel canto,* there now exists a center for the new electronic music. Maderna was one of the founders of the Studio di Fonologia Musicale at the Milan Radio. In his writings for conventional instruments he already showed the influence of Webern through a preference for restricted combinations of instruments. He is gifted with an Italian lyricism, but in spite of this has moved towards a constructivism which includes complex serial calculations. Pre-determination is primary. One of his earlier works, *Studies for the "Trial" of Kafka* (1950), shows an expressionist atmosphere. But more in keeping with his interest in total serialism is the *Serenata No. 2 for 11 Instruments* (1955).

Nono, a student of Maderna, espoused the twelve-tone system from the beginning. His early pieces were sparse in sound and texture, but he gradually moved to a more Italianate lyricism. In spite of this, he also moved towards total serialization. The dramatic lyricism found in the *Epitaph for Federico Garcia Lorca* (1952–54), found its ultimate realization in the opera *Intolleranza,* a work controversial because of its political implications.

Berio was associated with Maderna in the establishment of electronic music at the studio at Milan. He came under the influence of Dallapiccola at the Berkshire Music Center. But like Dallapiccola, there is a certain lyricism in his work. His has a strong feeling for instrumental color, and his interest lies within strong predetermination affecting not only the selection of sounds but their duration, intensity and timbre. *Nones* (1954), is a rigidly structured twelve-tone work. In its rigid, mathematical approach it is reminiscent of those academic contrapuntists of the Renaissance who tried to seek perfection within the purity of mathematics.

Xenakis, born in Roumania, has carried mathematical manipulation to the ultimate degree. He is not only a musician—his teachers included Honegger, Milhaud and Messiaen—but also an architect, having studied with Corbusier. His interest in architecture is not didactic; he designed the polytype of the French Pavilion at the Montreal Expo '67. Messiaen has called Xenakis "an architect, mathematician, logician, poet, and, above all else, a musician." If Messiaen is correct, then Xenakis represents in this day and age what Alberti meant to the Renaissance, and further may be the embodiment of the Pythagorean ideal of the oneness of music and mathematics. *Musique Stochastique* may or may not become the new term to describe current and future manners in music. This is Xenakis' term used to describe his concept of the grouping of masses. His *Atrées* (Hommage a Pascal), performed in Paris in 1962, utilizes the stochastic program.

The dividing line which once existed between composers of twelve-tone persuasion and tonal composers is vanishing, as is the dividing line between adherents of the new serialism and those of electronic music. In fact no longer is it easy to put a contemporary composer under a single classification. Milton Babbitt (1916–   ), Otto Luening (1900–   ) and Vladimir Ussachevsky (1911–   ) are representative figures of the composers whose interest in serialism has carried them well into the mathematical field of electronic music. To these men electronic composition has the neat feature of requiring no performing musicians who may get in the way of the production of pure sound.

Babbitt was the first exponent of the new serialism in America. His studies with Roger Sessions, and at Princeton, were the background for his earlier efforts in conventional pitch composition. But he has moved steadily through exploration of total serialization into electronic works. Now on the faculty at Princeton, he is one of the Directors of the Electronic Music Center operated jointly by Columbia and Princeton Universities. Here resides the RCA Synthesizer which makes it possible for him to carry out his experiments. One of his more conventional works is *Three Compositions for Piano* (1947).

Milton Babbitt at one of the keyboards of the Mark II RCA Electronic Sound Synthesizer (Courtesy of the composer).

Along with Babbitt, Luening and the engineer/composer Ussachevsky have contributed to important works in electronic media. Works jointly composed by Luening and Ussachevsky which have been recorded are: *Rhapsodic Variations for Tape Recorder and Orchestra,* and *A Poem in Cycles and Bells.*

EPILOGUE

In reviewing the material that has been presented in this chapter one is well aware that there has been much discussion of systems (and non-systems) of composition. Important as it is to know something of the methods of a composer in trying to understand what a composer is about—all information about a work helps one to become aware—nevertheless, in the last analysis a composer's methods are important to him only. His achievement must be judged for what it is.

We may find fascinating, in a discussion of American Colonial furni-ture-making, the fact that wooden pegs or dowels were used instead of nails. It is also fascinating to realize that at the heart of a composition is a mathe-matical equation which gives it order. Nonetheless we do not need to know the composer's system of order. The order in one way or another, without our knowing it at all, will invade the finished product and will be perhaps a part of its perfection. But the "system of order" will not guarantee the worth of the work anymore than a system of rhymes, rhythms, or meter will guarantee the worth of a poem. This must come from the inspiration of the creator which includes, pervades, and most of all, goes beyond his system.

It has yet to be established whether happenings, Third Stream, chance music, predeterminism, electronic calculations, random treatments of mate-rial in either jazz or art music can be meaningful experiences as art. The art-ist in each of the arts will—and must—constantly search for new means of expression. It is not within the province of this book to discuss a matter that properly belongs to aesthetics. The aesthetics of music has been a vexing philosophical problem for some time, and we can do no more here than make a suggestion. This book has been about the appreciation of music, and about the understanding of music. You may already have found that more under-standing can sometimes result in *less* appreciation. Certain works that were once favorites have lost their luster. Like a first love, they are remembered with some nostalgia, but as understanding develops tastes broaden. Your taste must continue to broaden and you should not only go back further in time, and dig deeper into certain areas, but keep your eyes—and especially your ears—towards the future.

Whether a new work becomes a part of the literature of the twentieth century only the future can tell. Rebellion is not enough. The rebellion must be successful. Its success depends not only upon the overthrow of the old regime, which is certainly the first step, but most especially in putting in the place of the old authority a new authority. The standards of judging the worth of a work of art in any field have never been set to the satisfaction of the majority. These words of Aldous Huxley are to the point.

> The traditional distinction between the crafts and the fine arts is based among other things, on degrees of complexity. A good picture is a greater work of art than a good bowl or a good vase. Why? Because it unifies in one harmonious whole more, and more diverse, elements of human experience than are or can be unified and harmonized in the pot. Some of the non-representational pictures painted in the course of the last fifty years are very beautiful; but even the best of them are minor works, inasmuch as the number of elements of human experience which they combine and harmonize is pitifully small. In them we look in vain for that ordered profusion, that lavish and yet perfectly controlled display of intellectual wealth, which we discover in the best works of the "literary" painters of the past.*

Whether Huxley's view is valid is something that must be considered seriously. Whether you ultimately accept or reject his premise must be your decision. But let us make a final statement to the listener.

With regard to contemporary music, as with all contemporary art: (1) You must have an absolutely open mind. But at the same time: (2) You must not allow yourself to be "taken in." With reference to the first statement, do not judge new music by the values you have set on the old. And with reference to the second, do not conclude, as some extremists do, that because music is new and daring, it is good. One of the tests of a work is whether you can go back to it again and again. You do not have to be a musician or a critic or a philosopher to make this test. What you must do is listen.

---

* Aldous Huxley, *On Art and Artists* (New York: Harper & Row, Publishers, 1960), pp. 301 and 302.

PART THREE

SCORE PROFILES

THE EYE AND THE SCORE

The score

A COMPLETE SCORE MAY include any number of *staves,* depending on the number of instrumentalists or singers involved in its performance. On the next page are the first four measures of a complete score as the conductor sees it.

The score profile

A Score Profile extracts the primary melodic elements from the complete score and represents them on one staff, occasionally more. Its purpose is to allow the listener to see the direction and shape of the primary melodic elements while listening to the whole.

The beginning of a Score Profile is shown here:

Example 1

Example 2

Following a Score Profile is not equivalent to reading music. Being able to read music means that one can either hear, identify, or reproduce precise pitches in the correct time in a musical flow. This requires applied musical training in depth over a considerable span of time.

To follow a Score Profile, the listener is required only to keep his place in the music. Then, by observing certain characteristics on the printed page, he gains added insights into the music that are not always possible in ordinary passive listening. By looking as well as listening he focuses on the main points of interest in the music. He finds *melodic contour* and *climax,* changes of *instrumentation,* varying *rhythmic patterns, tempo* changes, special *articulations,* and *dynamic* levels.

Strictly speaking, learning to follow a score is not essential for gaining a love of music. But it does hasten music appreciation and most certainly deepens it. When the listener grafts a topographical knowledge of a score to the pure listening experience, he gains a new dimension of appreciation; the "how" of music composition. He learns how the piece of music is constructed; its *form,* its design. When he perceives that music has shape, direction, unity, contrast, and continuity, his appreciation of the composer's solutions to musical problems grows enormously.

USING THE SCORE PROFILE.   The Score Profile is a compression of the essentials of a full score. It is designed in such a way that you can easily and quickly locate any of its important elements.

The leading melodic line is most often found on a single staff. When two important melodic lines are sounding together, they will be seen either on the single staff or on two.

On the top of the staff will appear names of instruments and tempo indications only. Abbreviations side by side indicate that the melodic line is played by instruments in unison. Abbreviations in vertical position show the melodic line played by instruments in different octaves. Below the staff will appear all other performance indications, as well as analyses of the music by the authors. *Every* measure is numbered.

Occasionally, a Score Detail will be seen. These will always be located at the bottom right of the page. These show in greater depth important portions of the score.

To the left of the first page of the Score Profile will be found pertinent data on the music. There you will see a brief commentary on the music, a legend of instrumental abbreviations, and the type of formal structure used. *Before you listen* examine the Score Profile all the way through.

1. Circle all *instrumental abbreviations* and be certain that you know what they mean. (See legend on facing page of Score Profile.) This will give

you a schematic picture of the work's timbral structure; the way in which the combined instruments are made to produce varied orchestral colors.

2. Note all indications for *dynamics*. Know what they signify. *Translate.* Dynamics are used by the composer to intensify, to underline, to clarify. They, along with articulation signs, and tempo indications are the composer's chief way of telling the performer how his music is to be interpreted.

3. Translate the *tempo indication* at the beginning of the Score Profile. Scan the Score Profile for any possible change or changes of tempo.

4. Look at the *time signature*. The upper number will tell how many counts there are in each measure. Watch for possible changes of time signature later in the Score Profile.

5. Note the use of *clef signs*. The clef will often change, reflecting the actual register in which the leading line is heard.

6. Study the composition's structure as indicated by the formal analysis on the Score Profile, always above the staff.

Preliminary listening:

7. *Without looking at the Score Profile,* listen to the entire work several times through. Feel exactly what the tempo actually is. Count the number of beats in each measure. *Stay with the beat* even though there may be changes of tempo in performance.

Look While You Listen:

8. Now follow the Score Profile all the way through, again counting each beat out loud. *Each time you say "one," place your finger under the first note or rest after each bar line.* Repeat the above process several times, each time noticing more and more details on the Score Profile. After two or three times, you will not need to count out loud and can concentrate on important structural features of the composition, such as *points of arrival,* and *tension and relaxation.* Notice whether the notes go up or down. Climaxes usually occur high on the staff. Often you will be able to see a gradual rise of the melodic contour as the climax is approached. The more notes present in a measure the faster will each be played. Look for special articulations, especially those for legato and staccato.

Once you have thoroughly familiarized yourself with the composition in this way you will want to compare recordings or performances of the same work by different artists. Use the Score Profile to compare different interpretations. If the Score Profile represents a part of a larger work, listen to the other units in the overall structure. See and hear the music of the Score Profile in context. Move on to other Score Profiles; note how each composer manages his structural elements.

To help you get started with your first Score Profile, here are the first four measures, with essential "following techniques" indicated.

Example 3   *Symphony No. 1*, Op. 21, Movt. I, Beethoven

There are four beats in each measure.
In general, high-sounding instruments will be heard.

Beethoven, Symphony No. 1, Op. 21, Movt. I

Written in 1799–1800, this work suggests the style of Haydn and Mozart, but also shows much originality. The introduction, with the first cadence in the subdominant rather than in the tonic, is quite original, and surprised many when it was first heard.

Orchestra:

> 2 Flutes (FL)
> 2 Oboes (OB)
> 2 Clarinets (CL)
> 2 Bassoons (BN)
>
> 2 French Horns (HN)
> 2 Trumpets (TR)
>
> 2 Timpani (TIMP)
>
> Violins (VL 1, 2)
> Violas (VA)
> Violoncellos (VC)
> Contrabasses (CB)

Form: Sonata-allegro with introduction and coda.

Note: Other abbreviations or terms regularly used in the Score Profiles are:

WW	Woodwinds
BR	Brass
STR	Strings
TUTTI	All (or nearly all) instruments of the orchestra
TH	Theme

SCORE PROFILE

313

Listening notes

In overall structure and effect Beethoven's *Symphony No.* 1 harks back to the style of the high classical period, to the style established by Haydn and Mozart in their late symphonies. This can be verified by examining not only the typical classical orchestration—winds and percussion in pairs and full strings—but also in the character of the inner melodic materials. Themes such as those at *SP m. 13, m. 52,* and *m. 100* have a typical classical clarity and unambiguity. Each could have admirably served as the basis for a sonata-allegro structure within a Haydn or Mozart string quartet, sonata, or symphony.

Structural patterns in Beethoven's first movement also follows a traditional path. There is the formal slow introduction, followed by exposition–development–recapitulation with coda, so often seen in late eighteenth-century first movements. However, the work is filled with inimitable Beethoven touches, harbingers of what was to come in his later works in the form, and what was to follow throughout the romantic century. There is a characteristic Beethovenesque eruptive energy throughout. Even in the first measure, Beethoven presents the unexpected: there is a strong harmonic cadence in the key of F major, the key of the subdominant, not the tonic, C major. (See Example 2 for complete harmonic texture.) At *SP m. 77* one finds a dramatic sudden switch of register, dynamic, and key. The melody, up to the last moment carried forte in the whole orchestra in the luminous key of G major, suddenly drops to the cellos at the dynamic level of *pp* in the key of G minor. This is the essentially romantic Beethoven. And throughout the development section, *SP m. 110–177,* the thematic fragmentation, resulting in high compression of musical thought, gives tremendous expectation of climax and arrival. The climax of this development comes with the return of the complete theme 1 at *SP m. 178.* Compare the sound of the orchestra here with that of *SP m. 13.* The coda is brilliant, featuring towards its close (*SP m. 279–298*) the bright heraldic sound of trumpets and horns.

Schubert, *"Der Leiermann," from* Winterreise, *Opus 89, No. 24*

Winterreise is a cycle of 24 *lieder* written in the last part of the composer's life. It is his crowning achievement, occupying a similar place in the development of Schubert's style to that of the *Art of Fugue* in J. S. Bach's, or
the *"Choral" Symphony* in Beethoven's. The last song achieves universality
through simplicity and great pathos.

Voice part: baritone.

Form: modified strophic lied, A–A–Coda.

Poet: Wilhelm Müller.

SCORE PROFILE
PART A
Etwas langsam (rather slow)

Drü - ben hin - term Dor - fe

steht ein Lei - er - man und mit star - ren Fing - ern

dreht er, was er kann Bar - fuss auf dem Ei - se

wank ter hin und her, und sein klei - ner Tel - ler

bleibt ihm im - mer leer, und sein klei - ner Tel - ler

bleibt ihm im - mer leer.

PART A (repeated)

Kei - ner mag ihn hö - ren, kei - ner sieht ihn an,

und die Hun - de knur - ren um den al - ten Mann.

Und er lässt es ge - hen al - les, wie es will,

dreht, und sei - ne Lei - er steht ihm nim - mer still,

316

dreht, und sei - ne Lei - er steht ihm nim - mer still.

CODA

Wun - der - li - cher Al - te,

soll ich mit dir gehn? Willst zu mei - nen Lie - dern

dei - ne Lei - er drehn?

Listening notes

The open, bare interval of the fifth that forms the bass throughout the piano part suggests to the listener the drone of a small portable organ. Through its cold, almost hypnotic repetition, it perfectly portrays the numb, defeated state of mind of the spurned lover as he listens to the organ.

The vocal line itself is repetitious, and does not change in basic contour until *SP m. 55.* Listen for the last few notes sung where the line ends on an agonized cry of remorse.

Listen for the many dissonances occurring in the piano part, *SP m. 4, m. 5,* etc., reinforcing the feeling of utter anguish and desolation heard throughout.

FREE TRANSLATION

Up near the village stands an organ grinder cranking with cold fingers as well as he can. He is barefoot on the cold ground without a coin in his cup. No one notices the little old man but the snarling dogs. He doesn't complain but keeps turning and turning.
Oh wonderful old man, shall I join you? Will you play for my songs?

Schubert, "The Trout," Opus 32

This lied (1817) is a delightful example of Schubert's lyricism. The part for keyboard shows the composer's gift for musical imagery and is highly suggestive of the babbling of a stream.

Voice Part: high

Form: modified strophic lied, A–A–B–A′

Poet: Christian Schubart

Synopsis of poem: There darts a happy swift trout in a sparkling brook. A fisherman arrives. As long as the brook is clear the trout will not be caught. But the fisherman roils the brook and soon his fishing rod is bent. The trout is caught.

* Measure 6 is occasionally omitted in performance.
  The singer then begins in measure 5.

mun - tern Fisch-leins Ba - de im kla - ren Bäch-lein zu.

PART A

Ein

(repeated)

Fi - scher mit der Ru - te wohl an dem U - fer___ stand, und

sah's mit kal - tem Blu - te, wie sich das Fisch - lein wand, so

lang' dem Was - ser___ Hel - le, so dacht ich, nicht ge - bricht, so

fängt er die Fo - rel - le mit sei - ner An - gel nicht, so

PIANO

fängt er die Fo - rel - le mit sei - ner An - gel nicht.

Doch

PART B

end - lich ward dem Die - - be

320

die Zeit zu lang.

Er macht das Bäch - lein tü - ckisch

trü - be, und eh_____ ich es ge - dacht, so

zuck - te sei - ne Ru - te, das Fisch - lein, das

Fisch - lein zap - pelt' dran, und ich mit re - gem

Blu - te sah die Be - trog - ne an, und ich___ mit re - gem___

Blu - te sah die Be - trog - ne an.

SCHUBERT, "TROUT" QUINTET, MOVT. IV

325

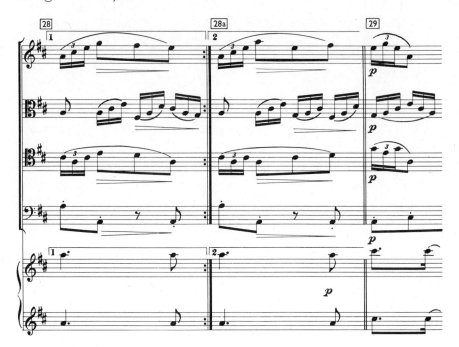

Listening notes

The song, "The Trout," is interesting on several counts. Not only does its use by the composer shed light on his predilection for song-like lyricism in general, but it is a masterpiece of its kind. The keyboard part, consisting of a fanciful broken-chord figure in the right hand with a springing bass in the left, is a charming bit of tone painting. To some it will represent the fisherman casting out his line; to others it may simply represent the rippling of the water as it tumbles over pebbles and stones. Whatever it is meant to represent, it serves as an admirable foil to the sprightly, folk-song-like melody in the voice. Note how the keyboard part at *SP m. 55* is tightened up considerably, reflecting the drama of the text in that stanza. It soon is changed entirely to exciting, repeated chords lasting until the climax of the song at *SP m. 66–67.*

The form of the song is simple but not uninteresting. It can be symbolized with the letters AAB. The first A spans *SP m. 1–26,* the second A, *SP m. 27–51,* and B, *SP m. 51–81.* The music for the first two stanzas is identical (AA) ; thus, that portion is strophic. The third stanza (B) is set to new music until **SP m. 68,** where a portion of the music of A comes back. Thus, the song is basically strophic with some modification.

The overall pattern then becomes:

	TEXT		MUSIC
First stanza:	(In einen Bächlein helle . . .)	A	
Second stanza:	(Ein Fischer . . .)	A	
Third stanza:	(Doch endlich . . .)	B with elements of A toward close.	

Movt. IV of the *"Trout" Quintet* consists of five variations on the melody of the song and a coda. The first three variations are ornamental, with the shape of the theme always evident. Variation IV, of the characteristic type, is highly suggestive of Beethoven's music at its stormiest. Note the change of mode from the bright, sunny D major of the theme to a fulminating, trenchant D minor in this variation.

Variation V is captivating because of its harmonic ambivalence, consisting of several shifts from major to minor and modulation to unrelated keys. The transition to the coda (Allegretto) is most effective.

A comparison between the song itself and the theme and variations derived from it is most rewarding. First, note the changes in the theme of the variations. Schubert scores it for the four strings, with the piano part conspicuously absent. He also tightens up its form considerably, probably feeling that a succinct, simple structural pattern would be best for the extremely figurative variations that follow. The theme becomes a classically proportioned binary form, **SP m. 1–8; B, SP m. 9–20.** Both sections are repeated.

Further note how the rhythmic pattern of the theme is transformed into a jogging pattern by the addition of dotted notes.

And although Schubert leaves out the keyboard figuration from the song here, he does not fail to introduce it later. The coda finds the theme tossed back and forth between violin and cello while in the background the original keyboard material is heard exactly as it was in the song, played mostly by the piano.

Verdi, "Addio del passato," Act III, La Traviata

Verdi's great drawing-room opera was written in 1853 and was first performed the same year in Venice. The libretto, by Piave, was based on a novel by Alexandre Dumas, son of the celebrated author of *The Count of Monte Cristo* and *The Three Musketeers*. Perhaps because the opera utilized a text reflecting the manners and morals of urban life (the original story was based on fact), it failed at first; only later did it become a standard fixture in the repertory.

Soloist: Lyric soprano (Violetto).

Form: Aria A–B–C with introductory recitative (recitative not included in Score Profile).

SCORE PROFILE

Listening notes

This, the first aria in Act III of Verdi's opera, *La Traviata* (*The Wayward One*), depicts Violetta's farewell to life and to her love for Alfredo. She has been abandoned by her lover and is now living with her maid, Annina, in a small flat in Paris. The doctor has just left, and Violetta knows without having been told that she is dying of consumption.

Note the poignant introduction in minor to the voice part, *SP m. 1*, as played by a solo oboe. Listen for the bittersweet quality it lends the music here and at *SP m. 19* and *SP m. 32*.

At *SP m. 12* Violetta sings of her love for Alfredo. Not only does the vocal line become more sensuous and passionate, but the voice is joined by the clarinet underlining the deep pathos of the situation.

Beginning with *SP m. 12,* when she asks God's forgiveness for her past life, the music changes to a major key and the melody soars to a touching climax.

Listen in this section for the throbbing, repeated chords in the orchestra.

FREE TRANSLATION

Farewell, happy dreams of yesteryear—already the color in my cheeks is fading. Oh how I miss Alfredo, the love and comfort he gave me! Oh God, forgive me! Grant that I may see you!

Haydn, Symphony No. 88, Movt. 4

This symphony, written around 1787, was one of the later symphonies. It was much admired by Beethoven, who especially was influenced by Movt. II, Largo. Movt. I is the "hunt" style because of the emphasis of theme 1 on the harmonic interval pattern, third-fifth-sixth.

Orchestra:

> 1 Flute (FL)
> 2 Oboes (OB)
> 2 Bassoons (BN)
>
> 2 French Horns (HN)
> 2 Trumpets (TR)
>
> Timpani (TIMP)
>
> Violins (VL 1, 2)
> Violas (VA)
> Violoncellos (VC)
> Contrabasses (CB)

Form: Rondo-Sonata.

SCORE PROFILE

REFRAIN

Allegro con spirito

Score Detail: m. 22–24

Note the strong half cadence, ending with a V chord. The key here is temporarily G minor, the tonic minor. The sudden darkening of the tonality adds immeasurable zest to the sunny character of the music.

(octave lower)

G minor: V6   I   +6   V

Melody also heard octave higher.

Modulation passage leading to _ _ _ _ _ _ _ _ _ _ _ _ _ _ _ _ _ _

from refrain

key of _ _ _ D major

D minor until measure 66

f D major

Timpani plays note "d" (V) in preparation for the tonic (I), soon to arrive.

Score Detail: m. 61–65
This progression is probably the most colorful in the movement. Note the many chromatics.

I   V

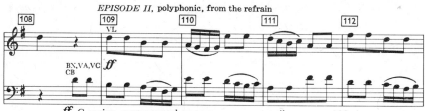

EPISODE II, polyphonic, from the refrain

ff G major, contrapuntal texture _ _ _ _ _ until measure 136.

B minor

VL 1

Unstable

key feeling

E minor

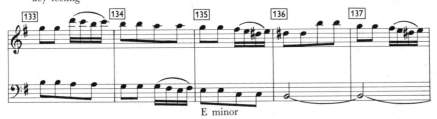

TUTTI

p

Note how the repeated "b", measures 140-143, is pivotal for modulation. It begins as the 5th of E minor and

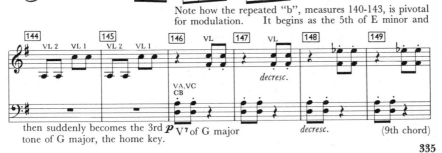

then suddenly becomes the 3rd p V^7 of G major *decresc.* (9th chord)
tone of G major, the home key.

335

FL
VL 1

add HN

pp

pp

pp

REFRAIN

FL

FL
VL 1
BN

p

BN

G major

p

B minor

TUTTI

OB, VL 1

f

p

FL, OB, VL 1

f

TUTTI

Cadence in D major

sf

FL
VL 1

p

G major

FL, OB, VL 1

f

CODA, from Ep. I

VL

Half cadence *f*

336

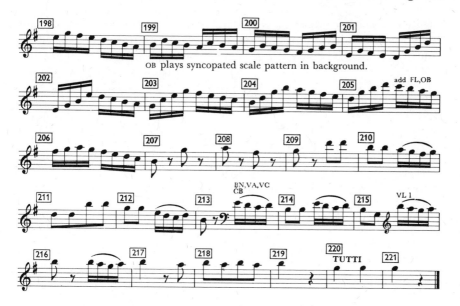

OB plays syncopated scale pattern in background.

Listening notes

Haydn's music is highly representative of traditional harmony. His life (1732–1809) spans the salient years of the classical period. The profile given here is particularly rewarding for assimilating the essential characteristics of chord structure, progression, and modulation.

First, to verify visually how important the triad is in all music displaying tonality, glance at the many outlined triads within the melody itself. Here are a few: *SP m. 4,* G major triad, starting on third of chord; *SP m. 16,* D major triad, starting on fifth of chord; *SP m. 92–93,* E minor triad starting on fifth of chord.

Also note the use of extended chords beginning at *SP m. 146.* The minor ninth chord at *SP m. 148* is typical of Haydn and also of Beethoven who was to use it later as a powerful agent for musical drama. (See the Score Profile on p. 368, *SP m. 610.*)

The keys used in the scheme of modulation are expected and fairly routine. They are:

1. G major (tonic) several times
2. D major (dominant)
3. B minor
4. E minor

Haydn also touches briefly on G minor, the tonic minor, *SP m. 20–23,* and D minor, the dominant minor, *SP m. 57–65.* These last provide a darkening element, setting off the sunny, zesty music to fine advantage.

Tchaikovsky, Symphony No. 6, Op. 74, Movt. II

Written and first performed in 1893, this is Tchaikovsky's last complete symphony. It is known by the name "Pathétique," although the title was not originated by the composer. It stands, with Tchaikovsky's *Fourth* and *Fifth Symphonies,* as among the most popular of orchestral works. The first performance in St. Petersburg was conducted by the composer.

Orchestra:

3 Flutes (FL)
   including Piccolo (PIC)
2 Oboes (OB)
2 Clarinets (CL)
2 Bassoons (BN)

4 French Horns (HN)
2 Trumpets (TR)
3 Trombones (TB)
1 Tuba (TU)

3 Timpani (TIMP)

Violins (VL 1, 2)
Violas (VA)
Violoncellos (VC)
Contrabasses (CB)

Form: Ternary, with coda.

SCORE PROFILE
PART A

Th. 1
Listen to effect of pizzicato strings against melody in woodwinds.
WW

Th. 1

arco

FL. OB
CL. BN

TR
TB

VL
VA *f* The distinctive triplet is

TB
TU

missing in the brass version of the theme.

The triplet returns

PART B
Th. 2, B minor
TRIO FL. VL
VC

p
con dolcezza e flebile

Pedal point continues in lower
instruments to measure [95]

(p)

VL
VA

sf *p*

341

Pedal point concludes

Pedal point resumes on D and continues to the end of the movement.

Listening notes

The accents in $\frac{5}{4}$ are usually grouped in either of two ways: 3 + 2, or 2 + 3. The two strong accents in each measure would be shown then as

$$| \, | \, | \, | \, | \quad \text{or} \quad | \, | \, | \, | \, |$$
$$(12312) \quad (12123)$$

The accent is cleverly disguised in **SP m. 1** and in alternate measures thereafter by the placement of a triplet exactly in the middle of the measure. If this figure were continued, the effect would be that of five beats without a duple pulsation, but in **SP m. 2** and in later measures the accent of $| \, | \, | \, | \, |$ is clearly established.

Note how the uneven duple rhythm gives an interesting lilt to the movement. This "con grazia" rhythmic pulse and the key of D major provide excellent contrast to the first movement in B minor.

Note the extra sparkle given to the texture by the violins and violas in **SP m. 33,** playing pizzicato in octaves above the theme now being played by all of the woodwinds.

In **SP m. 49** the theme is "straightened out" by the trumpets and trombones in ascending octaves as the upper strings move into a countermelody.

But the strings take over again in *SP m. 53* to end this section with the original distinctive figure.

The Trio at *SP m. 57* abandons the triplet and assumes a more thoughtful mien. This is enhanced by the pressing repeated notes. The pressing is indicated by the short dashes over the notes and creates a more intense sound. The quick crescendo-diminuendo in each measure adds to the intensity.

The Trio section from *SP m. 57* through *SP m. 95* is characterized by a pedal point of repeated *D*'s in the basses. See if you can hear the effect this gives, and the change when the pedal point discontinues at the return of the first theme in *SP m. 96*. The pedal point is resumed at the coda at *SP m. 152* and continues to the end of the movement.

Brahms, Academic Festival Overture, Op. 80

"Will you write us a Doctoral Symphony for Breslau? We expect a Festal Ode at the very least."

This question was contained in the letter of congratulations Brahms received from Breslau University several days after it had conferred upon him a doctoral degree. In the following year, 1880, he informed the University that he had completed the *Academic Festival Overture*. Brahms spoke of the *Overture* as a medley of student songs.

Orchestra:

1 Piccolo (PIC)
2 Flutes (FL)
2 Oboes (OB)
2 Clarinets (CL)
2 Bassoons (BN)
1 Contrabassoon (CBN)

4 French Horns (HN)
3 Trumpets (TP)
3 Trombones (TB)
1 Tuba (TU)

3 Timpani (TIMP)
1 Bass Drum (BD)
1 Cymbal (CYM)
1 Triangle (TRI)

Violins (VL 1, 2)
Violas (VA)
Violoncellos (VC)
Contrabasses (CB)

Form: Modified Sonata-Allegro, with Coda.

SCORE PROFILE

Score Detail: m. 17–18

While the flutes are holding a long, soft A♭, the clarinets are articulating a broken chord. Also note the arched figure of the cellos.

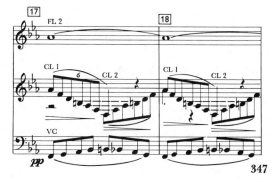

347

Score Detail: m. 63–70

The brass begins quietly, trumpets only. The other brass are gradually added —note the horn and trombone entrances. By m. 72 all the brass are playing and the flutes and oboes as well become part of the wind sound.

Score Detail: m. 174–178

While the bassoons take the original folk song, the violins play its free inversion above.

350

352

353

Listening notes

Although Brahms spoke of the *Academic Festival Overture* as a medley of tunes, it is less than a medley. It is also more than a medley—much more. It is less than a medley because it does not straightforwardly present a collection of songs or tunes with slight transitional or modulatory material between them. It is more than a medley because Brahms has incorporated the student songs into a cohesive whole. Certain thematic *ideas* of the songs are subject to development and mixture, and become integrated within the total concept.

The first figure of the opening theme, in C minor, **SP m. 1–13,** is reminiscent of a portion of the "Rakoczy March" of Berlioz in its rhythmic pattern,

Example 1 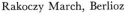 Rakoczy March, Berlioz

and it establishes the moderate tempo associated with ceremonial music. But as well, its vigorous rhythm suggests the joy of the festive day. This is superseded by the theme in C major, beginning at **SP m. 64,** which is based on the Thuringian folk song (a nod to a German students' association of the time) "Wir hatten gebauet."

Example 2 Wir Hatten Gebauet

Wir hat - ten ge - bau - et ein statt - lich - es Haus,

The basis of the theme beginning in **SP m. 129** is "Der Landesvater."

Example 3 Der Landesvater

Hört, ich sing das Lied der Lie - der hört es, mei - ne

deut- schen Brü - der, hall es, hall es wie - der fro - her Chor!

The brisk theme in G major that is begun by the bassoons at **SP *m. 157*** may be compared to the original version of the "Fuchslied."

Example 4   Fuchslied

Brahms returns to the opening key, C minor, at **SP *m. 241,*** but reverses his thematic materials in a quasi-recapitulation. The key changes to C at **SP *m. 290*** and fragments of the three songs are incorporated into the texture, with the final reference to the "Fuchslied" bringing us directly to the "Gaudeamus Igitur,"

Example 5   Gaudeamus Igitur

which may be termed a coda, but is more in the manner of a concluding symbolic statement, an apotheosis of the freedom of youth.

Brahms did not respond to the request for a Doctoral Symphony with a pompous, inflated work that might have impressed the faculty and the officials at Breslau, but chose instead to write what he termed a medley in the manner of von Suppé. The spirit of freedom—especially from the students' point of view—evidently appealed to Brahms. Note the text of "Gaudeamus Igitur."

> Let us now in youth rejoice,
> None can justly blame us;
> For when golden youth has fled,
> And in age our joys are dead,
> Then the dust doth claim us.

Beethoven, Leonore Overture No. 3, *Op. 72a*

Written in 1806, this overture is one of four written by the composer for his only opera, *Fidelio*. It was first used with the opera in March, 1806. It now is played primarily as a concert overture, the overture called *Fidelio*, Op. 72b, prefacing modern performances of the opera.

Orchestra:

2 Flutes (FL)
2 Oboes (OB)
2 Clarinets (CL)
2 Bassoons (BN)

4 Horns (HN)
2 Trumpets (TR)
3 Trombones (TB)

2 Timpani

Violins (VL 1, 2)
Violas (VA)
Violoncellos (VC)
Contrabasses (CB)

Form: Sonata-allegro, with introduction and coda.

SCORE PROFILE

Score Detail: m. 27

While the violins are sweeping up the scale and then down, the rest of the orchestra is holding an A♭ major chord with flutes on top and the contrabass anchoring the whole on the bottom.

357

EXPOSITION
Allegro Th. 1 – C major

Rhythmic background, first
in CB, then in the winds.

cresc. poco a poco

TUTTI

sempre ff

WW

WW

VL
VA

Rhythmic pattern heard in
woodwinds in background

358

Rhythmic pattern in
trumpets and timpani

DEVELOPMENT

from m. 32

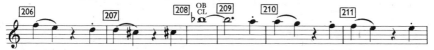

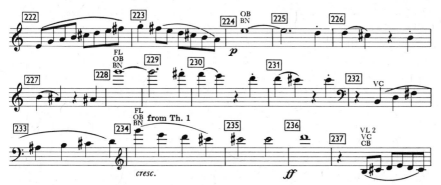

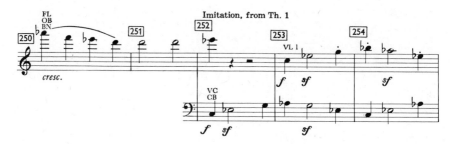

Imitation, from Th. 1

Rhythmic pattern in TR, HN

add WW

New theme
(tempo rubato)
TR(off stage)

Score Detail: m. 278–280

Background figures in the strings under the theme in the woodwinds.

363

cresc. poco a poco
Listen for strong
syncopations in background.

RECAPITULATION
Th. 1 — C major
TUTTI

ff

sempre ff

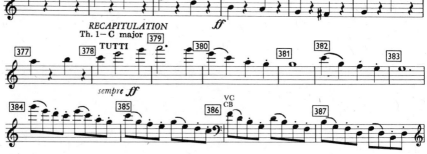

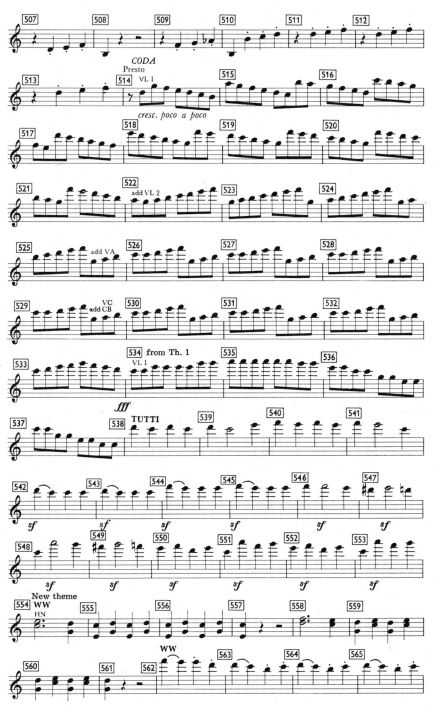

Score Detail: m. 606–613

Note the powerful sequence of chords leading to the searing minor 9th chord at m. 610. Note the dynamic indicated *fff* — extremely loud.

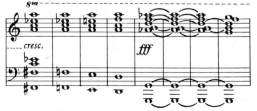

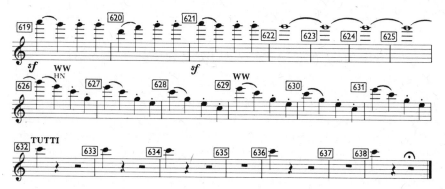

Listening notes

Rhythmically, this composition is one of the most exciting Beethoven ever wrote. Syncopation is very prominent.

Note how the syncopated rhythmic pattern,

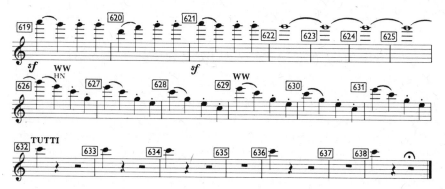

underlying the main theme of the allegro, *SP m. 37,* crops up in so many places: *SP m. 106*—where a dynamic accent, sfp, underscores the syncopation, *SP m. 254*—in the winds, as background to the theme in the strings, *SP m. 546*—where the rhythmic pattern is completely isolated from the original melody, *SP m. 614*—where a dynamic accent is placed on a different note of the rhythmic pattern than before,

Other exciting syncopated passages can be heard beginning at measures 169, 360, 452, and 570.

Another important rhythmic pattern, this time of a nonsyncopated nature, occurs in the trumpet solo section beginning at *SP m. 278.* The pattern

is used as background in the strings and bassoons to the theme in the winds. It is interesting to note both the derivation and later usage of this rhythmic pattern. It is taken from the first few notes of the trumpet call itself, *SP m. 272.*

Later it re-enters in the timpani, *SP m. 481,* as quiet background for the section leading to the rushing scales introducing the final Presto, *SP m. 514.*

Requiem Mass K. 626, "Kyrie" from Section I, Mozart

The Requiem was commissioned anonymously by Count Walsegg to be presented as his own composition in memory of his wife. It was Mozart's last work, written in Vienna in December, 1791. Although he did not live to complete it, it is a part of his crowning achievement. The entire Section I was Mozart's, and Süssmayer, a disciple of Mozart, who completed the work after Mozart's death, saw fit to conclude the Requiem in the hand of Mozart rather than his own. So the Kyrie fugue may be heard again as the concluding section of the "Agnus Dei."

Orchestra:

2 Basset Horns
2 Bassoons (BN)
2 Trumpets (TR)
3 Trombones (TB)

2 Timpani (TIMP)

Violins (VL 1, 2)
Violas (VA)
Violoncellos (VC)
Contrabasses (CB)

Organ

Voices:

Soprano
Alto
Tenor
Bass

Process: Fugue.

SCORE PROFILE
Fugue Exposition

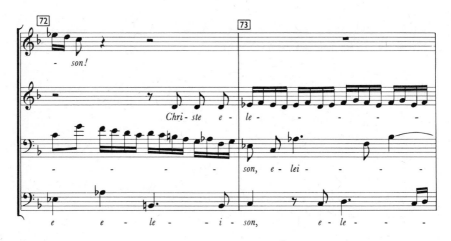

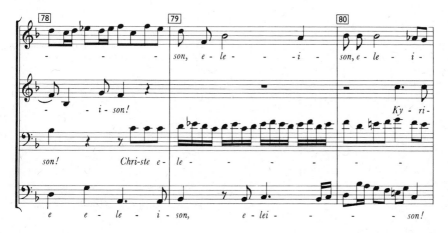

376

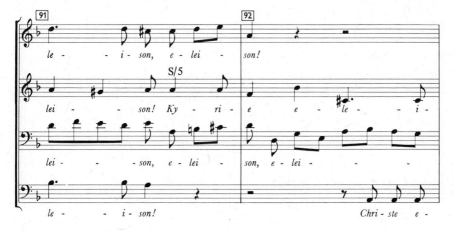

378

Listening notes

The opening measures of the *Requiem,* in fugato style, prepare the way for the "Kyrie" fugue, which forms the second part of Section 1, *SP m. 49.* In our previous analysis seen directly on the Score Profile, the subject is symbolized by both a letter and number. Thus at *SP m. 49,* S/5 stands for the subject beginning on the 5th scale step within the key of D minor. Follow the Score Profile, first watching for and listening to the voice carrying the subject. The subject, as is expected, is heard mostly in the minor key. The use of the stark interval of the diminished seventh, *SP m. 53,* from 2nd note to 3rd note, heightens its dramatic force. But at *SP m. 64, SP m. 75* and *SP m. 77* it is heard in the major, effecting strong contrast. The last entrance of the subject is heard in the tonic at *SP m. 91.* The fugue closes with a strong authentic cadence in a powerful homophonic texture, *SP m. 98–100.* The final chord, without third, suggests earlier polyphonic sacred choral music where the harmonic intervals of the octave, fifth, and fourth were prominent.

Debussy, Prélude à "L'Après-midi d'un Faune"

This *Prélude* was to have been the first of three sections of a work originally titled, *Prélude, Interlude, et Paraphrase Finale pour "L'Après-midi d'un Faune,"* but Debussy abandoned the second and third sections, which had not gone beyond some initial sketches. The entire work had been planned for a concert early in 1894, but Debussy, extremely meticulous, withdrew it for revision. Finally, in December of that year, the *Prélude* was performed. Its success was immediate.

Orchestra:

> 3 Flutes (FL)
> 2 Oboes (OB)
> 1 English Horn (EHN)
> 2 Clarinets (CL)
> 2 Bassoons (BN)
>
> 4 French Horns (HN)
>
> 2 Antique Cymbals
> 2 Harps (HARP)
>
> Violins (VL 1, 2)
> Violas (VA)
> Violoncellos (VC)
> Contrabasses (CB)

Form: Free, suggestive of ternary. A–B–A'–Coda

SCORE PROFILE

PART A

Très modéré

Th. 1

Score Detail: m. 1–2

Outlining the tritone C♯–G suggests vagueness and instability. In the older, or traditional, tonal sense, it could suggest a resolution to D. In m. 3, however, Debussy makes the first reference to E major.

Score Detail: m. 11

The first note of the melody is the seventh degree of the D major scale. Note the effect of different harmonizations used later in the composition.

Score Detail: m. 26

A fresh harmonization of the flute melody. Listen for the harps in the background.

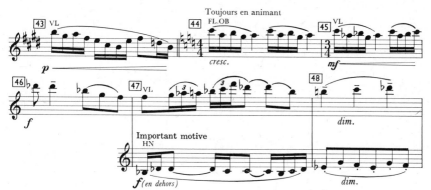

Score Detail: m. 55–56

Note the melody in the woodwinds, pentatonic in color, set against a tritonic bass line.

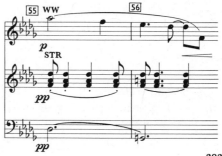

Score Detail: m. 62–63

In the woodwind melody at m. 62, note the use of the whole-tone scale.

Listening notes

The tonal center of *L'Après-midi* is E major, but this is not apparent in the opening two measures of the work. Note that the unaccompanied flute solo outlines an interval, G–C-sharp, that does not exist in the scale of E major. Also, it is the tritone, the interval of instability. Whatever suggestions of resolution there may be in this interval are not carried out, and in *SP m. 3* the G-natural is cancelled and the tonic chord of E major is stated. Not until *SP m. 13*, however, does Debussy reinforce this harmonically.

One of the many striking features of this original work is the suggestion of no less than four scales: the diatonic, pentatonic, whole-tone, and chromatic.

Diatonic usage: *SP m. 67–73*
Pentatonic usage: *Sp m. 37–38, 55–57, 63–65*
Whole-tone usage: *SP m. 32–33, 35–36*
Chromatic usage: *SP m. 1–2, 11–12*

What results is a broadening of color which adds to the already ubiquitous, diffuse cast of the work as a whole. And of course one does not speak of the Debussy orchestra without taking into account the delicate yet ravishing timbral brush strokes. Note how the solo entrance of the flute at *SP m. 1*, without accompaniment of any kind, lends immediate mystery and magic to the piece. Then, at *SP m. 4*, where the horn and harp join in, the sudden unfolding of timbral sonority is as warm and reassuring as the sun filtering through the foliage of a verdant forest. Each time theme 1 re-enters Debussy adds a new touch of instrumental color.

Thus does Debussy, through musical means, evoke the dreamlike atmosphere of Mallarmé's poem, which depicts the "sensuous, passionate" faun, half-man and half-animal with cloven hoof.

L'APRÈS–MIDI D'UN FAUNE
Eclogue

LE FAUNE

Ces nymphes, je les veux perpétuer.

                         Si clair,
Leur incarnat léger, qu'il voltige dans l'air
Assoupi de sommeiles touffus.

                   Aimai-je un rêve? . . .
"Que je coupais ici les creux roseaux domptés
"Par le talent; quand, sur l'or glauqe de lointaines
"Verdures dédiant leur vigne à des fontaines,
"Ondoie une blancheur animale au repos:
"Et qu'au prélude lent où naissent les pipeaux
"Ce vol de cygnes, non! de naiades se sauve
"Ou plonge . . . ."

                             —Mallarmé

Free Synopsis:

THE FAUN

Nymphs, do not go, you who float in air
drowsy with deep sleep—has this been a dream?

Upon a cut-reed I bestow the gift of sound;
in the green and gold of the distant fountains
a white flesh rests. The swans—no! naiads—
run or plunge at the sound of my air.

Appendices

APPENDIX I

A short guide to the fundamentals of music

PITCH. **Pitch** is the term used to designate the "highness" or "lowness" of a particular sound. Technically, pitch refers to the *number of vibrations per second* of a particular musical tone. The more vibrations per second, the higher pitched is the tone; the fewer vibrations, the lower pitched. The number of vibrations per second is more compactly spoken of as the *frequency*. For example, the frequency of "orchestra *A*" (the pitch to which an orchestra tunes) is 440, that is, 440 vibrations per second. This pitch is commonly referred to as *"A 440."*

Example 1   Octave Reference Chart

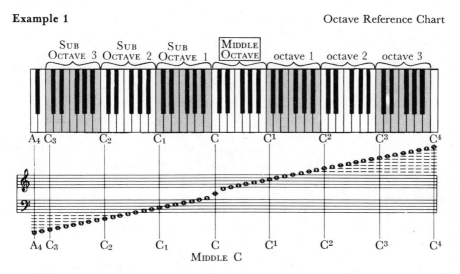

The term **octave**, abbreviated **8ve**, refers to a span of eight notes. Thus, C^2 is spoken of as being an octave higher in pitch than C^1.

THE STAFF. The musical graph in use today consists of five lines and the adjacent spaces. This is known as the *staff*. A staff may be used for high, middle, or low register voices or instruments.

In the evolution of notation, an 11-line staff evolved for keyboard instruments, because of their great range. Visual orientation to 11 lines and their spaces was difficult, however, and the necessity for something simpler resulted in the system that is in use today. It is a modification of the 11-line system. The middle line of the 11 is left out except when the note on that

391

line is needed, and then only a short segment of the line is used; enough on which to write the note. This short line is called a *leger line.* Leger lines and their adjacent spaces are used above or below the staff.

Example 2

G clef locates G above MIDDLE C → TREBLE STAFF

MIDDLE C

F clef locates F below MIDDLE C → BASS STAFF

The **G clef** and the **F clef** shown in their proper positions on the Great Staff are stylized versions of the actual letters G and F. These are the two clefs most commonly in use today, but there is a third clef that is used in orchestral scores in writing for instruments in the middle register. This is the **C clef,** and locates **middle C.** It is used with two different five-line staves, the alto staff and the tenor staff.

Example 3

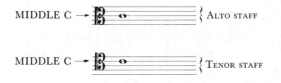

MIDDLE C → ALTO STAFF

MIDDLE C → TENOR STAFF

SHARPS, FLATS, NATURALS. The Octave REFERENCE CHART shows that the lines and spaces of the staff coincide with the white notes of the keyboard. The distance between any two adjacent notes on the keyboard, *considering both black and white notes,* is a **half-step** (also called **semitone**). In Example 4 the half-steps are shown by the arrows. The distance between two adjacent white notes is a **whole step** (also called a **whole tone),** with the exception of *E* to *F* and *B* to *C*.

Example 4

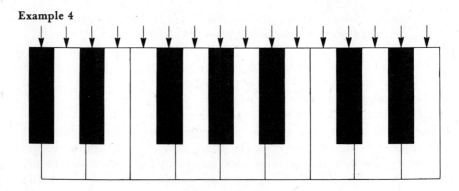

When it is desired to raise the pitch of a tone by a semitone, a *sharp* (♯) is placed in front of the note.

Example 5

When it is desired to lower the pitch of a tone by a semitone, a *flat* (♭) is placed in front of the note.

Example 6

ENHARMONICS. When one pitch has two designations, such as *C-sharp* and *D-flat,* either of these designations is the **enharmonic** of the other. Composers use enharmonics to facilitate notation during modulation, or to simplify certain key signatures.

At certain times in the course of a composition, it is necessary to raise by a semitone the pitch of a tone that is already sharped. For this, the **double-sharp** (𝄪) is used.

Example 7

F double-sharp is the enharmonic of *G*. To lower a note that is already flatted, the **double-flat** (♭♭) is used.

Example 8

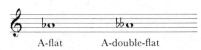

The natural (♮) cancels the effect of any sharp or flat, including double-sharps and double-flats, returning the note to its pitch unsharped or unflatted.

Duration

Example 9

Example 10

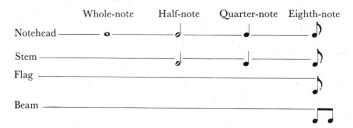

THE TIE AND THE DOT.   The binary system of the division of note values does not contain within itself any way to denote a duration three quarters of the given value of a particular note. If three quarters of the length of a whole-note is desired, this problem in notation is solved by joining a half-note and a quarter-note by means of a *tie.*

Example 11

In the evolving "shorthand" of notation, the tied quarter ultimately became a *dot.*

Example 12

The dot in this case equals a quarter-note, which is half the value of the half-note preceding. In certain English and other editions of music, this shorthand dot representing the tied quarter is still written with the spacing shown in Example 12, but modern usage has moved the dot closer to the note it follows, so that rather than Example 13 we have Example 14. From this evolved the general rule that *the dot placed after any note or rest adds to it half its value*. Thus; see Example 15.

Example 13

Example 14

Example 15

NOTES   RESTS

TRIPLETS AND DUPLETS.   Where there are duple and triple divisions within main accents, this is taken care of by a special notation. When three notes are wanted in place of two, a *triplet* is written and bracketed as shown below.

Example 16

TIME SIGNATURE.   At the beginning of each piece of music, a *time signature* is placed on the staff (directly after the key signature) to show the method of measuring that particular piece of music.

Vertical *bars* (or *bar-lines*) placed on the staff throughout the piece divide the music into *measures*. The lower number of the time signature designates what note value is to be the measuring unit; the upper number designates how many of these will be in each measure. Thus, the time signature **²⁄₄** ("two-four") specifies that a quarter (note or rest) is the measuring unit, and that there are two in each measure. No bar-line is necessary at the beginning.

Example 17

Any combination of note values or rests that equal two quarter-notes may, of course, appear in each measure.

Example 18

Intervals

An *interval* is the distance between two tones. The distance between two tones sounded together is referred to as a *harmonic interval.* When the two tones are sounded in succession, the distance is referred to as a *melodic interval.*

Example 19

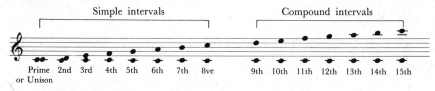

Transposition is the exact reproduction (in writing or in sound) of any pattern of tones at a different pitch level.

DIATONIC AND CHROMATIC INTERVALS. The Greek word *diatonic* means *across the tones,* and refers in practical usage to the letters of the tones as they stand in succession, omitting none and repeating none. The white-note pattern *C D E F G A B C* is a diatonic pattern. Thus, a diatonic semitone consists of an interval that uses two letters that stand in succession. *E* to *F* and *B* to *C* are diatonic and semitones as well as minor seconds. Further, *C* to *D-flat* and *F-sharp* to *G* are diatonic semitones. *C* to *C-sharp,* however, is a *chromatic* semitone. *Chroma,* also from the Greek, means *color;* and so the term *chromatic* has been applied to the alteration of a tone by raising or lowering it with the application of an **accidental.**

An accidental is a sharp, flat, or natural that alters the pitch of a tone standing in a diatonic succession.

INTERVAL INVERSION.   The **inversion** of an interval takes place when the positions of the two notes on the staff are reversed so that the lower note becomes the upper. This is accomplished by raising the lower note, or lowering the upper note, the distance of an octave. Thus, the interval $\frac{C}{F}$ becomes $\frac{F}{C}$.

Example 20

CONSONANCE AND DISSONANCE.   Consonance and dissonance help create the effects of tension and release in a composition.

> **consonance.** A combination of tones regarded as stable and not requiring resolution.

> **dissonance.** A combination of tones creating tension and requiring resolution.

Scales

A *scale* is a theoretical abstraction of the tones used in a piece of music. Named from the Italian word *scala,* meaning ladder, it is an arranged series of notes. The normal scale consists of the diatonic tones used in a particular **mode.**

MODES.   Music during the Middle Ages and the Renaissance, until about 1600, was written in what are called the **modes.** Each of these modes may be represented by a **diatonic scale** that uses only the white notes of the piano keyboard, and is represented by the lines and spaces of the staff.

There were originally four authentic modes—the Dorian, Phrygian, Lydian, and Mixolydian—to which were added the Aeolian, Locrian, and Ionian. It can be seen in the next example that the distinguishing feature of each mode depends upon the particular arrangement of the whole-steps and half-steps.

Example 21

AUTHENTIC MODE	SCALE STEPS	HALF STEPS OCCUR

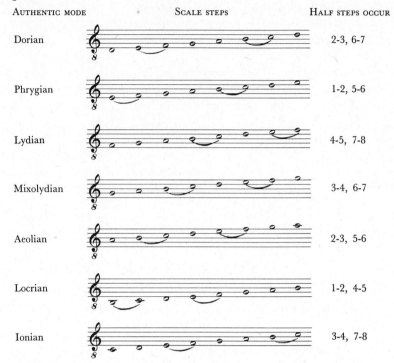

Dorian	2-3, 6-7
Phrygian	1-2, 5-6
Lydian	4-5, 7-8
Mixolydian	3-4, 6-7
Aeolian	2-3, 5-6
Locrian	1-2, 4-5
Ionian	3-4, 7-8

MAJOR AND MINOR MODES. With the constant changing of pitches by the application of accidentals and the "growing art" of harmony, the Ionian and Aeolian modes emerged to become the two modes that since have been the basis of harmony of Western music until the twentieth century, when their hegemony began to diminish.

With only two modes in common usage, the old mode-distinguishing names gradually went out of general use, and the two modes were referred to by the specific difference in pitch of the third scale-step as related to the tonic. Thus, the Ionian mode became the *major mode,* and the Aeolian mode became the *minor mode.*

The *key signatures* of all the major keys and their relative minor keys may be illustrated in the Circle of Fifths, as shown on page 400.

Major Scales, Keys with Sharps

KEY OF		KEY SIGNATURE SPECIFIED AS
C	C D E F G A B C	—
G	G A B C D E F♯ G	1 sharp
D	D E F♯ G A B C♯ D	2 sharps
A	A B C♯ D E F♯ G♯ A	3 sharps
E	E F♯ G♯ A B C♯ D♯ E	4 sharps
B	B C♯ D♯ E F♯ G♯ A♯ B	5 sharps
F♯	F♯ G♯ A♯ B C♯ D♯ E♯ F♯	6 sharps
C♯	C♯ D♯ E♯ F♯ G♯ A♯ B♯ C♯	7 sharps

Major Scales, Keys with Flats

KEY OF		KEY SIGNATURE SPECIFIED AS
C	C D E F G A B C	—
F	F G A B♭ C D E F	1 flat
B♭	B♭ C D E♭ F G A B♭	2 flats
E♭	E♭ F G A♭ B♭ C D E♭	3 flats
A♭	A♭ B♭ C D♭ E♭ F G A♭	4 flats
D♭	D♭ E♭ F G♭ A♭ B♭ C D♭	5 flats
G♭	G♭ A♭ B♭ C♭ D♭ E♭ F G♭	6 flats
C♭	C♭ D♭ E♭ F♭ G♭ A♭ B♭ C♭	7 flats

Example 22

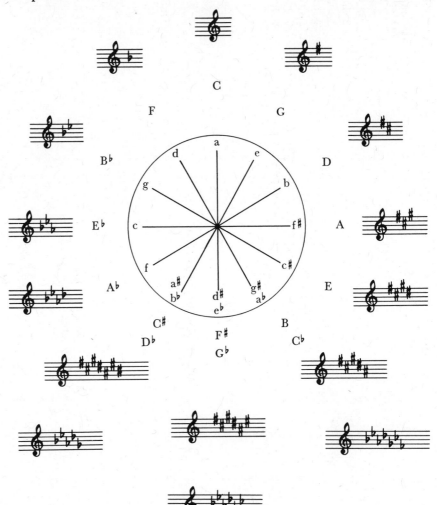

The major keys and their relative minors are paired around the circle, the major keys outside and the minor keys inside. The important enharmonic keys are shown. Clockwise motion represents key relations in ascending perfect fifths; counterclockwise, in descending perfect fifths. Proceeding around the circle of fifths clockwise from C shows the sharp keys in succession, with each succeeding key note a perfect fifth higher than the preceding one. Proceeding from C counterclockwise shows the flat keys in succession, with each key note a perfect fifth lower than the preceding one.

Tonality

Tonality embraces the concept of key or mode, but it is not synonymous with either. It is a larger concept. It is perhaps best to think of tonality as a *process,* that, with one single tone as the central tone, constantly departs from it in exploration of other tones and their relationship to it and ultimately returns to it.

The essence of tonality in the *Classical period* is that the key center may shift while the basic tonal center remains unchanged. In other words, there may be modulation to closely related or distantly related keys, *but the exploration of these keys is always in relation to the basic tonal center,* which ultimately returns. This is true not only throughout a symphonic movement, but throughout the entire symphony. There is always the connecting thread between even the most distant key center and the basic tonal center. The new key center amounts to an exploration or a side excursion. The concept of tonality embraces the idea that there will be a return to the basic tonal center.

A diagram of the first movement of Mozart's *Symphony No. 41* will illustrate this (Example 23).

Note that the basic key center is adhered to for slightly more than half of the first section, and then that the dominant becomes the key center throughout most of the second and third sections until the repeat sign, which is the end of the exposition. The strong relationship of the dominant to the tonic is illustrated by the fact that upon repetition of the exposition no modulation of any kind is needed. The dominant just "falls into" the tonic.

In the recapitulation, there is a brief excursion into the subdominant. And then back onto the main road, the basic tonality, until the end of the movement. Inspection or analysis of the other movements should only make it clearer that Mozart's *Symphony No. 41 in C Major* is not in the key of C major, but in the "tonality of C major." That is to say, *C* as the central tone and major as the mode provide the tonal center for the entire work. Note that Sir Donald Francis Tovey speaks of Schubert's *String Quartet in C Major* as "one of the greatest of all essays in tonality." Whatever the analogy—an essay, a journey, a quest—the point is that tonality is at the core of an experience that lasts a certain length of time.

Example 23

Symphony No. 41 ("Jupiter"), K. 551, Movt. I, Mozart

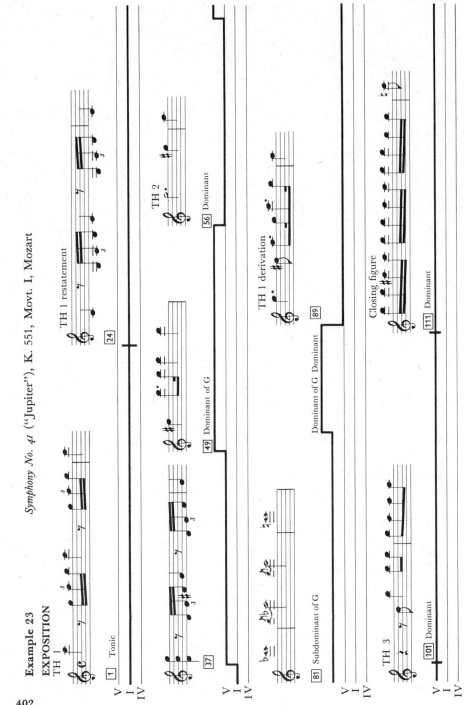

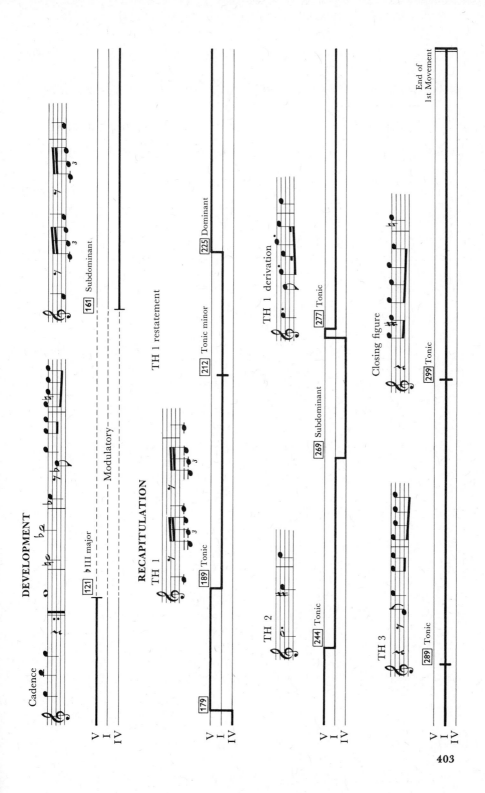

DEVELOPMENT

Cadence

121 ♭III major

Modulatory-

161 Subdominant.

V
I
IV

RECAPITULATION

TH 1

189 Tonic

TH 1 restatement

212 Tonic minor

225 Dominant

179

V
I
IV

TH 2

244 Tonic

269 Subdominant

277 Tonic

TH 1 derivation

V
I
IV

TH 3

289 Tonic

Closing figure

299 Tonic

End of
1st Movement

V
I
IV

403

TYPE OF METER	BEATS PER MEASURE	TIME SIGNATURES
Simple { duple	2	$\frac{2}{1}\ \frac{2}{2}\ \frac{2}{4}\ \frac{2}{8}\ \frac{2}{16}\ \frac{2}{32}$
Simple { triple	3	$\frac{3}{1}\ \frac{3}{2}\ \frac{3}{4}\ \frac{3}{8}\ \frac{3}{16}\ \frac{3}{32}$
*Common**	4	$\frac{4}{4}$ also: **C**
Compound†	6 or 2	$\frac{6}{1}\ \frac{6}{2}\ \frac{6}{4}\ \frac{6}{8}\ \frac{6}{16}\ \frac{6}{32}$
	9 or 3	$\frac{9}{1}\ \frac{9}{2}\ \frac{9}{4}\ \frac{9}{8}\ \frac{9}{16}\ \frac{9}{32}$
	12 or 4	$\frac{12}{1}\ \frac{12}{2}\ \frac{12}{4}\ \frac{12}{8}\ \frac{12}{16}\ \frac{12}{32}$
*Asymmetrical***	5 or combinations of 2's and 3's	$\frac{5}{1}\ \frac{5}{2}\ \frac{5}{4}\ \frac{5}{8}\ \frac{5}{16}\ \frac{5}{32}$
	7 or combinations of 3's and 4's	$\frac{7}{1}\ \frac{7}{2}\ \frac{7}{4}\ \frac{7}{8}\ \frac{7}{16}\ \frac{7}{32}$
Mixed	Alternating combinations usually of 2's, 3's or 4's	$\frac{3}{4} + \frac{2}{4}$ (typical)
Polymeter	Any number of beats, but heard simultaneously with different beat groups	$\frac{6}{8}$ (typical) $\frac{3}{4}$
Changing	According to the measure of the moment	Any combination at any time

*Meters in 8 are usually multiples of common meter.
†Compound meters can have higher beat numbers: 15, 18, etc.
**1) Higher beat numbers are possible: 10, 11, 13, etc.
   2) Inner combinations—other than 3's or 4's—are possible:

Ex.:

of Meters

EXAMPLE	SUGGESTED LISTENING
(musical notation example in $\frac{2}{4}$)	Beethoven, Movement 4, Symphony No. 1 meter: $\frac{2}{4}$
(musical notation example in $\frac{3}{4}$)	Tchaikowsky, Movement 3, Symphony No. 5 meter: $\frac{3}{4}$
(musical notation example in $\frac{4}{4}$)	Beethoven, Movement IV, Symphony No. 5 meter: **C** ($\frac{4}{4}$)
(musical notation example in $\frac{6}{8}$)	Brahms, Movement 1, Symphony No. 1 meter: $\frac{6}{8}$
(musical notation example in $\frac{9}{8}$)	Tchaikowsky, Movement 1, Symphony No. 4 (Moderato con anima) meter: $\frac{9}{8}$
(musical notation example in $\frac{12}{8}$)	Tchaikowsky, Movement 2, Symphony No. 5 meter: $\frac{12}{8}$
(musical notation example in $\frac{5}{8}$)	Ravel, General Dance, from Suite No. 2, *Daphnis and Chloe* meter: $\frac{5}{4}$
(musical notation example in $\frac{7}{8}$)	Prokofiev, Movement 3, Piano Sonata No. 7 meter: $\frac{7}{8}$
(musical notation example in $\frac{3}{4}\frac{2}{4}$)	Bartok, *Mikrokosmos*, Vol. 6, Bulgarian Dance No. 1 meter: $4 + \frac{2}{8} + 3$
(musical notation examples in $\frac{6}{8}$ / $\frac{3}{4}$)	Mozart, Ball Scene, *Don Giovanni* meters: $\frac{3}{8}$ $\frac{2}{4}$ $\frac{3}{4}$
(musical notation example, varied meters)	Bartok; Music For Stringed Instruments, Percussion and Celesta, Movement 4 meter: varied

The table following presents the signs and symbols most commonly in use in music.

Signs and Symbols

TERM	MEANING	USAGE OR PLACEMENT
staccato mark	note so indicated played shorter than its value	dot placed above or below note
stacc. staccato	same as above, but applying to several notes	above or below note
"wedge" mark	not as short as staccato and accented	above or below note
accent	note so indicated to be accented	above or below note
marc. marcato	"marked," a slightly lighter accent than preceding entry	above notes at point of usage
legato	notes to be connected without separation; to be played smoothly	above or below notes
tie	two notes of same pitch to sound as one continuous tone	connects notes separated by bar-line, or of unequal values
tenuto mark	hold note full value, or even slightly longer; sometimes also means "slightly pressing"	above or below note
comma	short breathing space: it may or it may not interrupt the rhythmic pace	between two notes, especially between phrases
pause	short pause of silence	at end of phrase
pause, fermata, hold	longer pause of silence or sound	over bar-line (silence), over note (sound)
G.P. grand pause, general pause	silence for all instruments	over a measure of rest in all parts

Symbol	Term	Meaning	Description
⌢ G.P.	as above	as above, but the silence is held	as above
𝄎 (repeat sign)	repeat sign	repeat preceding measure	this sign may be used immediately again if preceding measure is to be repeated more than once
𝄎 2 (repeat sign)	repeat sign	repeat preceding two measures	this sign also may be used more than once; the "2" is only a precaution
(staff)	as above	as above	at end of a section of music (either D.S. or 𝄋 may be used without the other)
D.S.	dal segno	(go back) to the sign	at end of a section of music
D.C.	da capo	(go back) to the beginning	D.S. directs the player to go back to this sign
𝄋	the sign	having gone back, now go forward	this sign appears twice indicating the omission of music in between; the second sign indicates the beginning of the coda
⊕	coda sign	(go forward) to the coda	
al Coda		to the (place marked) coda	often used in conjunction with D.S. or D.C.
al Fine		to the (place marked) fine	often used in conjunction with D.S. or D.C.
al ⊕		to the ⊕	same as above
(repeat marks)	repeat marks	repeat music enclosed	beginning and end of a section of music
1. 2. (first and second endings)	first and second endings	the repeated section is played twice; the second time the second ending replaces the first ending	at the end of a repeated section

THE OVERTONE SERIES. It is one of the phenomena of nature that when any musical sound is produced there are present, in addition to the basic tone, **overtones** that, although not distinguishable separately by the human ear, constitute the color of the sound.

Example 24

APPENDIX II

Synoptic listing of the forms of music, with suggested listening for each

The instrumental and vocal forms that follow should not be considered mutually exclusive. Vocal music, more often than not, will include instrumental forces. And instrumental music, such as the symphony, occasionally will include vocal forces.

FORMS FOLLOWING THE SONATA PATTERN. A *sonata* is an aggregate form ordinarily consisting of three or four loosely linked movements, contrasted in tempo and style.

The solo sonata. The *solo sonata* is written either for a single instrument with complete range such as the piano, organ, or harpsichord, or for instruments such as oboe, violin, or cello with a keyboard instrument. Properly these last should be termed *duo sonatas.*

Suggested Listening: Beethoven, *Sonata,* Op. 81a, "Les Adieux," for piano; Hindemith, *Sonata for Bassoon and Piano* (1939).

The symphony. A *symphony* is a sonata for full orchestra. Symphonies are often more extensive than sonatas for solo or chamber ensemble. The term *symphony* (*sinfonia*) is also used in baroque music to define instrumental forms prefacing choral or instrumental works.

Suggested Listening: Bizet, *Symphony in C,* for orchestra.

Trio, quartet, quintet. Chamber music media such as the *trio,* the *quartet,* and the *quintet* ordinarily follow standard sonata patterns. Their charm comes from an intimate character, not unlike that of the solo sonata, combined with the subtlety of musical dialogue found in all ensemble.

Suggested Listening: Schubert, "*Trout Quintet,*" for violin, viola, cello, contrabass, piano; Debussy, *Quartet in G Minor,* Op. 10, for two violins, viola, cello.

The concerto. A *concerto* is a sonata for one or more soloists with orchestra. It is almost always in three movements. There is no scherzo or minuet. *Cadenzas,* brilliant sections for soloist alone, are featured. The *concerto grosso,* originating in baroque music, features a small body of

409

soloists, the *concertino*, set in opposition to a larger instrumental group, the *tutti (ripieni)*. A concerto for orchestra does not allow for any set type or number of soloists. Rather, any or all instruments in the orchestra may lead momentarily without being considered *the* soloist or soloists.

Suggested Listening: Mozart, *Concerto for Clarinet*, K. 622; Brahms, *Concerto for Violin and Cello*, Op. 102; Beethoven, *Concerto for Violin, Cello, and Piano*, Op. 56; Bloch, *Concerto Grosso No. 2* (1952); Bartók, *Concerto for Orchestra* (1943).

The sonatine. A *sonatine* (sometimes sonatina) is a sonata of reduced dimensions. **Sonatina form** means sonata-allegro with absent or truncated development section.

Suggested Listening: Ravel, *Sonatine for Piano* (1905).

VARIATION FORMS. Variation technique occurs in all forms. Whenever any musical element is repeated, with however slight change, it is varied. Variation forms may be complete in one movement, or part of aggregate structures.

Theme and variations. The theme and variation form is an additive structure consisting of a theme repeated an indeterminate number of times, each time varied. The last variation is often climactic and dazzling, following one of slow, meditative character.

Suggested Listening: Rachmaninoff, *Rhapsody on a Theme of Paganini*, Op. 43, for piano with orchestra.

Passacaglia and chaconne. The **passacaglia** and **chaconne** have an additive structure with a theme considerably shorter than that in theme and varitions. These forms are often only a few bars in length. The passacaglia features an opening theme in the bass. Both tend to be more contrapuntal than theme and variations. **Ground** and **ostinato** are structures nearly identical with passacaglia, both suggesting a short figure in the bass overlaid with variations for each repetition. The notes of the ostinato usually do not change, and it may be heard in registers other than the bass.

Suggested Listening: Brahms, *Symphony No. 4*, Op. 98, Movt. IV (Chaconne); Copland, *Passacaglia* (1922), for piano.

Chorale prelude. The **chorale prelude** is an instrumental form, usually for organ and based on the **chorale**, a vocal form (see below). In one common version, individual phrases from the chorale are separated by transitions. These transitions continue as polyphonic commentary to the chorale phrases themselves. It is primarily a contrapuntal form.

Suggested Listening: J. S. Bach, *Wachet auf, ruft uns die Stimme,* for organ (see analysis of this in Chapter Five) .

FREE FORMS.   Many forms, both single and aggregate, have specific functions but are quite diverse in their use of structural pattern. For example, a rhapsody may be in the style of a rambling free improvisation, or it may follow strong classical structural patterns. The *Rhapsody in G Minor,* Op. 79, for piano, by Brahms, for example, is cast in a powerful sonata-allegro form; and the *Rhapsody on a Theme of Paganini* by Rachmaninoff is set as a theme with 24 variations.

Prelude.   The **prelude** can be either functional, as a preface to another piece, or independent. Many structural patterns are possible.

Suggested Listening: Shostakovich, *24 Preludes and Fugues,* Op. 84, for piano (functional) ; Puccini, *Prelude to Act II* of *Tosca* (functional) ; Chopin, *24 Preludes,* Op. 28, for piano (independent) ; Debussy, *Prélude à l'Après-midi d'un Faune,* (1892–94) , for orchestra (independent) (see Score Profile, p. 381) .

Overture.   The **overture** is similar to the prelude, but usually for full orchestra and substantial in dimensions. It is often cast in sonata-allegro form.

Suggested Listening: Functional Overture: Beethoven, *"Leonore" Overture No. 3,* Op. 72b, for orchestra (see Score Profile, p. 357)`; Concert Overture: Brahms, *Academic Festival Overture,* Op. 80, for orchestra (see Score Profile, p. 347) .

Fantasie.   A **fantasie** is a work in free form, resembling an improvisation. In baroque and pre-baroque music it is sometimes prefatory to a fugue.

Suggested Listening: Vaughan Williams, *Fantasie on a Theme by Tallis* (1910) , for orchestra; J. S. Bach, *Fantasia and Fugue in G Minor,* for organ.

Rhapsody.   A **rhapsody** is a work cast in any of many forms, usually quite imposing and substantial. The term is not used consistently by composers. It refers more usually to style rather than to form.

Suggested Listening: Liszt, *Hungarian Rhapsodies,* for piano.

Character piece.   A **character piece** is a work displaying one mood, emotion, or idea. Such pieces are often programmatic. Typical titles are **Im-**

promptu, Intermezzo, Song Without Words, Album Leaves, and *Ballad.* The form is often ternary.

Suggested Listening: Bernstein, *Four Anniversaries* (1948), for piano.

Tone poem. A **tone poem** is a substantial single-movement composition, usually orchestral, of programmatic content. The sonata-allegro form is much used, but others are common.

Suggested Listening: Richard Strauss, *Death and Transfiguration,* Op. 24, for orchestra.

Suite. A suite is any aggregation of pieces loosely bound together and contrasted to one another in style. Typical is the **dance suite.** This last, in the Baroque, consists primarily of dances such as the minuet, **gavotte, gigue,** and is variously called **French suite, English suite, partita,** or simply suite.

Suggested Listening: J. S. Bach, *Suite No. 2,* for flute with strings; Bartók, *Dance Suite* (1923), for orchestra; Vaughan Williams, *Folk Song Suite,* for military band.

Opera and ballet suite. The **opera** or **ballet suite** is a selection of characteristic music from opera or ballet, arranged in effective sequence.

Suggested Listening: Kodály, *Háry János Suite* (1926), from the opera *Háry János;* Stravinsky, *Firebird Suite* (1910), for orchestra, from the ballet *The Firebird.*

Incidental music. **Incidental music** is music written to accompany a play.

Suggested Listening: Schubert, *Rosamunde,* Op. 26, for orchestra.

Divertimento. A **divertimento** is a suite of light, entertaining character. Other titles are **Serenade** and **Cassation.**

Suggested Listening: Ibert, *Divertissement* (1930), for orchestra.

Ballet. A ballet is an extended theater-piece for dance, often divided into acts or scenes. Ballet is similar to opera, with the text danced rather than sung. **Choreography** is the specific arrangement of steps and postures to the music.

Suggested Listening: Milhaud, *La Création du Monde,* with chamber orchestra.

CONTRAPUNTAL STRUCTURES. *Contrapuntal structures* do not segmentize easily and therefore are to be described according to contrapuntal technique rather than according to parts or sections.

Fugue. Fugue is the combination of two or more melodic parts, using techniques of imitation and motivic transformation.

Suggested Listening: J. S. Bach, *Well Tempered Clavier,* Books I, II, for keyboard.

Invention. An *invention* is a less extensive contrapuntal composition in two or three melodic parts (voices). A prominent feature is inversion of the parts. Inventions are often canonic.

Suggested Listening: J. S. Bach, *2- and 3-part Inventions,* for keyboard.

Canon. The *canon* is a contrapuntal form based on continuous imitation.

Suggested Listening: Franck, *Sonata for Violin and Piano,* Movt. IV.

Toccata. A *Toccata* is a primarily contrapuntal work originally for keyboard, but also for orchestra, featuring brilliant display work. In baroque music a toccata is sometimes appended to a fugue and occasionally divided into several movements.

Suggested Listening: J. S. Bach, *Toccata and Fugue in F,* for organ.

VOCAL MUSIC. While all intelligible music must possess form, form is less apparent and freer in vocal music. The sonata-allegro pattern is diffuse and ineffective without motivic transformation and a sturdy overall superstructure including exposition, development, and recapitulation. But a song or an aria may very well ramble on, its inner segments only loosely connected, and still be intelligible. What makes this possible, of course, is the text, which largely dictates what the structure will be. Unmetered prose set to music tends to produce loose structures, while poetry suggests closer-knit forms.

Each stanza of a poem is frequently set to the same music, as in a church hymn. This form is called *strophic.* When each stanza is set to different music, it is termed *through composed.*

SINGLE MEMBER FORMS. *Recitative* is a rhythmically free and melodically somewhat static setting of a narration or dialogue. The shape of the melodic line follows very closely the inflection of the voice. If the accompaniment (often played by harpsichord or organ) is minimal, it is called **secco;** if dramatic and elaborate (usually orchestral), it becomes **accompagnato.** It is seen mostly in opera, oratorio, and cantata. Instrumental recitative, as in the first section of Movt. IV in Beethoven's *Ninth Symphony,* is a simulation of the vocal recitative.

Suggested Listening: Mozart, Recitatives for *Don Giovanni;* Schoenberg, *Variations on a Recitative,* Op. 40 (1943), for organ.

Plain song, sometimes called **plain chant,** is a form used for settings of the liturgy. **Gregorian chant** is the setting of early Roman Catholic Church texts. Only gentle accents occur, with an undulating, gentle pulse. The melodic intervals are small, with conjunct motion primary.

Suggestive Listening: "Dies Irae" from the Requiem Mass of the Roman Catholic Church. (Also listen to utilization of this chant in: Saint-Saëns, *Dance Macabre,* Op. 40, for orchestra; Berlioz, *Symphonie Fantastique,* Op. 14, for orchestra; Rachmaninoff, *Rhapsody on a Theme of Paganini;* Liszt, *Totentanz,* for piano and orchestra.)

A *song* is a setting of a poetic text for solo voice. A *part song* is for several voices. Songs are often ternary in structure.

The true *folk song* is anonymously composed, and undergoes considerable modification as it is transmitted from singer to singer. Also, songs and airs, such as *Au Clair de la Lune,* written by Lully in the seventeenth century, and the simple songs of Stephen Foster have become folk songs with the passing of the years and through their immense popularity.

Suggested Listening: Copland, *Old American Songs* (1950–1954), for voice with orchestra or piano.

The **art song,** termed **lied** in German, and **chanson** in French, is a setting by a master composer of a fine poem. Because both text and music are often of the highest caliber, the form is one of the richest in the literature for the voice. Art songs are usually performed by a single voice with piano, but orchestra is sometimes used.

Suggested Listening: Schubert, song cycle *Winterreise.* (See Score Profile, p. 316, for last song of cycle, "Der Leiermann.")

An *aria* is a song occurring usually in a large aggregate work such as an opera, oratorio, cantata, or passion. Accompaniment is orchestral and the aria amplifies and comments on emotions suggested in preceding recitatives. **Aria da capo,** in early aggregate forms, is ternary with the final part not written out the second time. A loose ternary pattern is common for many other arias. A *concert aria* is not written as part of an aggregate work but otherwise follows the dimensions and structure of the above. An *arioso* is a hybrid between a recitative and an aria, showing considerable lyricism but tending to the rhetorical.

Suggested Listening: Verdi, "Addio del Passato" from *La Traviata.* (See Score Profile, p. 329.)

A *hymn* is a simple setting of a religious or patriotic poem, suitable to be sung by untrained voices. Hymns are usually strophic in structure.

Suggested Listening: Billings, *Chester.*

A *chorale* is an early hymn originating in the German Lutheran Church, and often seen in SATB arrangement as part of larger works such as the cantata and *passion.* The chorale consists of short musical phrases punctuated by cadences, each with a fermata. The chorale as used by J. S. Bach is a compendium of harmonic devices of his time and formed the cornerstone of traditional harmony until its dissolution in the twentieth century.

Suggested Listening: J. S. Bach, chorales in the *St. Matthew Passion.*

An *anthem* is a choral setting in English, usually of a religious text, accompanied often by church organ, but sometimes done a cappella or with other instruments.

Suggested Listening: S. S. Wesley, *Blessed Be the God and Father.*

A *motet* is a contrapuntal, choral setting of a sacred text, often in Latin, and frequently unaccompanied.

Suggested Listening: Byrd, *Ego sum Panis vivum,* unaccompanied.

A *madrigal* is a setting of a secular text for mixed vocal ensemble. It contains a mixture of chordal and contrapuntal textures.

Suggested Listening: Bennet, *Thyrsis, Sleepest Thou,* unaccompanied.

AGGREGATE VOCAL FORMS. A *song cycle* is a group of art songs loosely related musically, frequently on poems by a single author.

Suggested Listening: Mussorgsky, *Songs and Dances of Death,* for voice with piano.

An *opera* is a play set completely to music, with all the words of the text (called *libretto*) sung. It includes many sections, any of which may follow diverse structural patterns: overtures (or preludes), recitatives, arias, duets, ensembles, choruses, ballets, incidental music, etc.

Number opera features the above-mentioned individual forms. In *continuous opera,* the demarcation between and identification of these is not pertinent. There is a continuous flow of music closely following the dramatic development of the play.

Some opera, especially that in a lighter vein, contains considerable spoken dialogue, e.g. English *ballad opera, singspiel, opera comique,* and *operetta.*

Suggested Listening: Menotti, *The Telephone,* number opera; J. Strauss, Jr., *Die Fledermaus,* operetta with spoken dialogue; Richard Strauss, *Elektra,* continuous opera.

An *oratorio* is a setting of a religious text with a similar structure and with forms as in opera. There are no costumes, scenery, or ballet. The soloists are often in fours, SATB. A narrator singing recitatives is commonly seen.

Suggested Listening: Mendelssohn, *St. Paul,* with soloists, chorus, orchestra.

A *cantata* is similar to an oratorio. However, cantatas are not always on a sacred text and often shorter. Two kinds are the solo cantata and the choral cantata. A *passion* is an extensive cantata (or oratorio) on one of the Gospel accounts of the Passion of Christ.

Suggested Listening: J. S. Bach, *Cantata No. 211* ("Coffee Cantata"), for STB, flute, strings.

A *mass* is a setting in Latin of certain portions of the liturgy of the Roman Catholic Church. Five of these portions are, the Kyrie, the Gloria, the Credo, the Sanctus, and the Agnus Dei. A mass for the dead is called a *requiem* and includes a slightly different arrangement, including the dramatic portion, the Dies Irae. A mass that is more suitable for performance in the concert hall than in church is called a *concert mass.*

Suggested Listening: Schubert, *Mass No. 2 in G Major,* for soprano, chorus, and orchestra.

APPENDIX III

Table of foreign terms found in this text

Adagio: slow.

Allargando (abbr. *Allarg.*) : broadening.

Allegro: moderately fast.

Andante (abbr. *Andte*) : walking tempo.

Animato: animated.

Arco: with the bow (used after a pizzicato passage) .

Ben marcato: very marked.

Con brio: with brilliance.

Con dolcezza: with sweetness.

Con espressione (abbr. Con espress.) : with expression.

Con forza: with force.

Con grazia: with grace.

Con spirito: with spirit.

Crescendo (abbr. *Cresc.,* or $<$) : gradually growing louder.

Dans le mouvement avec plus de langeur: in the tempo but with more languor.

Diminuendo (abbr. *Dim.,* or $>$) : gradually becoming softer.

Dolce: sweetly.

Dolcissimo (abbr. *Dolciss.*) : very sweetly.

Dolente: sadly.

Doux: sweetly.

En animant: animated.

En dehors: from afar.

Espressif: expressively.

Espressivo (abbr. *espress.*) : expressively.

Etwas Lebhaft: somewhat fast.

417

Flebile: lamentably, tearfully.

Forte (abbr. *f*) : loud.

Forte-piano (abbr. *fp*) : loud attack, and suddenly soft.

Fortissimo (abbr. *ff*) : very loud.

Gestopft: stopped.

Glissando (abbr. *gliss.*) : sliding from one pitch to another.

Legato: connected articulation.

L'istesso tempo: the same tempo.

Maestoso: majestic.

Marcato (abbr. *Marc.*) : marked.

Même mouvement: same tempo.

Mezzo-forte (abbr. *mf*) : moderately loud.

Mezzo-piano (abbr. *mp*) : moderately soft.

Molto: much.

Morendo: dying away in sound.

Mosso: with motion.

Mouvement de début: return to first tempo.

Piano (abbr. *p*) : very soft.

Pianissimo (abbr. *pp*) : very soft.

Più: more.

Pizzicato (abbr. *pizz.*) : plucked.

Poco: somewhat.

Poco a poco: little by little.

Presto: extremely fast.

Rinforzando (abbr. *rf.* or *rfz.*) : played with a sudden increase of force.

Retenu: held back.

Rubato: flexible tempo.

Sempre: always.

Sforzando (abbr. *sf, sfz*) : forceful attack.

Sforzando-piano (abbr. *sfp*) : with force and suddenly soft.

Sotto voce: soft voice.

Staccato (abbr. *stacc.*) : detached articulation.

Subito: suddenly.

Tempo Primo (abbr. *Tempo I*) : recurrence of first tempo.

Très lent et très retenu jusqu'à la fin: very slowly and held back until the
  end.

Très modéré: very moderate.

Très soutenu: very sustained.

Tutti: all (or nearly all) of the instruments of the orchestra.

Un fil de voce: a thread of vocal sound.

Un peu plus animé: a little more animated.

APPENDIX IV

Glossary of technical terms

[Technical terms not defined in this glossary are explained in the text.]

Absolute symphony: a symphony existing solely for itself, avoiding extra-musical inferences.

Accent: an emphasis on single or simultaneous tones achieved in various ways: by dynamics, duration, pitch location, etc.

Accidental: an accidental is a sharp, flat, or natural that raises or lowers the pitch of a tone.

Added notes: non-chord tones added to tertian chordal structures.

Arpeggio: a chord whose individual tones are played successively, not simultaneously.

Articulation: how tones are played relative to clarity, or to legato/staccato.

Asymmetrical meter: a meter that is made up of unequal groups of beats, indicated by a time signature such as $\frac{5}{4}$, $\frac{7}{8}$, etc.

Atonal: music without key or tonal center.

Authentic cadence: a cadence ending with a dominant-tonic progression.

Bar: see *Measure.*

Bar line: vertical lines on the staff which indicate the beginning and end of a measure.

Beat patterns: conducting gestures which represent groups of beats as indicated by the time signature.

Bel canto: a singing style which emphasizes beauty of sound and line rather than dramatization of the text.

Blue note: refers primarily to the lowering in pitch of either the third or seventh scale step of the major scale.

C clef: the clef used for middle register voices or instruments.

Cadence: a short progression of chords that either holds back or terminates the flow of music.

Cadenza: the improvisation-like portion of a work, often of a brilliant character and usually rhythmically free.

Canon: occurs in a contrapuntal texture where one voice imitates another on a regular basis.

Cantus firmus: the established tune against which another voice is set.

Changing meter: occurs when different time signatures succeed each other.

Chord: the simultaneous occurrence of three or more tones.

Chord progression: the linear relationship of two or more chords.

Chromatic: characterized by the interval of the minor second.

Chromatic scale: a stepwise ordering of the twelve different tones within an octave.

Chromaticism: in tonal music, the use of tones not in the particular diatonic scale being used.

Clef: a symbol placed on the staff to specify exactly what pitch name each line and space is given.

Climax: the point during a composition in which the propelling forces reach their peak. In a simple melody this may be the highest note, but in a more complex situation other forces are also at work, such as harmonic rhythm, chord density, etc.

Closure: towards the end of a fugue, where the subject returns in the home key.

Composite organum: the two voices of organum doubled at the octave above.

Compound meter: any meter the basic beat of which may be subdivided into threes, such as $\frac{6}{4}, \frac{9}{8}$.

Conjunct motion: linear motion characterized by the interval of a second.

Consonance: a combination of tones regarded as stable and not requiring resolution.

Counterpoint: the planned setting of one melodic line against another.

Cross relation: melodic half-step change taken over by a different voice.

Descant: florid melody set against a cantus firmus.

Diatonic: referring to the natural tones of the modes; opposed to chromatic.

Diminished seventh chord: a four-tone chord built of minor thirds.

Dominant: the tone a fifth above the tonic.

Double-flat: used to lower a note that is already flatted.

Double-sharp: used to raise a note that is already sharped.

Double-stop: two notes played simultaneously on an instrument of the string family.

Double-tonguing: a technique that wind players, mostly brass, use to execute rapid passages with alternating articulation of "T" and "K."

Dynamics: pertaining to loudness and softness of tone.

Enharmonic: one pitch with two letter-name designations. Example: C-sharp and D-flat.

F clef: the clef used for low register voices or instruments.

Figured bass: numbers referring to intervals which, together with the bass line, provide the basis for a keyboard realization of the harmony.

Finite-canon: canon in which the imitation continues until it is broken by free counterpoint, in order to conclude the work.

Flat: a sign placed in front of a tone to lower the pitch by a half-step.

Flutter tongue: rapid fluttering of the tongue while producing a tone; it is similar to the German and French method of pronouncing the letter "R."

Free organum: organum in which the voices do not necessarily proceed in parallel motion.

Frequency: the number of vibrations per second of a tone.

Fugato: an imitative section in the style of the opening of a fugue.

Fugue: a polyphonic procedure in two or more voices in which imitation based upon a special subject or subjects is primary.

Fugue exposition: the opening of a fugue in which the subject is presented at least once in all voices.

G clef: the clef used for high register voices or instruments.

Gebrauchmusik: music for functional use.

Half-cadence: a progression of chords ending on the dominant.

Half-step: see *Semitone.*

Harmonic interval: two tones sounded together.

Harmonic minor: the scale resulting when the seventh step of the natural minor is raised a half-step.

Harmony: the relationships between chords.

Homophony: a texture where one predominant melodic part is supported closely by subsidiary harmonic elements.

Idée fixe: fixed idea; the cyclic theme representing "The Beloved" in *Symphonie fantastique* of Berlioz.

Imitation: one melodic part imitating another in close succession.

Improvisation: the performance of music by its composer or composers as it is created.

Infinite canon: a canon in which the imitation continues throughout until brought to a stop at some designated point; a round.

Instrumentation: the specific number and kinds of instruments which form the orchestra.

Interval: the distance between two tones.

Inversion: in an interval, two notes on the staff are reversed so that the lower becomes the upper.

Isorhythm: in early polyphonic music, the repetition of the same rhythmic patterns.

Key: the letter designation of a tonal center which can either be major or minor. Ex.: E-flat major, B minor.

Key signature: the grouping, at the beginning of a staff, of sharps or flats derived from the key to be employed. The sharps or flats are in effect for each following measure unless otherwise indicated by accidentals.

Leger line: short lines used above or below any staff when it is necessary to extend it.

Leitmotif: a leading motive often used in German romantic opera.

Major mode: the diatonic scale of the major mode contains half-steps between the third and fourth, and the seventh and eighth steps. Originally, Ionian mode.

Measure: the distance from one bar line to the next.

Mediant: the tone midway between the tonic and the dominant (the third scale step).

Melismatic: a style in which an extended series of tones are sung to one syllable.

Melodic contour: the shape or profile of a melody.

Melodic interval: two tones sounded in succession.

Melodic minor: the scale resulting when the sixth and seventh scale steps of the natural minor are raised a half-step.

Melody: a succession of single tones in time.

Meter: the regular accentuation of rhythmic groups on a predictable basis.

Metrical modulation: a process by which the tempo is adjusted through special metronomic designations for successive note values.

Minor mode: the diatonic scale of the natural minor mode contains half-steps between the second and third, and the fifth and sixth steps. Originally, Aeolian mode.

Mixed meter: occurs when measures in different meter alternate.

Mode: any one of various diatonic scales which may begin on any line or space on the staff.

Modulation: the process of transition from one key to another.

Monody: recitative-like melodic line sustained by block chords.

Motive: a short, germinal melodic idea.

Musica ficta: the use of chromatics, in early music, not written in the music but introduced by the performer.

Musique concrète: a type of composition which uses sounds (pitched or unpitched) transformed by various kinds of electronic manipulations.

Musique stochastique: clustered masses of sound, giving the amorphous effect of "clouds of sound," delineated in notation by lower and upper pitch limitations; this technique is evolved through sophisticated advanced mathematical methods.

Neumatic: a melodic style in plainsong, where two, three, or four tones are sung to one syllable. Also called *group style.*

Note value: the symbol which represents the duration of a tone.

Obbligato: a subsidiary melodic line set against another primary melodic line.

Octave: refers to a span of eight notes of different letter names.

Orchestration: the manner in which instrumental timbres are combined in an orchestra as specified by the composer's score.

Organum: in early music the coupling of a lower voice with upper in parallel motion.

Ornament: the addition of one or more tones above or below a specific melodic tone, indicated by various symbols, such as small notes.

Ostinato: a short melodic figure repeated indeterminately, often in the bass; a ground.

Pandiatonic: the seemingly indiscriminate use of several tones of a scale or mode melodically and/or harmonically.

Parallel chords: chords which keep the same intervallic structure as they move up or down.

Parallel motion: two melodic lines progressing in the same direction by the same numerical interval.

Pedal point: the continuous or repeated sounding of a tone, often while contrasting melodic and harmonic elements are sounding.

Pentatonic mode: a mode of five tones which have the relationship found in the tones C D E G A.

Phrasing: the manner in which a performer shapes the inner components of a melodic line or lines in terms of dynamics, tone connections, articulation and length of sound, and tempo.

Pitch: the highness or lowness of a particular sound.

Polychord: different chords sounding simultaneously.

Polymeter: two or more meters sounding simultaneously.

Polyphony: the combining and blending of two or more melodic lines.

Polytonality: two or more keys sounding simultaneously.

Punctus contra punctum: point against point. Origin of the term "counterpoint."

Pure minor (see *Minor mode*) : Another term for *natural minor*.

Quodlibet: the process by which two or more melodies that originally had separate existence are combined in a comprehensible manner.

Range: all the tones possible from the lowest to the highest notes that can be produced by a voice or instrument.

Register: the specific area within the total spectrum of sound, generally defined as Soprano, Alto, Tenor, or Bass.

Rhythm: everything pertaining to the duration of musical sound; specifically, the time spans separating successive musical impacts.

Rhythmic pattern: a varied group of repeated note values which becomes one of the unifying structural elements in a composition.

Root: the lowest note of a chord in its fundamental position.

Scale: a theoretical abstraction of the basic set of tones used in a piece of music.

Score: the musical graph upon which the composer notes all parts to be played or sung; each different instrument or voice is represented by the appropriate staff or staves.

Semitone: on the keyboard the distance between any two adjacent tones; a half-step.

Sequence: repetition of a melodic pattern, but beginning on a different note.

Serial technique: a system of composition in which the tones to be used (often 12) are arbitrarily put in a specific order or series, and are used in this order (or transformation of it), melodically and harmonically, throughout the work.

Sharp: a sign placed in front of a tone to raise the pitch by a half-step.

Similar motion: two melodic lines progressing in the same direction, but not always by equal numerical intervals.

Simple meter: meters with two, three, or four beats to the bar.

Sprechstimme: a type of singing in which the pitch is not maintained, but is barely suggested and immediately moved away from.

Staff: the five lines and their adjacent spaces which, with the appropriate clef, designate the register appropriate to the instrument or voice.

Stretto: refers to the overlapping of subject entries in a contrapuntal texture.

Strophic: in vocal music where each stanza of a poem is set to the same melody.

Subdominant: the tone a fifth below, or a fourth above, the tonic.

Subject: the specific term for the principal melodic idea of a fugue, and re-lated contrapuntal procedures.

Syllabic: a melodic style in which one syllable is sung to each tone.

Syncopation: the accentual deviation from the expected and regular flow of beats; stressing weak beats.

Tempo: the pace of the beats; the speed at which a piece is played.

Tertian harmony: chords built in thirds.

Tessitura: in vocal music, the basic operational area of the tones within a given register.

Thematic transformation: the result of simultaneous variation techniques where a motive or theme assumes a new guise.

Theme: a theme is a melodically striking component of a composition.

Tie: a curved line connecting two notes of the same pitch in order to con-tinue the sound without interruption.

Timbre: see *Tone color.*

Time signature: the double number at the beginning of the music placed after the clef sign: the lower number denotes beat unit, the upper number denotes the number of beat units per measure.

Tonality: the gravitation of several tones around and towards one primary tone.

Tone: a sound of specific pitch produced by an instrument or a voice.

Tone cluster: any vertical structure which consists of two or more adjacent intervals of a second.

Tone color: the distinguishing quality of sound of an instrument or voice; timbre.

Tonic: the key tone.

Tremolo: the quick repetition of the same tone on bowed string instruments.

Triad: a three-note chord built in thirds.

Triple tonguing: a technique that wind players, mostly brass, use to execute rapid passages in triplets with the articulations "T" "T" "K."

Triplet: the division of any note value into three.

Tritone: any interval spanning three whole tones.

Tritone switch: the alternation of chords with roots a *tritone* apart.

Tune: a simple melody easily played, sung, and remembered.

Twelve-tone row: see *Twelve-tone technique.*

Twelve-tone technique: a technique of organization in atonal music in which an arbitrary melodic ordering of all 12 tones within the octave is used as the basis for the entire harmonic, contrapuntal, and thematic structure.

Unison: a sounding of the same tone by two or more voices or instruments.

Up-beat: the last beat of the measure.

Variation: any alteration or transformation of a previous musical idea in composition; identity with change.

Whole-tone: the distance of two adjacent semitones, or half-steps.

Index

429